SPACESHIP EARTH 101

People, Planet & The Power of Money

NICK EGNATZ

Press On Publishing

Spaceship Earth 101: People, Planet & The Power of Money

Published by Press On Publishing
Munster, IN

ISBN: 979-8-218-49120-8
BUSINESS & ECONOMICS / Education

Cover design by Amanda Miller, copyright owned by Nick Egnatz.
Interior design by Bryan Canter, copyright owned by Nick Egnatz.

QUANTITY PURCHASES: Schools, companies, professional groups, clubs, and other organizations may qualify for special terms when ordering quantities of this title.
For information, go to nickegnatz.com

The People, Planet & the Power of Money Project would never have been possible without my beloved wife, Sue, our children, Erin and Nick, and our five grandkids, Tristan, Kedzie, Harrison, Maddie, and Leo, without whom I would be a lost soul and quite incapable of researching, writing about, and ultimately challenging the current debt-money system.

Whatever level of understanding this book is able to add to our knowledge of our money system is the direct result of the loving, nurturing environment that my parents, Louise and Nicholas Egnatz, MD, provided for me and my seven rambunctious brothers, Mike, Alex, Tom, Joe, Chris, John, Bill, and our wonderful sister, Lisa.

The People, Planet & the Power of Money Project is dedicated to the people and the planet we inhabit and derive our sustenance from, all of whom desperately need a better money system.

Contents

Preface

The *People, Planet & the Power of Money Project* is an educational project for everyday citizens, advocating for a system of publicly created money. It started as a single book, but eventually became three shorter books to properly tell the story of money creation to those of us, who like myself, have no formal economics training. But why on Earth should a project about how our money is created be of interest to those of us outside the academic community?

Because in 2018 a fifteen-year-old girl from Sweden, Greta Thunberg, took it upon herself to skip school and stand outside Parliament with a sign that read "School Strike for Climate."

We are told that we do not have enough money to address the crises of climate change, dying oceans, and plastic everywhere including in our hearts and brains. Nor do we have the money to ensure that all of our citizens have a decent social safety net to get by on if robots, another pandemic, or another financial meltdown like that behind the Global Financial Crisis/Great Recession decides to take our jobs. As citizens we are expected to accept this limitation of what our money system can do, without being told the truth about who really creates our money and how they do it.

Spaceship Earth 101 owes its title to American economist Kenneth

Boulding's 1966 paper *The Economics of the Coming Spaceship Earth.*[1] Dr. Boulding defined the American economy of the time as a *cowboy economy*, symbolic of the seemingly limitless American plains and associated with exploitative, reckless, violent, and unjustly romanticized behavior. In sharp contrast, he coined the term *Spaceship Earth*, in which Earth was viewed as a closed single spaceship, lacking unlimited resources that would allow us to extract and pollute indiscriminately. Within *Spaceship Earth*, humanity must find its place in a cyclical ecological system and adopt what we now refer to as a sustainable lifestyle. My own *Spaceship Earth 101* model adopts this and looks at the Earth as a closed system powered by the sun; one with finite resources. It expands the discussion to include the political and economic systems that the monetary system operates within, arguing that just as publicly created money rose to meet the challenges of the past, it can provide the necessary money to meet our environmental and social crises of today and tomorrow.

The hull of *Spaceship Earth* is our atmosphere, without it there would be no ecosystems composed of plants, animals, or lifeforms of any kind, including humans. Humanity has made the dreadful mistake of looking upon itself as the master of nature, instead of being a part of nature. In truth, we are absolutely dependent upon having a vibrant, thriving natural world to live in. Yet today we find our natural world in a crisis, from climate change to dying species, oceans and ecosystems. Our failure to prioritize the natural world is often the direct result of not having the money to properly take care of our planet.

The *People, Planet and the Power of Money Project* is an educational outreach that provides the information on how the one thing we all need to simply survive in modern society—money is presently created and information on an alternative system of money, that can better respond to the environmental and social crises that we know about today and those that will certainly appear on the horizon in the future.

The Project is composed of three books:

Money Creation 101
History of Money 101
Spaceship Earth 101

Book One: Money Creation 101 directly answers the question of who creates our money. It also takes the economics profession to task for being unable or unwilling to tell us who creates our money and how they create it. We hear from a Federal Reserve economist, university professors and others who have difficulty answering the question of who creates our money. We also listen to the pleas of economics students beseeching their university programs to simply teach the truth about who creates our money so that they will be properly equipped to respond to the existential crises facing humanity that they will be asked to solve after they graduate. After reading *Money Creation 101* you will be better informed on the question of who creates our money and how they create it than the two respected economists from top university programs, who were interviewed anonymously at their own request, for the *People, Planet & the Power of Money Project.*

Book Two: History of Money 101 takes us back to our civilization's birthplace—the Fertile Crescent, then to ancient Greece, Rome, the American colonies, the U.S. Revolution and the U.S. Civil War, examining examples of publicly created money that successfully met the challenges of their time. A basic understanding of this history makes it much easier for us as citizens as we decide whether or not we want to keep our present system of bank-created debt-money or change to a more democratic system of publicly created money. This short book is chock-full of the type of monetary history that economics students across the globe are now begging their own university programs to include in their education.

To more fully tell our story here, *Book Three: Spaceship Earth 101* broadens the discussion, including climate change, plastic pollution, dying oceans, species and ecosystems, Artificial Intelligence, rising levels of inequality, the battle for democracy in America in 2024, avoiding the capitalist/socialist divide, striving for a more perfect union, the rise of Solidarity in Poland of the 1980s, the breakup of the Soviet Union in the early 1990s, the independence of both Russia and Ukraine, the rise of dictator Vladimir Putin, and Putin's invasion of Ukraine; all within the context of privately-created debt-money vs. publicly created money.

In summary, almost all of what we use for money is created out of thin air by private banks when they make loans. This money exists only as a loan while we are in debt to the bank, paying huge amounts of interest to the bank for their privilege of creating the money we desperately need in the first place. The Federal Reserve System exists to facilitate and protect this system of bank-created debt-money. Because the job of the Federal Reserve is to continue the bank-created debt-money system, it has effectively shut down explanations of the present system and discussions of an alternative system. If we don't understand what we now have, we are much less likely to search and press for change. Since the one thing we all need to exist is money and money only exists when someone somewhere is in debt, the bank-created debt-money system has effectively made debt slaves of our people and country.

About 15 years ago, when I quite by accident stumbled across the existence of the bank-created debt-money system, I began to look for an alternative system of money. I found it in The NEED Act (National Emergency Employment Defense Act) that had been originally written as the American Monetary Act, by my soon to be colleagues at the American Monetary Institute.[2] It was put into Congress in 2011 as comprehensive legislation that would give us a seamless, overnight transfer to a system of publicly created money. It is explained in detail in *Money Creation 101*, Chapter 7. Throughout the *People, Planet & the Power of Money Project* we refer to ideas to update the NEED Act under the name the *NEED Act Revisited.* Colleagues at the Alliance for Just Money have written an update of the NEED Act, titled the American Monetary Reform Act of 2024,[3] covered in Chapter 6 of *Spaceship Earth 101.*

The three major and necessary reforms in the above monetary reform proposals are:

1. The federal government will become the sole creator of our money.
2. Banks will only loan us money that has already been created by our federal government. Bank creation of money as debt will be decisively stopped.
3. The Federal Reserve System will be slimmed down and put into the U.S. Department of Treasury.

The 101s in the book titles are a reference to my one college economics course—Econ101. When we reached the chapter on the Federal Reserve System, our instructor told us that we would skip it because only a handful of individuals in the entire country were capable of understanding how our money is created within the Federal Reserve System. I would discover many years later that our instructor in all probability had no idea that almost all our money was created by banks when they make loans, charging us interest for their privilege. And if he did understand this, then he should have been ashamed of himself for not explaining it to us.

---

1. Boulding, Kenneth E., "The Economics of the Coming Spaceship Earth," Sixth Resources for the Future Forum on Environmental Quality in a Growing Economy in Washington, D.C. on March 8,1966, http://www.ub.edu/prometheus21/articulos/obsprometheus/BOULDING.pdf
2. National Emergency Employment Defense Act (NEED Act), 112th Congress, Sept. 21, 2011, https://www.congress.gov/bill/112th-congress/house-bill/2990/text
3. Alliance For Just Money, "American Monetary Reform Act of 2024," chrome-extension://efaidnbmnnnibpcajpcglclefindmkaj/https://www.monetaryalliance.org/wp-content/uploads/AMRA2024.pdf

Author's Note

The first draft of the *People, Planet & the Power of Money Project* was written in 2020 during the COVID pandemic. Climate disasters and social issues may be commented on as they have occurred when writing and rewriting. By mentioning this now, it will hopefully avoid confusion if you see a reference to something mentioned in 2021, 2022, 2023, or 2024 but being placed earlier in the text than other things that may have occurred in 2020.

Climate change, dead zones in the ocean, nitrogen and phosphorus cycles run amok, and plastic pollution everywhere, including our bodies, are global problems, as is the tremendous level of inequality within human society. While individual nations may have their own money systems, we are all part of a global bank-created debt-money system, overseen by the Bank for International Settlement in Basel, Switzerland.[1] Since the end of the World War II the U.S. dollar has had a unique role as the world's unofficial reserve currency.[2] As such, it is America's responsibility to take the lead in changing to a system of just, sovereign, publicly created money—the immediate focus of the *People, Planet & Power of Money Project*. However, the change must extend across the planet and those who live outside the U.S. are encouraged to advocate for monetary reform in their respective countries. The information within these pages pertains to you and should be helpful to your understanding of a money system that was not designed to be understood, no matter what country or part of the globe you reside in.

The three separate books are all interrelated and you are encouraged to read all three. Although the *People, Planet and the Power of Money Project* books are numbered, they may be read in any order. The best place to get started is with the book in your hands. If you don't have one in your hands, those interested in history, might want to start with *History of Money 101.* Those interested in systems or how things work, might want to start with *Money Creation 101.* And those interested in environmental, social and political issues, might be more comfortable starting with *Spaceship Earth 101.*

I am a Vietnam vet who volunteered for the U.S. Air Force and then volunteered to go to Vietnam because I, uninformed at the time, supported the war. It was only after I was home and the war was over, that I discovered that I had been grossly misinformed about the history that preceded our war on the Vietnamese people. When I returned from Vietnam and the Air Force, I went to work, met and married my wonderful wife Sue, had children and later grandchildren, and lived a relatively normal, uneventful life.

After the attacks on the World Trade Center and the Pentagon on September 11, 2001, I became quite concerned when the George W. Bush Administration began to beat the drums for war in Afghanistan and Iraq. I began to do my research and became an activist against both wars, which I found immoral, illegal, and counterproductive to our national self-interest. This activism naturally led to support for social justice and environmental issues.

As an activist for more than the last two decades, I often use strong language to drive home a point. Throughout the *People, Planet & Power of Money Project*, I have made every attempt to use the strongest language possible to convey the utter depravity of our present money system, without overstepping the boundaries of truth.

When I say that this system of private bank-created debt-money is fraudulent, I mean exactly that. Merriam-Webster online dictionary describes fraud: "deceit, trickery, an intentional perversion of truth… an act of deceiving or misrepresenting… one that is not what it seems or is represented to be." The simple fact that almost all of us are uniformed about how the one thing we all need to survive in society (money) is created, is all the proof we need that 'fraudulent' is the perfect word to describe our present financial system.

Additional evidence is provided in *Money Creation 101.* Two university economics professors and a Federal Reserve macroeconomist were either unable or unwilling to explain how our money is created. If they can't tell us how it is created, how on earth are those of us without a PhD after our names expected to understand how our money is created? Yet, using the brave research of my mentor, the late Director of the American Monetary Institute, Stephen Zarlenga, along with Dr. Werner, Dr. Yamaguchi, Dr. Kumhof, Dr. Benes, the Monetary Analysis Directorate at the Bank of England, and other experts you will meet within these pages, a person like myself with a grand total of one college economics course, is able to explain money creation to you in language we can all understand.

All three books use expert witnesses to provide facts and tell our story. When quoting them and other sources, quotation marks or indented text is used. On occasion to clarify what is being discussed we use brackets for my explanations within their quotes.

In addition to the chapter titles in the Table of Contents, we provide a Subchapter Index in the back of the book to help readers find and refer back to specific information.

As your tour guide, I thank you for entering the world of the *People, Planet & the Power of Money Project.*

---

1. Bank for International Settlements, "Welcome to the Bank for International Settlements," https://www.bis.org/index.htm
2. IMF Blog, "Dollar Dominance in the International Reserve System: An Update," International Monetary Fund, June 11, 2024, https://www.imf.org/en/Blogs/Articles/2024/06/11/dollar-dominance-in-the-international-reserve-system-an-update

ONE

AI in the 21st Century—Friend or Frankenstein?

AI: A Threat to Both Jobs and Humanity

Spaceship Earth 101 was originally written in 2020 during the COVID Pandemic. It has been rewritten and updated many times since then. This has been done, partially because anything I write must be gone over, again and again and again. With the launching of ChatGPT in November 2022, Artificial Intelligence is now on everyone's radar. In 2020 when I started writing this chapter, I agonized over whether to write out the term "Artificial Intelligence" or to use the initials "AI." At the time I came down on the side of spelling the words out because not everyone would immediately know what AI was. Now that AI threatens so much more than just job losses, the abbreviation "AI" seems more appropriate. In this chapter, we will provide expert testimony that AI, capable of completely turning the world upside down, must be looked at as a threat to humanity itself.

Job Loss

The threat of job loss is terrifying for anyone. As the specter of Artificial Intelligence (AI) confronts us, a system of publicly created money would offer much-needed security to our threatened workforce. AI will not be quite as scary with a system of publicly created money put in place to provide for the needs of the people, who have lost their jobs or those who don't have jobs to lose and are presently left entirely out of the equation.

Most afternoons I take our dog Reba to the dog park. She loves seeing the other dogs and their owners, as do I. Reba's dog park is located at one of the more hopeful places in Northwest Indiana. Wicker Park is a township park that services the industrialized cities of Hammond, East Chicago, and Whiting, along with the towns of Munster and Highland. Wicker Park has playgrounds, splash pad, picnic facilities, golf course, driving range, social center, banquet hall, outdoor concert facilities, and a 2.5-mile walking/jogging/riding path. All this in addition to Reba's dog park. We make steel in Northwest Indiana and Wicker Park is as good an example as there is of successfully bringing all people together in what we like to refer to as a melting pot.

Northwest Indiana calls itself the Crossroads of the Nation. U.S. Highway 41, which runs adjacent to Reba's Wicker Park dog park in Highland, Indiana, traverses our country north to south from Copper Harbor, Wisconsin, to Miami, Florida. Just a couple of miles south of Reba's dog park, U.S. Route 41 crosses U.S. Highway 30, which spans the width of America, connecting the Atlantic Ocean from Atlantic City, New Jersey, to the Pacific Ocean in Astoria, Oregon. More recent interstate highway additions (only 50–70 years old), Interstate 65 and Interstate 80/94, intersect in Gary, Indiana, just a few miles east of us and also span the nation. They are now the more modern version of the Crossroads of the Nation. I remember in 1966, after I'd completed Air Force Basic Training and Air Traffic Control School, my dad and I went to buy an old Volvo PV 544 at a used car lot just a couple of blocks down the street from what is now Reba's dog park. I drove that old Volvo to my first duty station after training, all the way on U.S. Route 66 from Northwest Indiana to Norton Air Force Base in San Bernardino, California. The interstate highway system was still a work in progress then, and Route 66 was the way to sunny Southern

California, from neighboring Chicago to LA. There was even a TV series called *Route 66* about the experiences of two young guys traveling it in a Corvette.

Repurposing the Boxes

At the dog park, I can look across the street to the shuttered Ultra supermarket, a massive store that was once one of the busiest supermarkets in Indiana. It has been closed for several years now. But for more than thirty years it was wildly successful in giving people in Northwest Indiana and nearby Illinois a clean, well-stocked supermarket with reasonable prices. When our son and daughter were little, I worked nights tending bar in Chicago. My wife worked days in an office in Chicago. For years I did the grocery shopping at 2 AM after work at our twenty-four-hour Ultra supermarket. The Ultra going out of business sale a few years ago was heartbreaking to watch. It went on for a couple of months. I only went inside Ultra once during the final sale, and I couldn't bring myself to buy anything. It was all just too sad.

But the empty Ultra supermarket is hardly alone. Big box stores and little box small businesses are shuttering everywhere. These closures began long before the COVID pandemic put the shutdowns on steroids. However, some of the closed stores could be put to other uses. That requires a new purpose for which there is a demand and the money to get the ball rolling. The same publicly created money, that we proposed in *Money Creation 101* and provided historical examples of in *History of Money 101*, could be what allows us to transform these stores.

Chicago-based company Wilder Fields has a vision of turning some of the empty big box stores across the country into high-tech vertical farms using artificial intelligence and robotics to grow organic produce.[1] They are implementing this concept in an abandoned Target superstore in nearby Calumet City, Illinois—the creation of an indoor suburban organic agriculture wonderland. Perhaps there will be a similar urban agriculture future for the forlorn Ultra supermarket that I see every day while Reba plays at the dog park. Wilder Fields is estimating eighty new jobs at its former Calumet City Target location, which will also include a small retail facility.[2]

Jake Counne, the founder of Wilder Fields, explains, "In the footprint of an average living room, we can grow a football field's worth of produce, and we can do it at a cost on par with what's grown on the West Coast.... Our team created propriety hardware and software—we have multiple patents pending—that reduce the costs associated with energy and labor. These inventions also increase production growth because they make it possible to dynamically control the grown environment—a minute at a time—and to significantly reduce human contact."[3] While Wilder Fields believes they will create eighty new jobs, we assume these are to be people jobs and not robot jobs. How many agriculture jobs will be lost. Who can know for sure, but probably more than eighty.

The Scary Brave New World of AI

Artificial intelligence (AI) is a wide-ranging branch of computer science that designs and builds smart machines capable of performing tasks that require human intelligence. Builtin.com defines it as an interdisciplinary science that uses multiple approaches and is bringing about a paradigm shift in all sectors of the tech industry.[4]

President Barack Obama warned us in his farewell address that "the next wave of economic dislocations...will come from the relentless pace of automation that makes a lot of good, middle-class jobs obsolete."[5] It is not rocket science. Robots will take our jobs, not because the robots like to work or even because they want to see us unemployed, but because the capitalist economic system demands that work be done in the cheapest and most efficient manner.

Since that is our system, we had better make sure that we have a money system that can handle the workers displaced by AI. The bank-created debt-money system has already proven itself structurally incapable of this task. Within the debt-money system, our two political parties argue over whether we can afford to make badly needed investments in jobs and our future, without massively increasing our already monumental federal debt. With a system of publicly created money that argument does not exist, because we will be able to create and spend the money, debt-free, for the very programs that we desperately need.

Driverless Vehicles

The trucking industry is currently coming face to face with AI. As reported on *60 Minutes*, "Autonomous trucking [driverless trucks] is not an if, it's a when. And the 'when' is coming sooner than you might expect."[6] The estimate is that some two million U.S. semi-truck drivers will soon be in danger of being replaced by an AI driver.

On August 11, 2023, driverless taxis operated by Cruise and Waymo were given the green light to operate round the clock in San Francisco. Before this Cruise, owned by General Motors, restricted operations between the nighttime hours of 10 PM and 6 AM, and only to selected parts of the city. Waymo, owned by Google, could operate only with a human driver. That changed on August 11, 2023, when the California Public Utilities Commission, the states regulating body for self-driving cars, voted 3-to-1 to allow Waymo and Cruise to expand their operations.[7] The day after the approval, ten autonomous Cruise taxis stopped on a busy street with their hazard lights flashing, bringing traffic to a standstill for fifteen minutes. A few days later another Cruise taxi drove onto freshly poured concrete and had to be pulled out of the concrete. Soon after this a Cruise taxi then collided with a fire truck, injuring a Cruise passenger.[8]

On August 14, 2023, two driverless Cruise vehicles stopped alongside an accident in which a vehicle had struck a pedestrian. The fire department claimed that the two robo-taxis delayed the ambulance from timely transporting the victim, with critical injuries, to the hospital where the victim died 20 to 30 minutes after arriving. Cruise has claimed that there was a lane open, which the ambulance did finally take as it exited the scene. Cruise has agreed to cut its driverless taxi fleet in half, while the accident and incidents are being investigated.[9] How long it will take to get the kinks out of a driverless system is not known. Or even if we *can* get the kinks out at all. But there is little doubt that we are moving in the direction of driverless vehicles.

Jobs to Be Replaced by AI

Technology solutions provider Saviom lists twelve categories of jobs that AI will replace: customer service executives, bookkeeping, data entry, receptionists, proofreading, manufacturing, pharmaceutical, retail services, courier services, doctors, soldiers, taxi and bus drivers, market research analysts, and security guards.[10] Saviom also listed twelve jobs that AI can't replace: human resource managers, writers, lawyers, chief executives, scientists, clergy, psychiatrists, event planners, graphic designers, public relations managers, software developers, and project managers.[11]

Oxford Economics came out with a report in 2019 stating that robotics will replace 20 million worldwide manufacturing jobs by 2030.[12] The U.S. stands to lose 1.5 million manufacturing jobs during this period. This figure represents only manufacturing jobs lost and does not account for additional jobs outside of manufacturing that also may be lost to robotics. The states most vulnerable to losing jobs were listed as Oregon, Louisiana, Texas, North Carolina, and my own state of Indiana.[13]

AI-Piloted Fighter Aircraft

In May 2024 Secretary of the Air Force Frank Kendall flew in a F-16 jet fighter, piloted by AI. Secretary Kendall rode in the front seat and an Air Force pilot was in the back seat, just in case the artificial intelligence X-62A VISTA (Variable In-flight Simulator Test Aircraft) made a mistake. The one-hour flight went well and included a brief dogfight with another F-16 with a human pilot. The planes came within 1,000 feet of each other in their maneuvers.[14]

A grinning Kendal climbed out of the plane and said that he had seen enough on this flight that he would trust VISTA AI with the ability to decide whether to launch weapons in a combat situation. Despite this trust in the AI system, Secretary Kendal did say that when weapons are used there would always be human oversight.[15] The International Committee of the Red Cross warns:

> The use of autonomous weapon systems entails risks due to the difficulties in anticipating and limiting their effects. This loss of human control and judgement in the use of force and weapons raises serious concerns from humanitarian, legal and ethical perspectives.[16]

As an Air Force Air Traffic Controller in the Vietnam War, I can only wonder if enough pilots and air traffic controllers are replaced with AI robots, whether the human controllers left on the job will find themselves with AI robots as supervisors.

Chatbots

An example of technology that has replaced the need for human employees is chatbot software used to conduct an online or telephone conversation. Chatbots have a natural language processing engine that allows them to analyze what you are trying to say, all while you are pulling out your hair wondering why on earth you can't talk to a real live person. Chatbots are the product of a branch of AI called machine learning.[17] Chatbots are an advancement over the rudimentary and absolutely maddening telephone answering systems now used by almost every place of business in our country: press one for this, press two for that (and press three if you just want to scream). There are telephone systems that call to tell you your library book is waiting for you or to ask you to confirm your doctor's appointment. And there are chatbots to answer your customer service questions when you are absolutely dying to talk to a person. And chatbots do all of the above and more online.

Within the chatbot world, there is what is called a Sensibleness and Specificity Average (SSA). Real humans have the highest SSA ranking at 86%, followed by chatbots: Meena 79%, Mitsuku 56%, Cleverbot 56%, DialoGPT 48%, and Xiaoice 31%.[18]

For those who enjoy irony, there are chatbots that interview you after you have lost your job to a robot and another chatbot to assist you when you look for a new job. HR departments insist that chatbots are mainly used to screen your employment application by gathering information to send to human managers.[19] Perhaps a chatbot will dial you up to schedule you for a second interview, this time with another chatbot. Eventually you might talk to a real live person, provided of course that there is still one left in the office.

Estimating Job Loss from AI

Artificial intelligence is impacting all sorts of jobs. Estimates for the job losses are all over the place, as are also the estimates of jobs created. Gartner, Inc., considered by *Forbes* magazine the "world's leading research and advisory company,"[20] predicted in 2020 that 69% of a manager's routine work will be fully automated by 2024.[21] While in 2024, Gartner reports that 73% of managers are overwhelmed by expanding responsibilities and that 74% of "managers are not equipped to lead the change." [22] Gartner also found that 55% of Human Resource leaders believe their current technology solutions "do not cover current and future business needs… with 46% believing that their "current HR technology solutions hinder rather than improve the employee experience."[23]

McKinsey & Company is widely considered the world's most prestigious management consulting firm.[24] They published a study in 2017 concluding that almost half of global work activities have the potential for automation. Almost 5% of global jobs can be completely replaced and about 60% of jobs have the potential to be 30% automated. If we multiply the 60% of jobs by the 30% estimate of what portion they will be automated or lost, it equals an 18% loss of full-time jobs. Therefore, 23% of worldwide jobs are replaceable—the 5% off the top that can be completely replaced, plus the 18% that we just calculated. McKinsey says that globally, automation can affect 1.2 billion workers. McKinsey also states that automation will boost global productivity by 0.8–1.4% annually over the coming decades. McKinsey estimates that the U.S. could lose from 16 to 54 million jobs between 2016 and 2030.[25] My own math using McKinsey's forecasting: replacing 23% of 160 million U.S. jobs[26] comes to a possible 36.8 million U.S. jobs that could be lost to automation and fits right in the middle of the McKinsey estimate. No doubt that a scary, brave, new world of AI is confronting humanity.

While those are eye-popping numbers, McKinsey and others who have examined the effect of AI are quick to point out that this technology will also create human jobs. What is unclear is if the jobs created will make up for those lost. Economists Daron Acemoglu and Pascual Restrepo in their 2018 study *Artificial Intelligence, Automation, and Work* state that there should be "no presumption that adjustment to the changed labor market brought about by rapid automation will be a seamless, costless and rapid process."[27] We can make predictions using all manner of permutations and prognostications. But we have no idea how many workers, permanently displaced by artificial intelligence, will seamlessly find new replacement jobs created by AI.

AI Robots Have the Same Bad Habits We Have

Those of us that managed to stay awake in school, may remember that the capitalist system demands that work be done in the most inexpensive way possible. Well, at least that is always what the author was told. Maybe, just maybe that is not always the case. Maybe AI isn't exactly a free lunch. In 2024, we are told that AI and the data centers that these systems require use massive amounts of electricity. Three years ago, Google proudly announced that it would do its part to address climate change by going "net zero" (it would release no more greenhouse gasses into the atmosphere than it removes) by the year 2030. But in 2024, Google also told us that its emissions grew 19% from 2022 to 2023, and that its baseline emissions from 2019 when they started the zero emissions project to 2024 had gone up 48%.[28]

Given this, AI robots don't actually work for free, and may be every bit as harmful to the environment as humans have been.

Power Hungry AI & Crypto Schemes

The International Monetary Fund (IMF) uses the term "power hungry" to describe both the mining of crypto currency and creation and use of artificial intelligence. The IMF reports that a single Bitcoin transaction uses the same amount of electricity that is consumed in 3 years by the average person in Ghana or Pakistan.[29] Quoting one International Energy Agency forecast, the IMF tells us that the combined use of electricity by crypto schemes and AI data centers is projected to increase from an actual 2% in 2022 to between 3.5% – 6% of all global electricity use by 2027.[30] The energy required to make and operate the Bitcoin system, representing only one crypto scheme, is more than the all the electricity used by Argentina, a country of 45 million people.[31] Using all this electricity to power AI and crypto schemes, in addition to the tremendous cost incurred, pumps carbon into the atmosphere, straining our efforts to fight climate change and begin to drawdown the carbon and other greenhouse gasses in the atmosphere.

Both AI and crypto *currencies* have been marketed to us as an efficient way to get things done. While some AI robots are much cheaper to operate than people doing the same jobs, it certainly appears that the tremendous amounts of electricity needed to power the AI brain systems make them a horse of an entirely different color. What they are experimenting on with these horses of a different color will be explained further in the chapter.

Crypto schemes, such as Bitcoin, are nothing more than a hi-tech Ponzi scheme targeting the masses. They are not money or a money system and that is why we have chosen to italicize the word currency when it is used to describe crypto. The absolute test of whether or not something is money or currency, is its acceptance as a payment for taxes by the state (federal government). If it is accepted as a payment for taxes, the state recognizes it as a form of money. Since the state should be the sole creator and beneficiary of money, it would indeed be disastrous if Bitcoin or any other privately created crypto scheme was ever recognized by our government. Think of the various crypto Ponzi schemes as a lottery system or a trip to the casino. If you feel like gambling, please understand that is all you are doing when you purchase crypto. You are using your hard-earned money to get in on a con game that only pays off if a whole bunch of other suckers buy-in after you have made your purchase. Good luck with that.

The Bitcoin crypto scheme had a massive increase in price after Donald Trump won the 2024 Presidential Election. In one month, it went from a price of $69,374 to $103,713 upon Trump's victory.[32] While this was a huge windfall to those who own Bitcoins, what would it mean if Bitcoin was an accepted money system or a part of our accepted money system? Inflation at the rate of 29.5% in just one month or 354% inflation in one year. A good example of why the so-called crypto *currencies* are speculative gambling schemes, made to benefit those who got in at the ground floor and not you.

Collective Action Necessary to Deal with AI

How do we deal with events or situations that are simply too large and overwhelming for us to face individually? We need to act collectively as a society to deal with such formidable problems. Will the 36 million Americans who are forecast to lose their jobs to AI by 2030 all be individually able to successfully navigate the daunting process of training for and finding a new job? Not likely, but even in the statistically impossible event that our 36 million soon-to-be unemployed could seamlessly steer through the process of finding a new job, this is all predicated upon the supposition that there will be an equal number of new jobs to replace all the lost jobs—and that is a huge supposition.

The *People, Planet & the Power of Money Project* has been written to educate the public about how we can collectively handle 36 million additional unemployed people, retraining them for whatever new jobs that become available and humanely assisting those unable to quickly land in new AI generated jobs. The way forward is through a replacement of our present private bank-created debt-money system with a system of just, sovereign publicly created money, explained in greater detail in Book One: *Money Creation 101*. A system of publicly created money can create money, debt-free, in the amounts we deem necessary to confront a crisis of 36 million new unemployed, without raising taxes or borrowing. The NEED Act,[33] put into Congress in 2011 and completely ignored by Congress, was such a system.

Throughout the *People, Planet & Power of Money Project*, I have referred to an, as of yet unwritten update of it, which I call *The NEED Act Revisited* as a way to bring the NEED Act current. This new title would both honor the 2011 NEED Act and all those who worked on it, while also recognizing both the *Chicago Plan*[34] from the Great Depression and Michael Kumhof and Jaromar Benes's *The Chicago Plan Revisited*[35] from 2012. Colleagues at the Alliance for Just Money have drafted the American Monetary Reform Act of 2024, and it is discussed in Chapter 6.

Throughout the *People, Planet & Power of Money Project* we use expert witnesses to more fully tell our story. Our first expert provided a warning about what AI could become long before many of us had ever heard of Artificial Intelligence.

Expert Witness: Dr. Stephen Hawking

English theoretical physicist Stephen Hawking was widely viewed as one of the world's greatest living geniuses before he died in 2018. Dr. Hawking's major achievement was to effectively show that the Big Bang theory in which the universe began from a single point was physically possible.[36] In a 2014 BBC interview, Dr. Hawking gave the world an ominous warning about AI:

> The development of full artificial intelligence could spell the end of the human race.... It would take off on its own, and re-design itself at an ever-increasing rate.... Humans, who are limited by slow biological evolution, couldn't compete, and would be superseded.[37]

Professor Hawking's observations on AI come from the perspective of having lived since his early twenties with motor neuron disease (MND), also known as amyotrophic lateral sclerosis (ALS) or Lou Gehrig's disease. MND/ALS is a progressive, usually fatal neuromuscular disease that attacks motor neurons in the spinal cord and lower brain, which transmit signals from the brain to the voluntary muscles throughout the body.[38] Paralyzed and dependent on a wheelchair for much of his life, Hawking was intimately and progressively, from the time he became ill in his early twenties until his death, tied more and more to machines. After contracting pneumonia in 1985, Hawking had his trachea removed and lost the ability to speak. He learned to communicate through a speech synthesizer using a computer program to select words developed by American Walt Woltosz.[39] When a man who, for most of his life has been dependent upon machines to live, issues a warning about machines replacing humanity, we need to take heed.

AI Ups Its Game with ChatGPT

Except for the 2023 San Francisco driverless taxi, the Air Force fighter jet story, and the power-hungry AI and crypto schemes, the above discussion of AI was written in 2020 with only minor tweaking after that date. I had debated whether to us artificial intelligence or its abbreviation AI in the chapter title. I was not sure if using AI would be unfamiliar with some readers.

That hesitancy changed when research and deployment company Open AI released its newest chatbot ChatGPT on November 30, 2022. Suddenly AI was on the news day and night. It became apparent to me at least that there is a distinct possibility that yes, humanity is on a collision course with Professor Hawking's prediction that, "The development of full artificial intelligence could spell the end of the human race...."

Well, maybe Professor Hawking was just being a spoil-sport, throwing a wet-blanket on the tech sector of our free market paradise. After all, Open AI has told us that they are doing this for our benefit,

"Our mission is to ensure that artificial general intelligence—AI systems that are generally smarter than humans—benefits all of humanity."[40] So, the artificial general intelligence (AGI) systems/beings/creatures are smarter than us but have no fear, for they are here to benefit all of us.

Whew, I was worried for a moment. Although it does remind me of a 1962 Twilight Zone TV show, *To Serve Man*.

Expert Witness: Michael Chambers

Michael Chambers is a government encryption specialist, and he is neither a real person nor an AI robot. Michael Chambers, played by actor Lloyd Bochner, is a creation of two actual humans though: Rod Serling television producer of 1960s era The Twilight Zone TV show and screenwriter Damon Knight (although most of the Expert Witnesses featured in the *People, Planet & Power of Money Project* are real people, we retain the right to make substitutions as needed. And substitutes such as Mr. Chambers here and Professor Plastics, who you will soon meet in Chapter 4, are definitely not AI robots).

To Serve Man begins with an alien spaceship landing on Earth. At first, the aliens were ever so friendly and helpful. They offered to share their technology of limitless energy and the ability to transform barren deserts into gardens. People were lining up to be taken to their planet to see how they do it. The Kanamit aliens had inadvertently left a book with the humans with the title *To Serve Man* that was about all the great ways they would help us. Michael Chambers was involved with trying to decode or translate the book for our government. As the protagonist of the story, Mr. Chambers was already climbing on the spacecraft to go to the alien's planet, when his assistant yells to him as he is boarding the spaceship, that *To Serve Man* was a cookbook.[41] The alien then pushes Chambers up the steps to the ship and closes the hatch behind him.

Michael Chambers is shown on the spaceship in his room smoking (everybody smoked on TV in 1962) and refusing to eat, as the alien chided him that they didn't want him to lose weight. After the alien left the room, Chambers looks at the camera and says,

> "How about you? You still on Earth or on a ship with me. It doesn't make very much difference because sooner or later, we'll all of us be on the menu. All of us."[42]

Today the question is, will all of us be on the ChatGPT AI menu?

AI Gobbles Us Up Via Data Colonialism

The geniuses behind Big Tech want our data. With this data they can bombard us with advertising and make money off us. With this data Russia,[43] China,[44] the Republican Party[45] and Donald Trump[46] can saturate both social media and the mainstream media with lies, misinformation and propaganda to convince enough of us to give up our democracy for the wonders of a "unified Reich"[47] in our former democracy. It is bad enough that our data is being used to constantly sell to us and that Russia and China are using our data to damage our democracy, but junking our democracy for a dictator-on-day-one[48] is entirely on another level of treachery. Here we will focus on Big Tech using the Doctrine of Discovery legal device to consume your personal data and basically own you.

Doctrine of Discovery

The Doctrine of Discovery was discovered, so to speak, by the Catholic Church in the 15th century as they issued three separate papal bulls (edicts), proclaiming the right of Christian nations to take possession of non-Christian lands in the interest of saving the heathen souls of the non-Christians. The third of these bulls issued in 1493, after Christopher Columbus had discovered the so-called New World, specifically made clear that it was the duty of Christian explorers to Christianize the inhabitants by seizing their lands.[49]

I am more than a little embarrassed that I spent 12 years in Catholic schools, and that I didn't have enough sense at the time to object to this. I generally knew that some of these things were done, I don't remember being taught that the Catholic Church made the attempt to legally justify it. The Cornell Law School explains:

> The doctrine of discovery refers to a principle in public international law under which, when a nation "discovers" land, it directly acquires rights on that land. This doctrine arose when the European nations discovered non-European lands, and therefore acquired special rights, such as property and sovereignty rights, on those lands. This principle disregards the fact that the land oftentimes is already inhabited by another nation. In fact, this doctrine was used in order to legitimize the colonization of lands outside of Europe.
>
> More broadly, the doctrine of discovery can be described as an international law doctrine giving authorization to explorers to claim *terra nullius* – i.e. said inhabited land – in the name of their sovereign when the land was not populated by Christians.[50]

Expert Witnesses: Ulises A. Mejias & Nick Couldry - Data Colonialism

According to Ulises A. Mejias, Professor of Communication Studies at the State University of New York, Oswego and Nick Couldry, Professor of Media Communications and Social Theory at the London School of Economics and Political Science:

> The Doctrine of Discovery survives today in a seamless move from cheap land to cheap labor to cheap data, a phenomenon we call "data colonialism." The word "colonialism" is not being used metaphorically here, but to describe a very real emerging social order based not on the extraction of natural resources or labor, but on the continuous appropriation of human life through data. Data colonialism helps us understand

> today's transformations of social life as extensions of a long historical arc of dispossession. All of human culture becomes the raw material that is fed to a commercial AI machine from which huge profits are expected.[51]

Drs. Mejias & Couldry point out that generative AI is not just interested in plagiarizing the content of famous authors who are now owned by powerful media groups. They want your data and mine and they want all of it. In their book *Data Grab: The New Colonialism of Big Tech and How to Fight Back* they suggest borrowing the model used by Latin American and Latine activists: Simultaneous action on three levels.

1. Within the system: Work to regulate, anti-trust laws, consumer protection laws, mainstream politics, etc.
2. Against the system: Unionization, workers' rights, Indigenous data sovereignty, environmental organizing. Movements against using data technologies for wars, surveillance, apartheid, and the persecution of migrants.
3. Beyond the system: Creating ways of limiting data exploitation, redirecting data use toward more social and democratic goals. Requiring new technologies and new ways of rejecting present technology.[52]

Expert Witness: Dr. Geoffrey Hinton—Emeritus Professor, University of Toronto: Computer Science, Machine Learning, Psychology, Artificial Intelligence, Cognitive Science

In May 2018, Dr. Hinton was awarded what is referred to as the 'Nobel Prize in Computing,' the A.M. Turing Award by the Association of Computing Machinery with Yoshua Bengio and Yann LeCun.[53] With the award they were given the moniker "Fathers of the Deep Learning Revolution," along with a prize of one million dollars.

In May 2023, Dr. Hinton announced that he had resigned from his position as vice president and research fellow at Google. Dr. Hinton has also been called both the “father of AI”[54] and the “godfather of AI.”[55]

Technology Correspondent for NPR (National Public Radio) Bobby Allyn reports:

> In 2012, Hinton and two of his students at the University of Toronto built what's called a neural network. It's called that because it's a geeky computer system that kind of operates the way a brain works, like the way neurons work. You could feed it tons and tons of data, like photos, and it would learn how to identify, say, a flower from a dog. This breakthrough is the foundation of so many AI tools used in everything from analyzing MRI scans and hospitals to helping farmers understand crop yields and, of course, used in the hit service ChatGPT. But now Hinton has left Google and is sounding the alarm.
>
> He came to this position recently after two things happened. First, when he was testing out a chat bot at Google and it appeared to understand a joke he told it, that unsettled him; secondly, when he realized [an] AI that can outperform humans is actually way closer than he previously thought.[56]

Dr. Hinton resigned his positions at Google to sound the alarm about the future of AI. Dr. Hinton in a May 2023 interview on National Public Radio:

> These things could get more intelligent than us and could decide to take over, and we need to worry now about how we prevent that happening… I thought for a long time that we were, like, 30 to 50 years away from that. So, I call that far away from something that's got greater general intelligence than a person. Now, I think we may be much closer, maybe only five years away from that.[57]

Dr. Hinton does not blame Google or believe that they have acted irresponsibly:

> Actually, I left [Google] so that I could talk about the dangers of AI without considering how this impacts Google. Google has acted very responsibly.[58]

While believing AI can be used for many good things, Dr. Hinton has severe reservations about how AI may be used for the opposite:

> It's hard to imagine how you'd stop bad actors from using it [AI] for bad things.[59]

This is a conundrum. Are we to be left worrying which is worse: AI being used to do bad things by bad actors? Or AI being five years away from using its superior intelligence to overtake humanity and start setting our agenda, instead of doing our bidding?

AI's Next Leap Forward: Wetware Computing and Organoid Intelligence

It didn't take the AI bandwagon long to get to work solving the problem of the high cost of AI robot intelligence:

> Wetware computing and organoid intelligence is an emerging research field at the intersection of electrophysiology and artificial intelligence. The core concept involves using living neurons to perform computations, similar to how Artificial Neural Networks (ANNs) are used today. However, unlike ANNs, where updating digital tensors (weights) can instantly modify network responses, entirely new methods must be developed for neural networks using biological neurons…[60]

For a translation we turn to Russ Baker, Editor-in-Chief of WhoWhatWhy, an investigative journalist specializing in exploring power dynamics behind major events:

> AI was supposed to make things easier for humans, but it turns out the best way to do AI is with human brains. It's a no brainer… Because you can apparently get artificial intelligence more effectively, more cheaply, and with less environmental consequence — by using actual brain cells. Not yours, and not mine. No, they're growing brains to order in the lab.[61]

Training a single Large Language Model AI, like GPT-3, a precursor to GPT-4, demanded 10 GWh (gigawatts, each gigawatt is equal to 1-billion-watt hours of electricity). This is about 6,000 times the energy a human brain uses in a year. The human brain operates using 86 billion neurons while using only 20 watts of power.[62] There is a huge cost saving to be had making human brains from stem cells to do the heavy lifting for AI.

> Ethics statement:
>
> Ethical approval was not required for the studies on humans in accordance with the local legislation and institutional requirements because only commercially available established cell lines [stem cells] were used.[63]

Is it possible for humanity to come together and regulate AI? So as to guarantee that AI is here to actually serve our people and planet? And just perhaps, to do so without using hybrid wetware human brains? Or is the fate of people and planet, to be put on an AI dinner platter as was Michael Chambers in *The Twilight Zone*? The clock is ticking as *Spaceship Earth* travels through the heavens.

---

1. Wilder Fields, https://www.wilderfields.com/
2. Pate, Joseph S., "WATCH NOW: Company behind vertical farm in vacant Target hopes to roll out new technology nationwide," Northwest Indiana Times, July 25,

2020, https://www.nwitimes.com/business/local/watch-now-company-behind-vertical-farm-in-vacant-target-hopes-to-roll-out-new-technology/article_4a522a8f-e688-5b8f-9cba-ed16dd1da12f.html

3. *Ibid.*
4. BuiltIn.com, "What is Artificial Intelligence?", https://builtin.com/artificial-intelligence
5. The White House, "President Barack Obama's Farewell Address," Jan 10, 2017, https://obamawhitehouse.archives.gov/farewell
6. Wertheim, Jon, "Automated trucking, a Technical Milestone that Could Disrupt Hundreds of Thousands of Jobs, Hits the Road," 60 Minutes, August 23, 2020, https://builtin.com/artificial-intelligence
7. Bidarian, Nadia, "Regulators give green light to driverless taxis in San Francisco," CNN Business, Aug 11, 2023, https://www.cnn.com/2023/08/11/tech/robotaxi-vote-san-francisco/index.html
8. Lu, Yiwen, "A Bumpy Ride for San Francisco's Driverless Taxis," New York Times, California Today, Aug 22, 2023, https://www.nytimes.com/2023/08/22/us/california-autonomous-vehicles.html
9. Anguiano, Dani, "Self-driving car blocking road 'delayed patient care', San Francisco officials say," The Guardian, Sept 5, 2023, https://www.theguardian.com/us-news/2023/sep/05/san-francisco-cruise-robotaxi-death-ambulance
10. Deskmuckh, Dipayan, "12 jobs that robots (AI) will replace and 12 that won't," Saviom, March 22, 2021, https://www.saviom.com/blog/12-jobs-that-robots-ai-will-replace-in-the-future-and-12-that-wont/
11. *Ibid.*
12. Larderi, Alexa, "Robots Will Replace 20 Million Jobs by 2030, Oxford Report Finds," U.S. News & World Report, June 26, 2019, https://www.usnews.com/news/economy/articles/2019-06-26/report-robots-will-replace-20-million-manufacturing-jobs-by-2030
13. Cooper, Adrian, "How Robots Change the World," Oxford Economics, June 2019, https://cdn2.hubspot.net/hubfs/2240363/Report%20-%20How%20Robots%20Change%20the%20World.pdf?utm_medium=email&_hsenc=p2ANqtz--S_yv5LZTWzdC5IER_NtSl3PcknlmRKCRLWkiY7DXoc24tLeHNQmxbfIluLCA4PrkWMen4_J_hWSH49WG3OQvHF61Jlg&_hsmi=74013545&utm_content=74013545&utm_source=hs_automation&hsCtaTracking=07b1855a-24f4-4b99-bcb8-b0d2a13b715e%7C53b7a48e-9591-4179-8eab-694443190b4f
14. Copp, Tara, "An AI-controlled fighter jet took the Air Force leader for a historic ride. What that means for war," AP, May 3, 2024, https://apnews.com/article/artificial-intelligence-fighter-jets-air-force-6a1100c96a73ca9b7f41cbd6a2753fda
15. Copp, Tara, "An AI-controlled fighter jet took the Air Force leader for a historic ride. What that means for war," AP, May 3, 2024, https://apnews.com/article/artificial-intelligence-fighter-jets-air-force-6a1100c96a73ca9b7f41cbd6a2753fda
16. International Committee of the Red Cross, "ICRC position on autonomous weapon systems," May 12, 2021, https://www.icrc.org/en/document/icrc-position-autonomous-weapon-systems
17. Digital Marketing Stream, "The Holy Grail of the Digital Era -- Will Chatbots Replace Humans?" https://digitalmarketingstream.com/what-are-chatbots/
18. *Ibid.*
19. *Ibid.*

20. Forbes, "Gartner Inc.," Feb 7, 2018, https://www.forbes.com/sites/gartnergroup/?sh=614f0b116deb
21. Gartner, "Gartner Predicts 69% of Routine Work Currently Done by Managers Will Be Fully Automated by 2024," Newsroom Press Release, Mumbai, India, Jan 23, 2020, https://www.gartner.com/en/newsroom/press-releases/2020-01-23-gartner-predicts-69--of-routine-work-currently-done-b#:~:text=Artificial%20intelligence%20(AI)%20and%20emerging,69%25%20of%20the%20manager's%20workload.
22. Gartner, "Gartner Survey Finds Leader and Manager Development Tops HR Leaders' List of 2025 Priorities for Third Consecutive Year," Stamford Conn., Oct 15, 2024, https://www.gartner.com/en/newsroom/press-releases/2024-10-15-gartner-survey-finds-leader-and-manager-development-tops-hrleaders-list
23. *Ibid.*
24. Vault Rankings, "2021 Most Prestigious Consulting Firms," #1 McKinsey & Co., https://www.vault.com/best-companies-to-work-for/consulting/best-consulting-firms-prestige
25. McKinsey Global Institute, "A Future that Works: Automation, Employment, and Productivity," Overview of Select Recent Studies on the Impact of Automation and Future of Work, January 2017, https://www.mckinsey.com/~/media/McKinsey/Featured%20Insights/Digital%20Disruption/Harnessing%20automation%20for%20a%20future%20that%20works/MGI-A-future-that-works_Full-report.ashx
26. Statista.com, "Monthly civilian labor force in the United States from July 2019 to July 2020," https://www.statista.com/statistics/193953/seasonally-adjusted-monthly-civilian-labor-force-in-the-us/
27. Acemoglu, Daron & Restrepo, Pascual, "Artificial Intelligence, Automation and Work," National Bureau of Economic Research, NBER Working Paper No. 24196, January 2018, https://www.nber.org/papers/w24196
28. St. John, Alexa, "Google cites AI power needs for missing its climate target," Associated Press, Chicago Tribune, July 4, 2024, https://apnews.com/article/climate-google-environmental-report-greenhouse-gases-emissions-3ccf95b9125831d66e676e811ece8a18
29. Hebous, Shafik & Vernon-Lin, Nate, "Carbon Emissions from AI and Crypto Are Surging and Tax Policy Can Help," IMF Blog, Aug 15, 2024, https://www.imf.org/en/Blogs/Articles/2024/08/15/carbon-emissions-from-ai-and-crypto-are-surging-and-tax-policy-can-help?campaign_id=54&emc=edit_clim_20240820&instance_id=132197&nl=climate-forward&regi_id=155175712&segment_id=175643&te=1&user_id=bf4df3ddfeb87ff7c4b3b19f156eb65f&utm_campaign=4e8113dde1-CPdaily19082024&utm_medium=email&utm_source=CP+Daily&utm_term=0_a9d8834f72-4e8113dde1-110468110
30. *Ibid.*
31. Hinsdale, Jermey, "Cryptocurrency's Dirty Secret: Energy Consumption," State of the Planet, Columbia Climate School, May 4, 2022, https://news.climate.columbia.edu/2022/05/04/cryptocurrency-energy/#:~:text=But%20crypto%20has%20a%20dirty,of%20Argentina%2C%20population%2045%20million.
32. Grantham-Philips, Wyatte, "What's next for Bitcoin as it surpasses $100,000 in post-election rally?" PBS, Associated Press, Dec 5, 2024https://www.pbs.org/newshour/world/whats-next-for-bitcoin-as-it-surpasses-100000-in-post-election-rally,

33. National Emergency Employment Defense Act (NEED Act), 112th Congress, Sept. 21, 2011, https://www.congress.gov/bill/112th-congress/house-bill/2990/text
34. Paul H. Douglas, University of Chicago; Irving Fisher, Yale University; Frank D. Graham, Princeton University; Earl J. Hamilton, Duke University; Willford I. King, New York University; Charles R. Whittlesey, Princeton University, "A Program for Monetary Reform," July, 1939, https://faculty.chicagobooth.edu/amir.sufi/research/monetaryreform_1939.
35. Kumhof, Michael, & Benes, Jaromir, *The Chicago Plan Revisited,* International Monetary Fund, Working Paper, https://www.imf.org/external/pubs/ft/wp/2012/wp12202.pdf
36. Geach, James, "Stephen Hawking's PhD thesis crashed his website—here's what it says in simple terms," The Conversation, Oct 6, 2017, https://theconversation.com/stephen-hawkings-phd-thesis-crashed-its-host-website-heres-what-it-says-in-simple-terms-86351#:~:text=The%20major%20achievement%20of%20Hawking's,possible%20evolution%20of%20the%20cosmos.
37. Cellan-Jones, Rory, "Stephen Hawking warns artificial intelligence could end mankind," BBC News, Dec 2, 2014, https://www.bbc.com/news/technology-30290540
38. The Best Schools, "The 50 Greatest Living Geniuses," https://thebestschools.org/features/50-greatest-living-geniuses/
39. US National Library of Medicine, "An exceptional man," https://www.ncbi.nlm.nih.gov/pmc/articles/PMC1123440/
40. Open AI, "Planning for AGI and beyond," https://openai.com/blog/planning-for-agi-and-beyond#SamAltman
41. IMDb. "To Serve Man," Twilight Zone, 1962, https://www.imdb.com/title/tt0734684/
42. YouTube, "To Serve Man," Twilight Zone, 1962, https://www.youtube.com/watch?v=Zp_EhjlLGkQ
43. Kelly, Meg & Samuels, Elyse, "How Russia weaponized social media, got caught and escaped consequences," Washington Post, Nov 18, 2019, https://www.washingtonpost.com/politics/2019/11/18/how-russia-weaponized-social-media-got-caught-escaped-consequences/
44. Hsu, Tiffany & Myers, Steven Lee, "China's Advancing Efforts to Influence the U.S. Election Raise Alarms," New York Times, April 1, 2024.
45. CNN Staff, "Fact check: Trump makes more than 20 false claims in RNC Acceptance speech," CNN, July 19, 2024, https://www.cnn.com/2024/07/18/politics/fact-checking-night-4-republican-national-convention-trump/index.html
46. Corn, David, "Trump Is Running a Disinformation Campaign, Not a Political Campaign," Mother Jones, Oct 8, 2024, https://www.motherjones.com/politics/2024/10/donald-trump-is-running-a-disinformation-campaign/
47. Price, Michelle L., "Trump's social media account shares a campaign video with a headline about a 'unified Reich." AP, May 21, 2024, https://apnews.com/article/trump-election-2024-rhetoric-germany-antisemitism-31002afb91b642c0314223d19e51f427
48. Graham, David A., "Trump Says He'll Be a Dictator on 'Day One,'" The Atlantic, Dec 6, 2023, https://www.theatlantic.com/ideas/archive/2023/12/trump-says-hell-be-a-dictator-on-day-one/676247/

49. Mark, Joshua J, "Doctrine of Discovery," World History Encyclopedia, Oct 11, 2023, https://www.worldhistory.org/Doctrine_of_Discovery/
50. Cornell Law School, "doctrine of discovery," Legal Information Institute, https://www.law.cornell.edu/wex/doctrine_of_discovery#:~:text=This%20doctrine%20arose%20when%20the,already%20inhabited%20by%20another%20nation.
51. Mejias, Ulises A., & Couldry, Nick, "AI Companies Want to Colonize Our Data. Here's How We Stop Them." Truthout, April 1, 2024, https://truthout.org/articles/ai-companies-want-to-colonize-our-data-heres-how-we-stop-them/#:~:text=The%20Doctrine%20of%20Discovery%20survives,of%20natural%20re-sources%20or%20labor%2C
52. *Ibid.*
53. Association for Computing Machinery, "Fathers of the Deep Learning Revolution Receive ACM A.M. Turing Award," June 15, 2018, https://awards.acm.org/about/2018-turing
54. Geeks for Geeks, "Google Loses 'Father of AI' as Geoffrey Hinton Quits Google over Chatbot Concerns," May 5, 2023, https://www.geeksforgeeks.org/geoffrey-hinton-quits-google-over-chatbot-concerns/#
55. Corfield, Gareth, "Artificial intelligence will do 'real damage,' warns Microsoft chief," The Telegraph, May 3, 2023, https://www.telegraph.co.uk/business/2023/05/03/artificial-intelligence-will-do-real-damage-warns-microsoft/
56. Allyn, Bobby, "'The Godfather of AI warns of AI possibly outperforming humans," NPR WBEZ Chicago, May 27, 2023, https://www.npr.org/2023/05/27/1178575886/-the-godfather-of-ai-warns-of-ai-possibly-outperforming-humans#:~:text=Geoffrey%20Hinton%20is%20known%20as,about%20what's%20driv-ing%20his%20crusade.
57. *Ibid.*
58. Geeks for Geeks, "Google Loses 'Father of AI' as Geoffrey Hinton Quits Google over Chatbot Concerns," May 5, 2023.
59. *Ibid.*
60. Jordan, Fred D; Kutter, Martin: Comby, Jean-Marc; Brozzi, Flora & Kurtys, Ewelina, "Open and remotely accessible Neuroplatform for research in wetware computing," Frontiers Media, May 1, 2024, Technology and Code Article, https://www.frontiersin.org/journals/artificial-intelligence/articles/10.3389/frai.2024.1376042/full
61. Baker, Russ, "AI Industry Growing Human Brains in a Lab: Wetware," WhoWhat-Why, August 5, 2024, https://whowhatwhy.org/culture/ai-industry-growing-human-brains-in-a-lab-wetware/?utm_source=WhoWhatWhy+Now&utm_campaign=0700efce4a-EMAIL_CAMPAIGN_2_1_2021_16_41_COPY_01&utm_medium=email&utm_term=0_6b3f79a618-0700efce4a-251589449
62. Jordan, Fred D; Kutter, Martin: Comby, Jean-Marc; Brozzi, Flora & Kurtys, Ewelina, "Open and remotely accessible Neuroplatform for research in wetware computing," Frontiers Media, May 1, 2024, Technology and Code Article.
63. *Ibid.*

TWO

Unemployment, Bare Minimums, UBI and Basic Fairness

Occupy Movement

As *Spaceship Earth* travelled through the heavens on September 17, 2011, the occupation of Wall Street began. One thousand people descended upon New York's financial district to protest the direction in which our society was going and then stayed, refusing to leave, occupying nearby Zuccotti Park. Soon there were simpatico occupations in every major American city. The occupation of Wall Street's Zuccotti Park lasted 59 days and ended when New York City police forcibly evicted the occupiers shortly after midnight on Nov 15, 2011, for purportedly unsanitary and hazardous conditions.[1] Virtually all of the other occupations across the country were dealt with similarly.

Graphic designer Will Brown's poster of a ballerina posed atop the statue of the Wall Street bull under the question, "What Is Our One Demand?"[2] had helped to bring this multitude to Wall Street. While there were many demands among those that took part in the occupations across the country, many of them centered around the gross inequality in a nation that came into being with the words, "All men are created equal."

Before the Occupy Movement burst on the scene in 2011, there was almost no mention of 'inequality' on the nightly network or cable news shows. After the Occupy Movement, inequality began to be frequently mentioned nightly on most news shows. Although the Occupy Movement did not reach a consensus agreement on one single demand, reducing inequality was certainly considered as a very important issue by most occupiers. But instead of getting a reduction in inequality, we got a television discussion of a reduction in inequality with little or no actual reduction.

Our job as citizens is to turn that discussion into an actual reduction in inequality. Change Our Money – Change Our World is what the monetary reform of publicly creating money can do. It is the vehicle that can take us from our current gross level of inequality to a more equal society. It won't make us all exactly equal, but it will make us more equal. In addition to reducing inequality, publicly created money will give us the ability to properly fund climate action and the other environmental and social crises that confront us.

My own involvement with Occupy Chicago and my relationship with the man who became my mentor in monetary reform, Stephen Zarlenga, Director of the American Monetary Institute and author of *The Lost Science of Money*[3] is covered in Chapter 6 of *Money Creation 101*. Stephen was my guide into channeling my anti-war, social justice, and environmental activism into reforming our money system, which would give us the ability to fund the monumental projects that will make our world more peaceful, equal and livable.

U.S. Treatment of Unemployed & Low-Paid Workers

There could have been a silver lining to the COVID Pandemic, but only if we had used the treatment of our COVID unemployed workforce as a dry run for the millions of us that will be displaced over the next decades by AI.

Those unemployed as a result of the COVID pandemic and recession received a mixed bag of unemployment benefits. For their first twelve weeks, Americans received an extra $600 in weekly unemployment benefits as a result of the CARES Act (Coronavirus Aid, Relief, and Economic Security Act) passed by Congress and signed by President Donald Trump on March 27, 2020. The $600 per week expired on July 31, 2020. Congress passed a bill to extend the $600, but Trump and the Senate both balked, saying it was too expensive. Then Trump came up with the clever political move of signing an Executive Order to pay $300 weekly federal assistance for six weeks, if the states offered an additional $100. Many of the states balked, and Trump then backed down from even requiring their $100 contribution, thus begrudgingly allowing workers to get the $300 per week in federal assistance.

The legality of Trump's governing by fiat is questionable at best since the Constitution has given Congress the power of the purse. But it was a clever ploy on Trump's part. He refused to negotiate an agreement with Congress, and then signed an Executive Order that used fiat pronouncement in place of legislative negotiation, much like dictatorships do. Sticking his tongue out at the Constitution and Democrats alike, saying sue me if you can, while knowing that a lawsuit was not a political option for his Democratic Party opponents who supported the assistance, but also supported a legal, Constitutional path to getting it.

Trump then funded his executive order with money already appropriated for the Federal Emergency Management Agency (FEMA). On August 26, 2020, Hurricane Laura hit the Louisiana/Texas Gulf Coast with estimated 145 mph winds and a 10- to 20-foot storm surge. One half million people had been directed to evacuate and 20 million more were in its path. Without enough money in the FEMA cupboard for both unemployment payments and disaster relief, the states were then told to apply for only three weeks of unemployment payments. Trump had unilaterally approved the use of $44 billion in FEMA disaster money for the federal unemployment payments, after $30 billion was spent individual states began to be cut off.[4]

Hurricane Laura is long gone, as is the even more powerful Category 4 Hurricane Ida that hit the Louisiana Gulf Coast in 2021 on the sixteenth anniversary of Hurricane Katrina hitting the same region in 2005. While hurricanes in the Gulf of Mexico, Caribbean, and Atlantic Oceans are a normal occurrence, climate change has now made them three times more frequent than just a century ago and stronger than just forty years ago. This is evidenced by the percentage of Category 3 and higher hurricanes doubling since 1980.[5] We will more fully cover these natural disasters in Chapter 5.

The U.S. is a society in which our sense of worth is largely measured by what we do for a living. The extra $300/600 per week paid to the unemployed during the pandemic blatantly shows the inadequacy of our current system of state unemployment insurance. The maximum weekly benefit set by my state of Indiana is $390 per week, and the maximum period you can receive it is for 26 weeks,[6] but our lower-wage unemployed may only get $200 a week and our part-timers even less. The average payout for Indiana workers is $280 per week.[7] In Indiana, our highest-paid workers would have received $990 per week for 12 weeks ending in July 2020. But this is only because Congress stepped up to the plate to demand the additional $600 and only for the highest-paid workers. In a humming economy with full employment in which everyone receives a living wage, displaced workers might be able to get by on the current unemployment benefits compensation without the extra $600 per week from Congress. But only if they can quickly find new jobs. Unfortunately, this is far from reality for the unemployed in the U.S.

How do unemployed workers make ends meet when there is not a crisis compelling Congress to act? Martha Ross and Nicole Bateman in the Brookings Institution Nov. 7, 2019 report *Meet the Low-Wage Workforce* disclosed that before the COVID pandemic almost half of the workers in the U.S. were not paid a living wage, with 44% of U.S. workers making less than $15 per hour.[8] 2.2 million working people were paid the $7.25 per hour federal minimum wage, or less, and another 23 million were paid between $7.25 and $11 per hour.[9]

The Bare Minimum Wage Club

The states that belong to the bare minimum wage club of $7.25 per hour, that have not given their workers a raise since July 2009, are Alabama, Georgia, Idaho, Indiana, Iowa, Kansas, Kentucky, Louisiana,

Mississippi, New Hampshire, North Carolina, North Dakota, Oklahoma, Pennsylvania, South Carolina, Tennessee, Texas, Utah, Wisconsin, and Wyoming.[10]

Since 2024, the same 20 states are still at a minimum wage of $7.25. Using the Coin News inflation calculator, we have experienced 21.5% cumulative inflation after coming out of the COVID-19 Pandemic from 2020 to August 2024.[11] Yet, despite a cumulative 21.5% inflation rate over the last 4 years and a cumulative 46.6% inflation rate over the last 15 years, the 20 Bare Minimum Wage States have offered no increase in the minimum wage to their workers in 15 years! Much of this inflation was the result of quantitative easing in which taxpayers bailed out the over-extended big banks by buying their toxic financial assets through the Federal Reserve System, (explained in *Money Creation 101*: Chapter 8, "Financial Shenanigans & the Cultural Hegemony of Debt-Money").

Nationally in 2023, only about 1.1% of workers were paid the federal minimum wage of $7.25 or less,[12] but nearly 40 million workers (23%) are making less than $17 per hour.[13]

The 30 states with a higher minimum wage than the bare minimum club are led by the non-state District of Columbia, which provided a more livable minimum of $15.20/hour in 2021 and increased it to $17.00 in 2023. The District of Columbia adjusts the minimum wage every July 1 based on a set formula, as do Alaska, California, Florida, Michigan, Minnesota, Montana, Nevada, Ohio, Oregon and Washington.[14]

In 2024, the actual top ten minimum wage states are:

- Washington, $16.28
- California, $16.00
- Connecticut, $15.69
- New Jersey, $15.13 (seasonal and small employers less than 6 workers, $13.73)

- Massachusetts, $15.00, Maryland, $15.00, New York, $15.00 (New York City, Long Island and Westchester, $16.00)
- Oregon, $14.20 (Oregon pays $15.45 in Portland Metro Area and $13.20 in non-urban counties)
- Colorado, $14.42
- Arizona, $14.35.[15]

The next tier of minimum wage states:

- Maine, $14.15
- Hawaii, Illinois and Rhode Island, $14.00
- Vermont, $13.67
- Delaware, $13.25
- Florida, $13.00
- Missouri, $12.30
- New Mexico, Virginia, Nebraska, and Nevada, $12.00[16]

The last tier before the sorry Bare Minimum Club:

- Alaska, $11.73
- Arkansas, $11.00
- South Dakota, $11.20
- Minnesota, $10.85
- Ohio, $10,45
- Michigan, $10.33
- Montana, $10.30,
- West Virginia, $8.75.[17]

But even Arkansas ensures its workers a minimum wage of $11.00. Arkansas, with the second lowest cost of living of all the states, behind only Mississippi, manages to pay their workers a minimum wage of $11.00, while 26 other states, all with a higher cost of living, pay a lesser minimum wage.[18]

My guess is that the more comfortable one is in his or her own personal situation, the more likely one is to believe that low-income Americans, adding up to almost half the population, are being paid what they are worth and that there is no need to raise the minimum wage. Here is a pre-pandemic picture of the low-income American workforce compiled by Brookings Institution in 2019.

Meet America's Low Wage Workforce:

- 53 million people
- 44% of all U.S. workers ages 18–64
- More than half, 56%, are age 25–50, in their prime working years
- 43% of the 25–50, in their prime working years, are raising children
- 54% of low-wage workers are women, while women represent only 48% of the workforce
- Black and Hispanic people are disproportionately represented
- $10.22 median hourly wage
- $18,000 median annual earnings
- 14 million people, 26% of low-wage workers, with median earnings of $20,000, are the only earners in their families
- Another 13 million people, 25% of low-wage workers, live in families in which all workers are low-wage workers, with median family earnings of $42,000
- They are particularly concentrated in smaller places in the southern and western parts of the United States, making up larger shares of the labor force in areas with lower employment rates, concentrating in agriculture and hospitality[19]

Martha Ross and Nicole Bateman of Brookings Institution sum it up quite neatly: "Nearly half of all workers earn wages that are not enough, on their own, to promote economic security,"[20] indicating that the bank-created debt-money system only has enough money in the right places to pay slightly more than half of all workers a living wage providing economic security. Meaning that the debt-money system is a colossal failure, at least from the perspective of almost half our people. As of 2024, we do not have an update from Brookings to compare it to, but it seems unlikely the picture has improved. Wages have gone up, but so has the cost of living.

The Economic Policy Institute (EPI) made an analysis of the Raise the Wage Act of 2023 that would gradually raise the federal minimum wage to $17 an hour by 2028. The EPI analysis found that doing so would impact almost 28 million (19% of U.S. workforce), providing a total of $86 billion in annual wages for our lowest paid workers, the average affected worker receiving an additional $3,100 per year.[21] Unfortunately not a single Republican in the Senate supports the Raise the Wage Act of 2023 and it remains just a proposal to make life better for our low wage workforce.[22]

And the Real Unemployment Rate Is?

With the COVID Pandemic raging, the headline unemployment rate broadcast in our corporate news media for July 2020 was 10.2%.[23] But Shadowstats.com shows an unemployment rate during COVID of 30% through July 2020.[24] The unemployment figure reported on TV and in the newspapers is the U-3 rate that the Bureau of Labor Statistics uses. U-3 only counts people without jobs that have actively looked for a job during the preceding four weeks.[25]

The Bureau of Labor Statistics (BLS) does have a broader U-6 rate. This is the one they don't mention on TV. The U-6 rate includes the underemployed or part-time workers and the marginally attached, those who have looked for work in the last year but not the last four weeks.[26] While the U-6 rate is a little more representative of reality, it still leaves out a large number of people.

The ShadowStats.com Alternate Unemployment Rate is the U-6 rate plus the long-term discouraged workers that have not looked for work in the last twelve months that were formerly counted in government statistics but defined out of existence in 1994.[27] We all know people who have been unemployed for more than a year; *ShadowStats* counts them as unemployed. As a person who has been unemployed several times, I understand that once the unemployment benefits stop, most people stop reporting to the unemployment office that they are still looking for work and are much less likely to be counted in the statistics.

Should people be considered unemployed no matter when or why they stopped working? Is it important for us to know if our economy is generating enough jobs for everyone to exist? There are all sorts of reasons that people don't return to work, such as physical or mental health issues, caring for kids, the infirm, and the elderly. Also, drug use, legal issues, and credit problems all show up on background checks and keep people from being hired. Yes, and some of the unemployed are just not geared to working and able to survive by living off of family, friends, and whatever government programs are available. Universal Basic Income (UBI) is one way for society to address this latter group. It is discussed later in the chapter.

In addition to counting part-time workers as fully employed and not counting those who have not actively searched for work either in the last four weeks (U-3) or one year (U-6), there are other issues with the unemployment figures that the Bureau of Labor Statistics (BLS) releases. The BLS uses a monthly survey of 60,000 households to compile its findings. Respected *Economist* and *Forbes* contributor Robert Barone calls the monthly U-3 and U-6 employment data "notoriously volatile" because the number of households surveyed in relation to the total number of households is small. But he holds out his major complaint for the Bureau of Labor Statistics' seasonal adjustment of the data each month. These adjustments are not normally made public until January of the next year.[28]

What this seasonal adjustment means is that January's unemployment rate is recalculated each month throughout the year, or eleven times, February's is ten times, March's is nine times, etc. The public is normally not informed of any of the recalculations until the following January. Throughout the year, people are therefore making economic and business decisions based on the flawed monthly statistics. You might lose your job tomorrow if your employer makes a business staffing decision based on erroneous BLS unemployment figures that will not be corrected until next year.

Update: At some point the Bureau of Labor Statistics (BLS) began a process of revising and publishing the revised monthly unemployment figures for the first two months after the monthly report had been published. Robert Barone's critique of the BLS was written in October, 2012, so it must have been after that date. In August, 2025, I have been unable to find when this practice first began, just as I was when I originally wrote this five-years earlier.

When President Trump did not like the fact that the BLS released a jobs report in August, 2025 that showed large revisions downward to jobs growth in May and June (258,000 less jobs), he claimed the data was "rigged" without providing any evidence to back up his claim and fired Commissioner of the BLS, Dr. Erika McEntarfer.[29]

"President Trump is once again destroying the credibility of our government by firing expert and nonpartisan officials because he does not like the facts that they present… Governments that go down this path find themselves in ugly territory very quickly." Max Stier, CEO of the non-partisan Partnership for Public Service.[30]

Compounding the problem, Trump has nominated partisan economist E.J. Antoni to replace Dr. McEntarver.[31] This is a part of Trump's consistent attacks on science and truth. He began in 2016 by calling anything that was critical of him or his worldview *fake news*. In his second term he has fired scientists for their belief in vaccination and climate change, in spite of the fact that both are universally accepted by the scientific community.

July 2020 Unemployment Rate:

U-3 Rate – 10.2%[32]
U-6 Rate – 16.5%[33]
ShadowStats.com – 30.0%[34]

May 2021 Unemployment Rate:

U-3 Rate – 5.8%[35]
U-6 Rate – 10.2%[36]
ShadowStats.com – 26.0%[37]

July 2023 Unemployment rate:

U-3 Rate – 3.5%[38]
U-6 Rate – 7.1%[39]
ShadowStats.com – 25.0%[40]

July 2024 Unemployment rate:

U-3 Rate – 4.3%[41]
U-6 Rate – 7.8%[42]
Unable to find ShadowStats.com 2024 statistics

These statistics are all we need to know about the number of people out of work that need a job or some form of income. According to Mr. John Williams' Shadow Stats, the real unemployment rate during the COVID Pandemic in May of 2020 was 30% and came down to 26% in May 2021 and to 25% in July 2023.[43] Adding the 44% of our workers who are low paid to the 30% unemployed comes to 74% of the American people struggling in the summer of 2020 during the COVID-19 Pandemic and 70% struggling in May of 2021.

But let's assume that the Shadow Stats statistics are wrong, and that the U-6 rate represents the true unemployment picture. We still have 44% of our workforce as low paid plus the U-6 unemployment rate, which still leaves us with 60.5% in July 2020, 54.2% in May 2021, and 51.1% in July 2023 of our people struggling financially.

The Raise the Wage Act of 2023, with 150 original House co-sponsors and 29 original Senate co-sponsors is going nowhere with a Republican majority in the House of Representatives opposing it.[44] And it only raises the federal minimum wage to $17 by 2028.

Fight for $21 Is the Old Fight for $15

In 2012, two hundred New York City fast food workers walked off the job demanding union rights and a minimum living wage of $15.00/hour.[45] That was eleven years ago, and using the inflation calculator (based upon U.S. consumer price index), $15.00/hour in 2012 translates into $19.97 in 2023.[46] It ticks up another dollar in 2024, can we just round it off and today say, Fight for Twenty-One.

Publicly Creating Money: Bridging the Small Business/Minimum Wage Gap

Raising the minimum wage to $21 per hour generates legitimate concerns from some small business owners that it would put some of them out of business. As a former small business owner and operator, I am sympathetic with their concerns. Publicly created money provides a simple solution. The small business owners that can demonstrate through their financial statements and tax returns an inability to pay $21 per hour, would then pay either the old minimum wage or what new higher wage they can afford. The federal government would then step in, under a system of publicly created money such as *The NEED Act Revisited* and pay the employees the difference between what their employer is paying them and the new $21 per hour. When these small businesses become more successful and improve their financial position, they would then be required to begin paying their employees like everyone else.

Universal Basic Income—UBI

If we as a society cannot guarantee all our people a job at a living wage and a smooth the transition to new employment after a job loss, we should provide a basic income. Universal basic income would also provide dignity and income to those who toil without pay, such as those that care for children, the elderly, ill, and disabled.

Tech entrepreneur and 2020 Democratic presidential candidate

Andrew Yang advocated for what he called The Freedom Dividend. Yang started with the premise that one out of every three American workers will be at risk of losing their job in the next twelve years to the new technologies of robotics and Artificial Intelligence. And this time, new replacement jobs would not be able to outpace loses. He proposed a Freedom Dividend: a universal basic income for all American adults of $1,000 per month, with no strings attached, as a foundation to build a more just, stable society.[47] The Freedom Dividend was to be paid for with a value-added tax on technology companies, many of which now pay little or no income tax.[48]

Yang's Freedom Dividend is along the lines of the Citizens' Dividend proposed in the 2011 NEED Act. The amount discussed for the Citizens' Dividend was a one-time payment of around $12,000, although no dollar amount was included in the NEED Act. While it was a one-time payment, there was talk of considering making it a yearly payment. Let's call it the Citizens' Freedom Dividend and combine the two ideas. Have it cover all U.S. adults over the age of 18 and make it for the equivalent of $250 per week in 2020 when this was originally written. Any system should be automatically adjusted for inflation and doing so puts the Citizens' Freedom Dividend at $300 per week in 2024.

Detractors will say that we can't afford a Citizens' Freedom Dividend UBI and the tech company tax will never generate enough money for the program. Enacting a system of publicly created money, would allow us to make up for any shortfalls that might arise in Yang's proposed tech company tax. That is why it is important to have the publicly created money of *The NEED Act Revisited* available to fund any deficits from a tech tax.

Think of the Citizens' Freedom Dividend as representing a slight leveling of life's playing field, after centuries of inequality-creating, bank-created debt-money. For those who feel they do not need the Citizens' Freedom Dividend, there are many worthy charities and nonprofit organizations they could send their weekly payments to. This way no one falls through the eligibility cracks. Those of us, who are fortunate enough to not need a raise, can use the dividend to expand their own giving to the causes that they hold most dear. And importantly, making it universal to all adult citizens allows those who truly need it the ability to retain a measure of dignity while receiving it.

The Citizens' Freedom Dividend amounts to an income of $7.50 per hour to each citizen, assuming a 40-hour work week. Adding it to the present $7.25 minimum wage leaves minimum income workers just a quarter ($0.25) short of the $15 per hour that low-paid people have been fighting for. To keep it in perspective though, the $14.75 per hour this would give our $7.25 minimum wage workers is still a quarter short to the $15 that the New York fast food workers went on strike for in 2012. Can we walk and chew gum? Quoting former President Obama, "Yes, we can." raise the minimum wage and enact the Citizens' Freedom Dividend.

UBI Citizens' Freedom Dividend

If our federal government continues to refuse raising the embarrassingly low $7.25 minimum wage, we certainly need the twenty bare minimum states to step up to the plate and raise their individual minimum wages. Another option to consider is to enact both the $15 minimum wage and the UBI Citizens' Freedom Dividend, thus paying them $22.50 for their essential work in our economy and bringing them up to an amount that takes into account post-pandemic-inflation. Making our former low-wage workforce members much better able to live the American Dream. Whichever option we choose, automatic increases for inflation should also be built into both the minimum wage and the Citizens' Freedom Dividend.

Another way to look at it is: Why are our lowest paid workers currently working for less money than will provide life's basic necessities for themselves and their families? Could the answer be that they toil for peanuts so that we can have 801 billionaires in America?[49] Maybe just maybe, we need to change this equation. A UBI Citizen's Freedom Dividend under a system of publicly created money allows us to slightly level the playing field for those who need the help the most.

And guess what? The billionaires would still be billionaires. ($1billion = 1,000 x $1million)

Jobs & Infrastructure

While many of us want to ensure that as a society, we are able to assist those who have fallen out of the workforce or are otherwise unable to work, we also want good-paying jobs available to drive engagement in the workforce. Using statistics from the American Society of Civil Engineers, the US Conference of Mayors Water Council, the Association of General Contractors of America, the Federal Highway Administration, and the American Public Transportation Association, the 2011 NEED Act, that would have given us a system of publicly created money, would also have created more than 7.2 million new, full-time, good-paying jobs. This is more than 16,500 jobs for each U.S. Congressional District.[50] Today adding specific programs to target climate change and other environmental concerns should only increase these numbers.

Under the current debt-money system we are left with Democrats and Republicans fighting over spending agendas that really can't be paid for, regardless of which side wins. The level of federal debt is sure to rise whichever side wins. A system of publicly created money allows us to create the money necessary for the needs of the people and planet, all done without raising debt or taxes.

We are all passengers on *Spaceship Earth*. A slight leveling of the field after centuries of inequality should not hurt any of us who are presently more fortunate than our brothers and sisters are. The wealthy will still be wealthy as we travel together on *Spaceship Earth*.

---

1. CNN Wire Staff, "New York court upholds conviction of Occupy protesters," CNN U.S., Nov 16, 2011, https://web.archive.org/web/20140222134938/http://www.cnn.com/2011/11/15/us/new-york-occupy-eviction/index.html?hpt=hp_t1
2. Keats, Jonathan, "How Wall Street Was Occupied: Discover The Art Of Dissent At The Museum Of Design," Forbes, Oct 28, 2019, https://www.forbes.com/sites/jonathonkeats/2019/10/28/design-of-dissent/

3. Zarlenga, Stephen, *The Lost Science of Money*, American Monetary Institute, Valatie, NY, 2002.
4. Stein, Jeff, Rosenberg, Eli, "Trump's $300 unemployment funding is already running out, leaving millions in crisis again," Washington Post, Sept 11, 2020, https://www.washingtonpost.com/us-policy/2020/09/11/lost-wages-unemployment-assistance-expiring/
5. Ocko, Ilissa & Sun, Tianyi, "How Climate Change Makes Hurricanes More Destructive," Environmental Defense Fund, https://www.edf.org/climate/how-climate-change-makes-hurricanes-more-destructive
6. Indiana Department of Workforce Development, "Unemployment Insurance, Claimant Handbook," https://www.in.gov/dwd/files/Claimant_Handbook.pdf
7. Carden, Dan, "Indiana may distribute $300, not $400, in temporary extra assistance for some jobless," Northwest Indiana Times, Aug 19, 2020, https://www.nwitimes.com/news/local/govt-and-politics/indiana-may-distribute-300-not-400-in-temporary-extra-assistance-for-some-jobless/article_09653b72-a17f-5ac1-9ec7-b596ec4c6fbf.html
8. Ross, Martha, & Bateman, Nicole, "Meet the low-wage workforce," Brookings Institution, Nov 7, 2019, https://www.brookings.edu/research/meet-the-low-wage-workforce/
9. Georgetown Center on Poverty and Inequality, "Why We Need to Raise Wages for America's Lowest-Paid Families," http://www.georgetownpoverty.org/wp-content/uploads/2018/04/Bare-Minimum.pdf
10. Labor Law Center, "Minimum Wage Rates by State," https://www.laborlawcenter.com/state-minimum-wage-rates
11. Coin News Inflation Calculator, https://www.usinflationcalculator.com/
12. BLS Reports, "Characteristics of minimum wage workers, 2023," U.S. Bureau of Labor Statistics, https://www.bls.gov/opub/reports/minimum-wage/2023/
13. Malinsky, Gili, "The number of low-wage U.S. workers is dropping—but 23% still make less than $17/hr." CNBC, Make It, Jul 24, 2024, https://www.cnbc.com/2024/07/23/oxfam-report-low-wage-workers-still-make-up-23percent-of-us-workers.html
14. U.S. Department of Labor, State Minimum Wage Laws, updated July 1, 2024, https://www.dol.gov/agencies/whd/minimum-wage/state
15. U.S. Department of Labor, "State Minimum Wage Laws," updated July 1, 2024.
16. *Ibid.*
17. *Ibid.*
18. *Ibid.*
19. Ross, Martha, & Bateman, Nicole, "Meet the low-wage workforce."
20. Picchi, Aimee, "Almost half of all Americans work in low-wage jobs," CBS News, Dec 2, 2019, https://www.cbsnews.com/news/minimum-wage-2019-almost-half-of-all-americans-work-in-low-wage-jobs/
21. Zipperer, Ben, "The impact of the Raise the Wage Act of 2023," Economic Policy Institute, July 25, 2023, https://www.epi.org/publication/rtwa-2023-impact-fact-sheet/
22. Congress.gov, "S.2488 – Raise the Wage Act of 2023," 118th Congress (2023-2024), https://www.congress.gov/bill/118th-congress/senate-bill/2488/cosponsors
23. Bureau of Labor Statistics News Release, "The Employment Situation--July 2020," https://www.bls.gov/news.release/empsit.t15.htm

24. John Williams' Shadow Government Statistics, "Alternate Unemployment Charts," Through July 2020, http://www.shadowstats.com/alternate_data/unemployment-charts
25. Amadeo, Kimberly, "Real Unemployment Rate with Calculations," The Balance, Updated Dec 2, 2022, https://www.thebalancemoney.com/what-is-the-real-unemployment-rate-3306198
26. *Ibid.*
27. John Williams' Shadow Government Statistics, "Alternate Unemployment Charts"
28. Barone, Robert, "Why Jack Welch Has A Point About Unemployment Numbers," Forbes, Oct. 16, 2012, https://www.forbes.com/sites/greatspeculations/2012/10/16/why-jack-welch-has-a-point-about-unemployment-numbers/?sh=6025b2f86554
29. Casselman, Ben & Romm, Tony, "Trump, Claiming Weak Jobs Numbers Were 'Rigged,' Fires Labor Official" New York Times, Aug 1, 2025, https://www.nytimes.com/2025/08/01/business/economy/trump-bls-firing-jobs-report.html
30. Kopack, Steve, Alba, Monica & Strickler, Laura, "Trump fires labor statistics boss hours after the release of weak jobs report," NBC News, Aug 1, 2025, https://www.nbcnews.com/business/economy/trump-orders-firing-bls-commissioner-weak-jobs-report-rcna222531
31. Burns, Tobias, "Trump stuns Wall Street, Washington with controversial BLS nominee," The Hill, Aug 17, 2025, https://thehill.com/business/5453833-trump-ej-antoni-bls-pick/
32. Bureau of Labor Statistics News Release, "The Employment Situation--July 2020," https://www.bls.gov/news.release/empsit.t15.htm
33. U.S. Bureau of Labor Statistics, Table A-15. "Alternative measures of labor underutilization," U-6 Total Unemployed, https://www.bls.gov/news.release/empsit.t15.htm
34. John Williams' Shadow Government Statistics, "Alternate Unemployment Charts," July 2023, 25%, http://www.shadowstats.com/alternate_data/unemployment-charts
35. Bureau of Labor Statistics News Release, "The Unemployment Situation -- May 2021," https://www.bls.gov/news.release/pdf/empsit.pdf
36. Federal Reserve Economic Data, "U-6 Unemployment Rate," May 2021, https://fred.stlouisfed.org/series/U6RATE
37. John Williams' Shadow Government Statistics, "Alternate Unemployment Charts," May 2021, 26.0%.
38. Bureau of Labor Statistics, "News Release: The Employment Situation—2023," U.S. Department of Labor, Aug 4, 2023, chrome-extension://efaidnbmnnnibpcajpcglclefindmkaj/https://www.bls.gov/news.release/pdf/empsit.pdf
39. FRED Economic Data, "Total Unemployed, Plus All Persons Marginally Attached to the Labor Force, Plus Total Employed Part Time for Economic Reasons, as a Percent of the Civilian Labor Force Plus All Persons Marginally Attached to the Labor Force (U-6)," July 2023, Federal Reserve Bank of St. Louis, https://fred.stlouisfed.org/series/U6RATE
40. John Williams' Shadow Government Statistics,
41. Bureau of Labor Statistics, "Table A-15. Alternative measures of labor underutilization," https://www.bls.gov/news.release/empsit.t15.htm
42. *Ibid.*
43. John Williams' Shadow Government Statistics, "Alternate Unemployment Charts," May 2021, 26.0%.

44. Education & the Workforce Committee Democrats, "Labor Leaders Introduce Bill to Raise Minimum Wage," July 7, 2023, https://democrats-edworkforce.house.gov/media/press-releases/labor-leaders-introduce-bill-to-raise-minimum-wage#:~:text=The%20Raise%20the%20Wage%20Act%20of%202023%20has%2029%20original,Van%20Hollen%2C%20Warren%2C%20Welch%2C
45. Fight For $15, https://fightfor15.org/about-us/
46. Coin News Inflation Calculator, https://www.usinflationcalculator.com/
47. Yang, Andrew, "The Freedom Dividend, Defined," Yang2020.com, https://www.yang2020.com/what-is-freedom-dividend-faq/
48. Holmes, Aaron, "From Amazon to GM, here are all the major tech and transportation companies who avoided federal income tax expenses last year," Business Insider, Nov 24, 2019, https://www.businessinsider.com/tech-companies-dont-pay-federal-income-taxes-amazon-gm-2019-11
49. Collins, Chuck, "801 U.S. billionaires hold a combined $6.22 trillion in wealth," Inequality, Sept 17, 2024, https://inequality.org/great-divide/billionaire-wealth-keeps-growing/#:~:text=September%2017%2C%202024&text=There%20are%20now%20801%20billionaires,Forbes%20Real%20Time%20Billionaire%20List.
50. American Monetary Institute, "Fact Sheet -- Infrastructure Jobs Numbers," https://www.monetary.org/wp-content/uploads/2011/10/revised-Fact-Sheet-plus-Job-Numbers-for-NEED1.pdf

THREE

Reclaiming the Ancient Lost Power to Heal Our Planet & Ourselves

At some point as *Spaceship Earth* has been journeying the heavens, money came into being. How it originated becomes very important if we currently are using a money system that claims its legitimacy on a false origin. The so-called bible of capitalism and modern economics makes such a claim.

The Wealth of Nations

In 1776, Adam Smith wrote *The Wealth of Nations,* "that became a foundational study in the history of economics and the first formulation of a comprehensive system of political economy." (Britannica)[1] Investopedia hails, "The publishing of *The Wealth of Nations* marked the birth of modern capitalism as well as modern economics."[2] The publication of Mr. Smith's book is considered such a seminal event in economics that, "The Adam Smith Institute is one of the world's leading think tanks, recognised as the best domestic and international economic policy think-tank in the UK and ranked 1st in the world among Independent Think Tanks by the University of Pennsylvania."[3] Even the Artificial Intelligence AI Overview that now magically appears at the top of Google searches reports that *The Wealth of*

Nations is referred to as the "bible of economics" and the "bible of capitalism."[4]

Yet in spite of its foundational position in modern economics, Mr. Smith's *The Wealth of Nations* was dead wrong on how money came into existence. Smith described butchers, bakers, and brewers in ancient societies bartering their goods with each other and coming to the discovery that if they named something money, such as gold and silver coins. They could all be more productive in their own right if they used money to purchase the exact things they needed, instead of finding another tradesperson who wanted what they made and also had what they needed (double coincidence of wants). Smith depicts money as being an outgrowth of private tradespeople moving from bartering their own goods and services with each other to developing money. Thus, becoming a much more efficient economics community. An entertaining story, but it doesn't match up with the evidence presented by anthropologists that money was originally a creation of the states in the Fertile Crescent.

This early money was in the form of a credit system, regulated by the ancient temple societies in the Fertile Crescent. The credit system made advances of agriculture products such as seeds and grain to farmers, who in turn repaid these loans, plus interest, to the temple at harvest.

Expert Witness: Dr. David Graeber (1961-2020)—American Anthropologist, London School of Economics

Dr. Graeber's *Debt: The First 5,000 Years* was an examination of debt that found no anthropological evidence of any barter societies existing over the 5,000 years the book covers. In *Debt: The First 5,000 Years*, he quotes the definitive anthropological work on barter, by Cambridge anthropologist Caroline Humphrey:

> No example of a barter economy, pure and simple, has ever been described, let alone the emergence from it of money; all

available ethnography[a] suggests that there never has been such a thing.[5]

The *People, Planet & Power of Money Project* vigorously takes issue with the consensus position of the economics profession that money developed from ancient societies using barter, instead agreeing with Drs. Graeber and Humphrey above and Kumhof, Benes and others below, that there is no evidence of ancient societies using barter.[6] Personally, I now take these positions even though I was raised as a conservative Republican and began my economics education and indoctrination into capitalism by reading Mr. Smith's *The Wealth of Nations* in my late teens.

Well, if money didn't originate as an extension of private tradespeople bartering, where did it originate?

Expert Witnesses: Drs. Michael Kumhof & Jaromir Benes

Drs. Kumhof[b] and Benes were at the International Monetary Fund (IMF) when they wrote their 2012 International Monetary Fund Working Paper, *The Chicago Plan Revisited*:

> The monetary historian Alexander Del Mar (1895) writes: "As a rule political economists do not take the trouble to study the history of money; it is much easier to imagine it and to deduce the principles of this imaginary knowledge." Del Mar wrote more than a century ago, but this statement still applies today.

---

a Branch of anthropology that studies individual cultures.

b When this was written in 2012, Dr. Kumhof was the Deputy Chief of Modeling Division of the International Monetary Fund. He is now with the Bank of England. Your author has had the pleasure of meeting Dr. Kumhof on two occasions at American Monetary Institute Annual Conferences and confesses to being completely tongue-tied and intimidated by him, certainly through no fault of his. I was just learning about money from an activist and social justice perspective and did not know what to say to him after hearing him give presentations that mostly went way over my head. But we all have to start our monetary journey somewhere, and every monetary reformer I know is very interested in assisting beginners in their journey.

> An excellent example is the textbook explanation for the origins of money, which holds that money arose in private trading transactions, to overcome the double coincidence of wants problem of barter. As shown by Graeber (2011), on the basis of extensive anthropological and historical evidence that goes back millennia, there is not a shred of evidence to support this story. Barter was virtually nonexistent in primitive and ancient societies, and instead the first commercial transactions took place on the basis of elaborate credit systems whose denomination was typically in agricultural commodities, including cattle, grain by weight, and tools. Furthermore, Graeber (2011), Zarlenga (2002) and the references cited therein provide plenty of evidence that these credit systems, and the much later money systems, had their origins in the needs of the state (Ridgeway (1892)), of religious/temple institutions (Einzig (1966), Laum (1924)) and of social ceremony (Quiggin (1949)), and not in the needs of private trading relationships.

Why is it important that early money systems were created by the state, as Kumhof and Benes report, and not by private individuals using barter, as Adam Smith related? Kumhof and Benes provide us with the answer:

> Any debate on the origins of money is not of merely academic interest, because it leads directly to a debate on the nature of money, which in turn has a critical bearing on arguments as to who should control the issuance of money. Specifically, the private trading story for the origins of money has time and again, starting at least with Adam Smith (1776), been used as an argument for the private issuance and control of money. Until recent times this has mainly taken the form of monetary systems based on precious metals, especially under free coinage of bullion into coins. Even though there can at times be heavy government involvement in such systems, the fact is that in

practice precious metals tended to accumulate privately in the hands of the wealthy, who would then lend them out at interest. Since the thirteenth century this precious-metals-based system has, in Europe, been accompanied, and increasingly supplanted, by the private issuance of bank money, more properly called credit. On the other hand, the historically and anthropologically correct state/institutional story for the origins of money is one of the arguments supporting the government issuance and control of money under the rule of law [publicly created money]. In practice this has mainly taken the form of interest-free issuance of notes or coins, although it could equally take the form of electronic deposits.[7]

Modern Civilization Begins in the Fertile Crescent

Modern civilization began in the Fertile Crescent around 11,000 BC with the birth of agriculture, as humanity began to domesticate both plants and animals. Other areas of early plant and animal domestication also allowed humans to distance themselves from the wild food webs of our hunter-gatherer past in Northern China, Southern China, New Guinea, India, Africa's Sahel Region, South America, Mesoamerica, and eastern North America.[8] But our modern civilization began in the Fertile Crescent, the crescent shaped area that arched across the Middle East from the Nile River valley in the south on Egypt's Sinai Peninsula to the southern edge of Turkey on the north, bounded by the Mediterranean Sea to the west and the Persian gulf to the east. It includes parts of modern-day Egypt, Israel, Palestine, Jordan, Lebanon, Syria, Iraq, along with the southeastern part of Turkey and the western edge of Iran.

Expert Witness: Dr. Fritz Heichelheim

Dr. Heichelheim was a young professor, lecturing on ancient history at Justus Liebig University in Giessen, Germany in 1933. Although a brilliant historian, he was also a Jew and was fired from his university position during the Nazi purge of Jews. His listing survives today on the *Hitler Black Book War Records*.[9] Fortunately for posterity Dr. Heichelheim was able to escape Nazi Germany for England where he lectured at Oxford and University College in Nottingham. He then spent the last twenty years of his life in Canada at the University of Toronto, lecturing on ancient economic history until his death in 1968.

Dr. Heichelheim called the organization of society in the Fertile Crescent the "Ancient Oriental System," with the:

> concept of a living King as the divine representative and savior of the whole human race, who had the power to organize the welfare of the whole world.[10]

This confused me when I first read about it, because I identified Oriental as referring to China and its neighboring countries. But what Dr. Heichelheim was referring to was the Fertile Crescent area of the Middle East and the kings and pharaohs who ruled in the ancient world. Think of them as a kinder, gentler version of Adolf Hitler who had taken over Dr. Heichelheim's 1930s Germany, or of Donald Trump, who is doing his best to imitate der Führer in America today.

Kumhof and Benes informed us that as the societies grew over the millennia, they developed into temple societies with elaborate credit systems of money, represented in agricultural commodities, livestock, and in some societies, tools.[11] These temple societies discovered that this accounting system of money was a power of the state that allowed them to better organize and grow their societies.

Dr. Heichelheim suspected that early lending may have begun around 5000 BC:

> Dates, olives, figs, nuts, or seeds of grain were probably lent out… to serfs, poorer farmers, and dependents to be sown and planted, and naturally an increased portion of the harvest had to be returned in kind… [Also] animals could be borrowed too for a fixed time limit, the loan being repaid according to a fixed percentage from the young animals born subsequently… So

> here we have the first forms of money, that man could use as a capital for investment, in the narrower sense.[12]

Dr. Heichelheim informed us that this changed in Babylonia in the 18th Century BC:

> The main ancient oriental innovation in this field was that inorganic materials were treated as if they were living organisms with the means of production.[13]

He was describing the introduction of gold and silver as a metal by weight form of money as a commodity that was not alive and could not reproduce. And charging interest on loans that were made in barren metal that could not beget more metal presented a problem. Since the money owed was the amount borrowed (principal) plus the interest charged and the supply of money available was only the total amount of principal, it soon became impossible to repay both the principal and interest of the loans without increasing the amount of gold and silver and thus the supply of metal.

Dr. Charles Goodhart Introduces Our Next Expert Witness

To introduce our next expert witness, we begin with an assessment from Dr. Charles Goodhart. Dr. Goodhart is Emeritus Professor of Banking and Finance with the Financial Markets Group at the London School of Economics, former Chief Adviser to the Bank of England and former outside independent member of the Bank of England's Monetary Policy Committee. Dr. Goodhart on Dr. Michael Hudson:

> Michael Hudson is the foremost expert on the financial and monetary systems of the antiquarian Western/Near Eastern World, from Mesopotamia to the Fall of the Roman Empire.[14]

I had the privilege to shake hands with Dr. Hudson when he made a presentation to an American Monetary Institute Annual Conference on

Monetary Reform in 2012 or thereabouts. I was early in my monetary education, and Dr. Hudson's talk focused on the danger of financial derivatives, which certainly got my attention, since I had become quite concerned that financial derivatives, largely ignored in mainstream news, could crash our entire financial system. This topic is discussed in Chapter 7 of *Money Creation 101*, "Financial Shenanigans & the Cultural Hegemony of Debt-Money."

Dr. Hudson made a recent appearance at the American Monetary Institute's 19th Annual Conference on Monetary Reform in September, 2024. He had a new book that was just in the process of being released to the public, *Temples of Enterprise: Creating Economic Order in the Bronze Age Near East.* I bought it and put off reading it until I had finished *Spaceship Earth 101* and sent it to my copy editor. Big mistake, I should have read Dr. Hudson's book first. Not only does *Temples of Enterprise* clear up some of the misconceptions about the Fertile Crescent societies, it brings this understanding forward to focus on how we reached the gross level of inequality we have in the 21st Century. This has sent me back to the drawing (writing) board to incorporate Dr. Hudson's expertise into *Spaceship Earth 101.*

Expert Witness: Dr. Michael Hudson

> Money, interest-bearing debt, land tenure and rent originated in the temples and palaces of Mesopotamia and Egypt in the third millennium BC [3000-2000 BC]. Recognition of how these large institutions created the basic elements of market exchange and economic enterprise dispels the myth of individuals inventing money and markets simply by bartering and lending with each other without government playing any positive role.
>
> Even more antithetical to mainstream financial mythology is the fact that the archaic structuring of credit was accompanied by royal "restorations of order" [debt foregiveness] that freed realms from an overgrowth of debt. The success of these acts seems anomalous to economic historians who oppose

> public regulation ("interference in free markets") and focus only on the helpful and productive role of credit [today's bank-created debt-money system]. Today's ideological claim that pro-creditor laws are natural and should be universal avoids acknowledging how Bronze Age [3500-1200 BC] rulers saved their realms from widespread impoverishment by rolling back debts, and how subsequent economies from classical antiquity to today have failed to protect their increasingly indebted populations.
>
> The Western historical continuum is depicted as originating only in classical Greece and Rome, "free" of royal Clean Slates [debt forgiveness]. Despite five centuries of Greek and Roman revolts advocating debt cancellations and land redistribution, their oligarchies amassed wealth by driving debtors into debt bondage, monopolizing the land and using their economic power to avoid paying taxes, bringing on economic polarization, austerity and a fiscal crisis. That is the fate that Bronze Age rulers managed to avert. But their success in protecting the resilience of debtors (that is, most of the population) instead of creditor claims clashes with modern preconceptions...[15]

Let's breakdown the systems Dr. Hudson is beginning to describe.

Antiquity's Western Historical Continuum vs.	Fertile Crescent Reality
Barter led to money	Money created as credit advances to farmers
Bank-created debt-money system	Credit system of grain/silver
Debt forgiveness is interference in free market	Debt forgiveness keeps status quo in society
Greece/Rome ignore debt forgiveness	Fertile Crescent regular Clean Slate debt forgiveness
Modern day debt slavery	Fertile Crescent prosperity for millennia

Beginning in the 3rd millennium BC, agricultural settlements began to take form and organize into temple societies of the Fertile Crescent, which was blessed by rich, alluvial soil formed by nutrient-laden deposits of sediments carried by their rivers. They organized under the "concept of a living King as the divine representative and savior of the whole human race, who had the power to organize the welfare of the whole world." What Dr. Heichelheim had labeled the Ancient Oriental

System.[16] Labor was at a premium and there was an understanding that the laborers and their families had to be able to have decent lives in order for society as a whole to thrive and prosper.

The laborers were given land tenure on plots of ground that they farmed. They were loaned grain for planting which they repaid at harvest along with a payment to the palace or temple for the use of the land. Hudson also informs us that the laborers also ran up tabs at the local alehouses, which again was repaid at harvest. This credit system of money was based on grain and agricultural products and was only possible because they had developed a system of weights and measures, which in turn was only possible because they had also developed the thirty-day calendar.

Although the soil was great for agriculture, it was lacking in metals, stone and hardwood, necessitating the need for trade with neighboring states outside the Fertile Crescent. As such, the temples took in orphans and war widows who were unable to survive on their own. They gave them jobs in the temple making garments and handicrafts that then could be traded with their neighboring states, enabling their society to get the needed metals and hardwood. This trade with outsiders was largely conducted in silver, hence the need for silver money, the shekel. But the silver shekel was originally a certain weight of silver and it was only much later that shekel coins were developed.

Thus, a bi-monetary system was used with 1 silver shekel (8 grams) equaling to 1 gur (80 gallons) of grain. Both grain and silver could be used throughout the economy for settling fees, taxes, rents and other official debt balances.[17] Although the bi-monetary system was used, it is doubtful if the farmer/laborers ever used anything but the credit system of grains through the temples.

The king or pharaoh gave each laborer land to farm on a system of tenure, in return he was expected to give the ruler a portion of her crops, military service as needed and his labor as needed to build temples and pyramids. This kind of arrangement is referred to as corvée labor and was an integral part of the Ancient Oriental System. Natural disasters, such as floods and droughts, occur and can cause a poor harvest or no harvest at all. The farm laborers who had been existing on credit from the temple throughout the year would have been subject to expulsion from their land if a natural disaster or other calamity caused them to lose their crop and they were unable to pay their debt.

Clean Slate Debt Jubilees

The kings and pharaohs had enough sense to understand that this would have been unsustainable. Their laborers, indebted and unable to pay would have simply left for another temple society. There would have been no food for the palaces, no soldiers for the military and no workers to build the temples. As such, the rulers deduced that Clean Slate debt forgiveness was necessary to keep the society functioning, to keep the ancient oriental power system intact—the king at the top of the heap and the laborers growing the food, serving in the military, building the temples and being able to drink a beer or two in the alehouses after work. There was no effort to make the lives of the workers better or worse. Clean slates were given throughout much of the Bronze Age, successfully maintaining the status quo of power. They were given whenever a new king or pharaoh took office and as otherwise needed.

A very important facet of the regular Clean Slate debt jubilees granted by the likes of King Hammurabi in Babylonia and others was that the debts were only forgiven on the grain side of the monetary system. Debts in silver, largely used by traders, were not forgiven. The credit monetary system of grain and agricultural products, along with the metal silver system for trade was created as a way to organize society. The same can be said for the 30-day per month calendar and the system of weights and measures created in the Fertile Crescent, all done to organize society.

Yet today in the 21st Century AD, we remained saddled with a bank-created debt-money system that creates an ever-expanding level of inequality between the wealthy millionaires and billionaires and the rest of society: A system of money with no regular Clean Slate debt jubilees that were regular fare in the ancient Bronze Age Fertile

Crescent. Instead, we are left with a Federal Reserve System that jacks up interest rates during times of inflation. Thus, inflicting a double whammy on the poor and working class, who are forced to pay both higher prices and to borrow at higher interest rates to simply survive. While this is going on for most of us, the billionaires rake in more loot. But the Federal Reserve System was not put in place to provide Clean Slate debt forgiveness to huge swaths of people in debt slavery, just as it was not put in place to ensure that we have a system of money that can provide for the needs of society — publicly created money. The Federal Reserve System was created to oversee and back-up the bank-created debt-money system.

Classical Antiquity: Greece & Rome

What we now refer to as classical antiquity began in Greece and Rome in roughly 750 BC. Dr. Hudson informs us that the major difference between these societies and those of the Fertile Crescent was that Greece and Rome failed to organize society around the concept that only a society that worked for everybody would be sustainable for the long haul. While classical antiquity in Greece and Rome did implement many of the commercial practices from the Fertile Crescent societies that preceded them, the wealthy Greeks and Romans delegated the responsibility of wealth to underlings and neglected to implement regular Clean Slate debt jubilees:

> It is now recognized that most of the techniques that would become basic commercial practices in classical antiquity were developed already in the third millennium BC in the temples and palaces of the Bronze Age Near East — money, along with the uniform weights, measures and prices needed for account-keeping and annual reports, the charging of interest, and profit-sharing arrangements between palaces, temples and private merchants, ranging from long-distance trade to leasing land, workshops, and retail beer-selling concessions. Assyriologists now apply the term *entrepreneur* broadly to Assyrian and

Babylonian *tamkarum* "merchants" from early in the second millennium BC down to the Egibi and Murashu families of Babylonia in the 7th through 5th centuries BC, who created sophisticated commercial strategies to manage estates and provision the palace and its armed forces.

These practices initially were developed to produce an export surplus of textiles, metalwork, and other labor-intensive handicrafts to obtain the stone, metal, and other raw materials lacking in southern Mesopotamia (what is now Iraq). During the second millennium these commercial techniques diffused westward via Ugarit[c] and Crete to Mycenaen Greece. After the long Dark Age,[d] seafaring merchants brought these commercial systems to Greece and Italy, where they were adopted circa 750 BC in a context with fewer institutional checks and balances on debt, dependency and economic polarization. Clientage[e] came to be viewed as a natural state of affairs economic as attitudes changed from those in the Near East.

Wealthy Greek and Roman families controlled handicraft production, trade, and credit directly rather than coordinating these activities for temples and palaces. Yet classical antiquity's aristocratic attitude viewed commercial enterprise as demeaning and corrupting. The details of trade, enterprise, and money lending typically were left to outsiders or to slaves and other subordinates acting as on-the-spot managers, organizers, and middlemen for their aristocratic backers. Most enterprising

---

[c] Ugarit is an ancient port city in northern Syria.

[d] Greek Dark Age (c. 1200 to 800 BC), Mycenaean Civilization fell and their writing system was lost.

[e] Clientage refers to the relationship between a patron and his client. While it did not have to involve property, it usually did. Similar to the feudal system of serfs and the lords of the manor. The patron ruled and provided some protection and land to live on and farm. The client or serf shared his crops with his patron and was also required to provide military service for his patron. The big difference between this relationship and that in the Fertile Crescent, is that in the Fertile Crescent the obligation was to the temple, and in the Clientage system the obligation was to an individual. Hudson indicates that the temples treated their laborers better than the Greek and Roman patrons did, including through the regular debt jubilees.

individuals were drawn from the bottom ranks of the social scale, typified by the fictional but paradigmatic freedman Trimalchio in Petronius's comedy dating from the time of Augustus [31 BC-14 AD]. "The greater a man's *dignitas*, the more likely that his involvement (in business) was indirect and discreet, camouflaged behind that of an undistinguished freedman, – client, partner, 'front man,' or 'friend,'" and leaving management of his affairs to slaves or other subordinates. When such lower-status individuals were able to accumulate fortunes of their own, they aspired to high status and prestige by sinking their money into land and obtaining public office.[18]

Greece and Rome Develop Publicly Created Metal Money

Greece and Rome both created systems of publicly created money in the 8th century BC, Beginning with King Lycurgus of Laconia (Sparta) and followed by King Numa of Rome.

Lycurgus used iron bars that derived their name, Pelanors, from the small cakes they resembled. The Pelanors were dipped in vinegar while red-hot and thus deprived of their value as iron because they could no longer be reworked into another iron implement.[19] In Rome, Numa used bronze, which was primarily copper, which was plentiful, mixed with a little tin and a smidgen of lead. When Numa became king in 716 BC, crude lumps of bronze (*Aes rude*) were already being used in trade by weight. The Aes rude bronze lumps evolved into thin strips of bronze, cut by weight to exact amounts. The Roman Aes (also called asses or aces) referred to the Roman pound of 12 ounces. They progressed from lumps, to cut strips, to stamped, cut strips. Only much later were bronze coins made.[20]

In contrast to money systems in which the money derives its value from its worth as a commodity, such as gold and silver; the early Greek and Roman systems derived their value from the power of the state to create a medium of exchange. The term fiat money has been used as a pejorative, yet the term fiat simply means that money is a legal creation of a nation-state's Rule of Law. The Greek philosopher Aristotle provides us with the best definition of money:

> All goods must therefore be measured by some one thing… now this unit is in truth, demand, which holds all things together… but money has become by convention a sort of representative of demand; and this is why it has the name *nomisma* — because it exists not by nature [as gold or silver], but by law [nomos]...[21]

"Lycurgus transformed the Spartan state to one of simplicity and equality for Spartans. By law, Spartan citizens were not allowed to take part in any profession except that of warrior; someone else had to perform all the mundane tasks necessary for society to function. The class of people that did the work in the towns was the *perioikoi.* Further out in the rural areas were the *helots*, slaves or serfs bound to the land. The reforms of Lycurgus had given the Spartans an early proto-socialist lifestyle. However, this lifestyle existed for them only because there were two classes of servants or slaves to do their work for them. Therefore, any successes they may have achieved toward equality and socialism must be filtered through the lens of their dependence upon the involuntary labor of others. Before we chide Sparta too harshly for this shortcoming, it must also be considered that at least some level of slavery and serfdom was common at the time within all the advanced societies of the Mediterranean basin."[22]

The paragraph above is from *History of Money 101*, published in 2023. Today I would temper the last sentence a bit after reading Dr. Hudson's *Temples of Enterprise*: Adding that the system of corvée labor used in the Fertile Crescent was not slavery, at least in the way we would compare it to pre-Civil War slavery in America.

Rome's exclusive use of fiat, publicly created, bronze money ran from King Numa in 716 BC through when the last Roman king was overthrown in 509 BC. It continued as the Roman Republic flourished as a "representative democracy"[23] until about 212 BC during the Punic Wars when silver also began to be used as money within Rome. Rome had begun to reward their conquering generals with silver as war booty. Compounding this mistake, Rome then allowed their generals to take their silver war booty to the mint and mint the silver into coins at a 500% markup to their stamped value.[24 25]

The profit from the creation of money is called "seigniorage." Only the state should be able to profit from the creation of money. Roman generals should have been paid by the state and if necessary, given a bonus by the state. But to give the generals silver war booty and then let them create the currency of the realm from this at a 500% markup was a recipe for disaster that contributed to the fall of the Roman Republic and the beginning of the Roman Empire under Augustus in 27 BC.

Rome successfully used a publicly created money system for five centuries, from 716 BC until 212 BC. Sparta had successfully used a publicly created money system for about three centuries, from some time before 700 BC until around 415 BC when they regressed into using silver and gold money to pay their armies outside of Sparta.[26] What Dr. Hudson has presented in *Temples of Enterprise* is that even using (what I refer to as) publicly created money in Greece and Rome was not enough for successful, sustainable society, because of the absence of both an overall spirit that society should leave no one behind and the Clean Slate debt forgiveness that helped to make it possible. One notable exception was King Solon in Athens who came to power in the early 6th Century BC by proposing a partial debt forgiveness called *seisachtheia* (shaking off of burdens).[27] Unfortunately, Solon's *seisachtheia* was only a one-time event; the failure to construct societies that enabled all to be successful in ancient Greece and Rome is their unfortunate legacy to us today.

Expert Witness: Adam Smith

The Wealth of Nations

While Mr. Smith got barter as the precursor to money dead wrong, he did quite surprising to me, get something very important, right:

> ...If, on the contrary, instead of sheep or oxen, he had metals to give in exchange for it, he could easily proportion the quantity of the metal to the precise quantity of the commodity which he had immediate occasion for.
>
> Different metals have been made use of by different nations for this purpose. Iron was the common instrument of commerce among the ancient Spartans, copper among the ancient Romans, and gold and silver among all rich and commercial nations.
>
> These metals seem originally to have been made use of for this purpose in rude bars, without any stamp or coinage. Thus we are told by Pliny upon the authority of Timaeus, an ancient historian, that, till the time of Servius Tullius, the Romans had no coined money, but made use of unstamped bars of copper, to purchase whatever they had occasion for. These rude bars, therefore, performed at this time the function of money.[28]

Here Mr. Smith acknowledges the early forms of publicly created money in ancient Sparta and Rome. Sparta used iron that had no value as a commodity, because it was dipped in vinegar after it was cast, thus depriving the *pelanors* the ability to be melted down and recast for another use. Rome used bronze bars which were essentially copper with a smidgen of lead that also had little commodity value. The early bars bore no markings, but as the system progressed, markings were added. This is all covered in detail in *History of Money 101*. Because I just stumbled across this recently rereading *The Wealth of Nations*, I had failed to mention in *History of Money 101* that Adam Smith chronicled these early uses of publicly created money in Sparta and Rome that have been widely ignored by history and today's economics community.

Processing Climate Change through the Lens of the Cold War

Who wants to think about the disastrous results of climate change? I certainly don't and I assume you probably don't either. Yet, it looms on the horizon, and it isn't going away. Even if we immediately take drastic action, we can never go back to the days before we began pumping massive amounts of carbon and other greenhouse gasses into our atmosphere, the hull of *Spaceship Earth.*

Nuclear war is something that is looming out there too. We used to have duck and cover drills in which our precious school children would practice climbing under their desks to protect themselves from a nuclear war. I believe the drills stopped when we realized that the desk would offer no protection from the nuclear cloud that would blanket *Spaceship Earth* should such a disaster occur. Climate change is a reality, the only variable is how much we can limit the effects. Nuclear war is not a certainty, until it happens. This story is an attempt to consider them both.

Spaceship Earth is us, our planet and all the life forms on it. The forecast for *Spaceship Earth*, as a result of human-caused climate change, is so bleak that the natural reaction is to push all thoughts of our fate out of our minds. To give us a way to look at what climate change unchecked could possibly do, let's take a look at a somewhat comparable catastrophe that was averted thirty-nine years ago. This narrowly avoided catastrophe was kept secret for years, and even when it was revealed it was so terrifying that the power structures within our society thought it best to just quietly ignore it. The hero, instead of being given a parade and medal, was given a reprimand and fired.

On September 1st, 1983, at the height of the Cold War, the Union of Soviet Socialist Republics (Soviet Union) shot down a Korean Airliner that had inadvertently drifted into their airspace. All 269 people on board died, including a U.S. Congress member, Dr. Larry McDonald of Georgia. This naturally led to a sudden escalation of tensions between the two nuclear-armed superpowers.[29]

Expert Witness and Hero: Lieutenant Colonel Stanislav Petrov

A little more than three weeks later, Lieutenant Colonel Stanislav Petrov was the officer on duty in charge of the Soviet Union's Air Defense Forces at a Soviet early warning site near Moscow. It was in the early morning hours of September 26, 1983, when the siren howled, and the computer system reported that the U.S. had launched a nuclear-armed intercontinental ballistic missile. Then, the siren howled again, and the computer reported the U.S. had launched a second missile, then a third, a fourth, and a fifth.

Lieutenant Colonel Petrov related, "The siren howled, but I just sat there for a few seconds, staring at the big, back-lit, red screen with the word 'launch' on it."[30] Listening to the siren and looking at the computer screen with the word "launch" flashing back at him, Colonel Petrov knew that it was his duty to immediately warn his military and civilian superiors. If they followed procedure, it would be their duty to immediately move up the line to superiors until a Soviet counterattack was launched. But Colonel Petrov was suspicious that just maybe, the newly installed computer system might be prone to mistakes. He was also concerned because ground radar had not picked up the attack yet. He also wondered why the U.S. would only launch five missiles and not more. Today the current U.S. capability includes 400 on-alert, land-based Minutemen missiles, along with unknown numbers of sea- and air-based nuclear missiles.[31] In 1983 we had a stockpile of 23,000 nuclear warheads[32] and in all probability had at least a comparable number ready to fire at a moment's notice, as the 400 plus we have today.

Colonel Petrov made the decision to do nothing. He said he felt there was a 50/50 chance he was right, so he told no one except his superiors; not even telling his wife about the incident until ten years later. He said:

> "There was no rule about how long we were allowed to think before we reported a strike. But we knew that every second of procrastination took away valuable time; that the Soviet Union's military and political leadership needed to be informed without delay. All I had to do was to reach for the phone; to raise the direct line to our top commanders—but I couldn't move. I felt like I was sitting on a hot frying pan."[33]

Colonel Petrov was right not to act. The alarm, that he never sounded and could very well have resulted in nuclear Armageddon, was just a glitch in the Soviet air defense system. However, instead of receiving a medal and becoming a national hero for averting nuclear war, Colonel Petrov was mildly reprimanded for incorrectly filling out his duty log and soon after he suffered a nervous breakdown.[34]

This story is included because it was kept completely silent until after the breakup of the Soviet Union a decade later and because nuclear annihilation represents a somewhat similar level of threat to Earth and humanity as climate change does today. Ironically, as a result of Colonel Petrov's courage to do nothing in response to the threat he thought we faced forty years ago that avoided a nuclear war, we now have the opportunity to do something in response to the threat that climate change presents to us today. *Spaceship Earth* and its passengers are all deeply indebted to Colonel Petrov. A debt we can best repay by beginning to treat our natural world like the protector of all life on our planet that it is.

The Ancient Lost Power for the Needs of Today

A question I am often asked is, "How can publicly created money lessen the effects of climate change and the economic fallout from huge disruptions like the COVID pandemic?" Some form of the NEED Act would put the Money Power—the power to create money with the people through our elected government, to fund what we perceive as the needs of the nation. This gives us the ability to create money in the amounts needed and then direct this money to programs that will heal our planet and ourselves.

This *NEED Act Revisited* will give us the power to create and spend new U.S. Money into existence, debt-free, for the programs that we collectively think will best stop the release of carbon into the atmosphere and nitrogen into oceans. It gives us the power to say let's take another look at plastic. Plastic has many uses, but it should only be made in a manner in which it can be reused and eventually recycled. This starts with the types of plastic we make. Do we really need to use plastic that cannot be broken down without creating all types of dangerous toxins? We should then consider the design of plastic goods. Are they designed to be easily recyclable? Or are they and our recycling systems incompatible, forcing us to throw most of it into the garbage? Are our recycling systems up to the task of managing our plastic waste in the first place? The next chapter takes a closer look at these questions.

In addition to rebuilding our environmental infrastructure in a manner that is sustainable for *Spaceship Earth*, publicly created money can be used to improve our human infrastructure. We can create money to introduce a true all-inclusive national health care program, public university education, a full-employment economy, and a form of universal basic income to ensure that no one in our society falls through the cracks. We can do all these things without borrowing or increasing taxes. We can do these things because we will have the Money Power that allows our government to create money without borrowing it from banks or foreign countries. Because publicly created money is not destroyed after its first use, as the present debt-based money is (Chapter 6 provides a more fulsome explanation of how our money is created, as does *History of Money 101*). Some of the publicly created money will remain in the economy, strengthening it. While some of the money will remain with those workers who do the essential work of society, allowing them to begin to develop financial security. And some of that money will flow back to the government through taxes, to again be spent on programs benefiting the people and planet.

Climate Change

Climate change represents an existential crisis. When assessing this ongoing catastrophe, our brains tend to hit a default button that switches the subject to something that we have more individual control over. This is a normal human reaction. However, experts say that there are ways for us to stop what we are currently doing and begin to draw down the level of carbon and other gases that cause climate change.

The March 2021 Yale University survey, *Climate Change in the*

American Mind, reported on American attitudes about climate change. The survey found that 70% of Americans understand that global warming exists, while only 15% do not believe it is happening. 57% think global warming is caused by humans, while only 30% think it is caused by natural changes in the environment. 65% of Americans feel a personal sense of responsibility to help reduce global warming. Americans are also quite worried about environmental hazards in their own local areas: 73% are worried about water pollution, 72% about air pollution, 68% about extreme heat, 65% about agricultural pests and diseases, 61% about droughts, 56% about water shortages, 56% about flooding, and 53% about tornadoes.[35] All of these concerns are made worse by climate change.

In 2024, four years later, a Yale University survey reported that 62% of registered voters would prefer to vote for a candidate who supports action on global warming, 15% would vote for a candidate who opposes action, and 23% believe that it doesn't matter either way. Among all registered voters, 62% support action on global warming, 23% believe it doesn't matter either way, and 15% support candidates who oppose action on global warming.[36] And then on Nov. 5, 2024, Americans voted climate change denier, Donald Trump into office as the President.[37]

This contradiction may indicate that even though most Americans understand that climate change is real, the lure of putting the responsibility with an authoritarian strongman like Donald Trump was preferable to a deciding number of voters, than was actually solving the seemingly unsolvable environmental issues that confront *Spaceship Earth*. Battling climate change will require huge monetary expenditures on two fronts. The first is to initiate a host of programs to reduce carbon and other greenhouse gas emissions to zero and to expand natural carbon sinks in the environment, thus, bringing us to negative net greenhouse contributions; that point where we begin to *reduce* levels of carbon and harmful greenhouse gases in the atmosphere – this is the work of Project Drawdown, discussed further below.

The second front is to help those whose homes and livelihood have been destroyed or damaged by natural disasters such as floods, wildfires, hurricanes, and tornadoes that have become more frequent and severe, including the massive relocation of millions of people whose homes are now repeated targets for these climate-induced disasters.

The NEED Act Revisited, as explained in the Preface is an aspirational rewrite of the 2011 NEED Act, which was legislation put into Congress, which would have given us a system of publicly created money. It can be designed to provide debt-free public money to fund these two fronts of climate action and climate disaster remediation. The debt-money system is structurally incapable of doing so without putting both our government and people in ever greater debt bondage to the banking system. Presently, there is scant political will to deal with the two fronts of disaster remediation and greenhouse gas drawdown by borrowing and increasing debt. In 2024, climate change is the primary existential threat confronting us. But there are significant other environmental crises that also demand our attention, such as dying oceans, species and ecosystems. The one thing we can be sure of in the future is that as we struggle to deal with these crises, new ones will appear, and we will also need publicly created money to deal with them.

The scientific community is almost unanimous in its understanding that the Earth's temperatures are rising due to the human population. NASA Global Climate Change reports:

> Multiple studies published in peer-reviewed scientific journals show that 97 percent or more of actively publishing climate scientists agree: Climate-warming trends over the past century are extremely likely due to human activities. In addition, most of the leading scientific organizations worldwide have issued public statements endorsing this position.[38]

The Intergovernmental Panel on Climate Change has told us that the net damage costs of climate change will be significant and will only increase over time if we kick the can down the road.[39] The time to act is now and the best way to start is by passing a form of *The NEED*

Act Revisited that gives us the power to create the money we will need for the crisis.

NASA Global Climate Change predicts the future effects of climate change will continue through this century and beyond. Temperatures will continue to rise, with frost-free and growing seasons lengthening. There will be changes in precipitation patterns, with more droughts and heat waves. Hurricanes will become stronger and more intense and sea levels will rise 1–8 feet by 2100, with the Arctic likely becoming ice free.[40]

Climate change deniers in power have to be willfully ignorant when 97% of publishing climate scientists agree that human activity is warming the planet, and many hold on to this ignorance for political reasons. But our ignorance of money creation is not willful and unfortunately is held by both political parties. It is the result of a misinformation and disinformation campaign that has gone on for more than a century. As we demonstrated in Book One: *Money Creation 101*, this misinformation and disinformation campaign has succeeded in confusing economists at both the Federal Reserve and on the university level.

The Local Weather Effects of Climate Change in the U.S.

According to the U.S. Global Change Research Program:

In the Northeast, heat waves and heavy downpours combined with rising sea levels will pose growing challenges to multiple aspects of life. Many of the states and cities are already incorporating climate change into their planning.

In the Northwest, expect disruptions in water supplies, increasing wildfires, insect outbreaks, tree disease and widespread die-offs. Rising sea levels, erosion, and inundation will all cause risks to infrastructure, and increasing ocean acidification poses a major threat to fisheries.

In the Southeast, rising sea levels will pose wide-ranging and unremitting threats to the region's environment and economy. Extreme heat will impact all aspects of life, including health, energy, and agriculture. Decreased availability of fresh water will have a negative impact on both the economy and environment.

In the Midwest, we can anticipate that our infrastructure, health, agriculture, forestry, transportation, air quality, and water quality will all be influenced by the extreme heat, heavy downpours, and flooding from climate change. The nation's greatest source of fresh water, the Great Lakes, will also be impacted.

In the Southwest, climate change will continue to cause increased heat, expanding droughts, and insect outbreaks. These in turn will continue to increase the number and intensity of wildfires. Expect reduced water supplies, declining crop yields, health impacts in cities due to heat, flooding and accelerating erosion in coastal areas.[41] [42]

Viewing Climate Change through Antonio Gramsci's Theory of Cultural Hegemony

Here we will focus on solving the climate change crisis and not merely reciting the litany of horrors awaiting us. This is a somewhat similar to the approach we have taken with money: we don't just complain about how dysfunctional the bank-created debt-money system is by putting and keeping us in debt, we provide an alternative system of publicly created money. This requires us to step outside the box of a blind adherence to our present money system and consider an alternative system with an open mind. In *Money Creation 101*: Chapter 8, we discussed Antonio Gramsci's theory of cultural hegemony.

Mr. Gramsci's theory of cultural hegemony is that the free-market capitalist state eventually rules by the automatic consent of the governed through the institutions of society. What this means is that after being immersed in our free-market capitalist system over the years, our social, educational, political, economic institutions begin to accept the free-market capitalist system we have without question. Our free-market capitalist system is the automatic default system. When a crisis arrives (such as the 1929 stock market crash and the ensuing Great Depression or the 2008 Global Financial Crisis/Great Recession), how did our society respond? Did we have a national debate about the merits of free-market capitalism? Did we have a national debate about switching from a system of bank-created debt-money to a system of publicly created money? No, instead of a public debate about whether or not we should change or modify our monetary system, we automatically responded by propping up (bailing-out) the failing banks and financial institutions that caused the crises to begin with.

Hegemony means domination, ultimate domination. Merriam-Webster Online Dictionary uses all caps to define hegemony—DOMINATION.[43] Cultural hegemony is the absolute DOMINATION of an economic or money system over a society, so much so that even when these systems gravely fail society, they are automatically rescued without debate or question. Now that climate change literally threatens the future of humanity on Earth, we are told that we do not have enough money to respond to the challenge of immediately beginning to transfer to a sustainable energy loop that stops putting carbon and other greenhouse gasses into our atmosphere. Instead of taking a look at the publicly created money system, the NEED Act,[44] that was put forward and ignored in 2011, it is not even considered. That is cultural hegemony—absolute domination of thought. No outside the box thinking is allowed within the capitalist bank-created debt-money system.

Expert Witness: Paul Hawken and Project Drawdown—Rallying for a Planned Solution to Climate Change

In 2001, environmentalist, entrepreneur, and author Paul Hawken asked authorities in the fields of the environment and climate a question: "What do we need to do to arrest and reverse global warming?" He was looking for a shopping list, so to speak, of solutions to global warming, along with price tags on the individual items or solutions. Hawken was surprised that there was no such list, much as I was when I began to write this book. I knew global warming was a huge challenge. I just thought, and still do, that putting a system of publicly created money in place would be able to fund the solutions. I had no idea that before Paul Hawken there was no overarching plan in place to stop and reverse global warming and save *Spaceship Earth.*

What Hawken was searching for was a comprehensive overall strategy to stop pumping carbon, methane, and other greenhouse gases into the atmosphere, and also be able to draw down the excess gases that are already there. In 2013, after several climate reports further alarmed Hawken, he began Project Drawdown: referring to the point in time when greenhouse gases in the atmosphere peak and begin to decline on a year-to-year basis.[45]

The term "Green New Deal" was originally coined by newspaper columnist Thomas Friedman in 2007.[46] But the Green New Deal always reflected an overall aspiration of confronting climate change, rather than the nuts and bolts of how to do it, to say nothing of an accounting of the costs. It took me a little while until I found an actual plan — Project Drawdown: an overall plan to stop the existential threat of climate change to humanity's future. This is hardly meant to disparage all those who have fought for the environment over the years. Rather, Project Drawdown is a place for concerned citizens and activists to go, gather, and rally together to implement a planned solution to climate change. Project Drawdown attacks climate change on three fronts:

1. Reduce the sources of climate change. Stop putting CO2, methane, and other greenhouse gases into the atmosphere.
2. Support natural ecosystems in the form of carbon sinks, where carbon is naturally stored.
3. Improve society: increasing equality and justice can naturally benefit the climate. For example, improved education for women results in women having fewer children and thus putting less stress on the environment and less carbon in the air.

Project Drawdown was originally comprised of 70 researchers from 22 countries, all with advanced degrees and more than half with PhDs from many of the world's most respected universities. They first identified the sources of the carbon, methane, and other greenhouse gases in our atmosphere: Electricity generation, 25%; Food, Agriculture & Land Use, 24%; Industry, 21%; Transportation, 14%; Buildings, 6%; Other, 10%.

Instead of devising a plan on their own, they looked across the globe for solutions, utilizing the collective wisdom of humanity for the answers. They narrowed the solutions to those with the greatest potential to reduce carbon emissions and sequester carbon from the atmosphere. The solutions put forward would lead to regenerative economic outcomes that create security and jobs, improve health, save money, facilitate mobility, eliminate hunger, prevent pollution, restore soil, clean rivers, and more. Hawken suggests that we not look upon global warming as something that is happening to us, but rather consider:

> Global warming is happening for us—an atmospheric transformation that inspires us to change and reimagine everything we make and do—we begin to live in a different world. We take 100 percent responsibility and stop blaming others. We see global warming not as an inevitability but as an invitation to build, innovate, and effect change, a pathway that awakens creativity, compassion, and genius. This is not a liberal agenda, nor is it a conservative one. This is the human agenda.[47]

Project Drawdown's mission is to assist the world in reaching Drawdown—that point in the future when atmospheric greenhouse gas levels stop increasing and begin to steadily decline, as quickly, safely, and equitably as possible, decisively stopping catastrophic climate change.[48] Project Drawdown offers 82 specific categories of solutions to achieving Drawdown. The following are a few examples.

Abandoned Farmland Restoration:

Is the process for restoring degraded, abandoned land to productivity and bio-sequestration (net removal of CO2 from the atmosphere by plants and microorganisms and its storage in vegetative biomass and soil). Worldwide there are an estimated 400 million hectares [1 hectare = about 2.5 acres] of farmland abandoned due to degradation. Drawdown estimates that 189–296 million hectares could be restored and converted to regenerative or other carbon-friendly farming. From 2020–2050, this would result in 12–20 gigatons of CO2 either reduced or sequestered from the atmosphere. One gigaton represents 1 billion metric tons. The savings here equals 12–20 billion metric tons of CO2 removed from, or otherwise not added to the atmosphere. Implementing the plan will initially cost $98–$160 billion. The net operational savings are projected to be from $3.2–$5.2 trillion, with a 30-year lifetime net profit of $2.7–$4.3 trillion. Project Drawdown states that it is "somewhat embarrassing for humanity that we continue to clear land for agriculture while leaving degraded, once-fertile lands behind in an abandoned state."[49]

Distributed Energy Storage:

Is the necessary supporting technology for many of the other solutions to reduce our greenhouse gas emissions in the production of electricity. If we can't store electricity, we are forced into a system in which it must be consumed only as it is made, instead of storing the solar energy and using it as needed to, say, recharge your car's battery for the next day or power your home's electrical needs during the evening. As storage technologies are discovered and developed, homeowners will then be able to sell their surplus energy from solar rooftop panels, etc., back into the grid. The grid will then store and make available the surplus energy as it is needed by society. Presently, we only have battery storage. While batteries have tremendously improved, other solutions are waiting to be discovered.[50] Publicly created money could be used to develop these needed solutions.

Coastal Wetland Protection:

Is critical in the sequestration of carbon. Coastal wetlands have the capacity to store five times as much carbon as tropical forests. Within the coastal wetlands are mangrove forests, comprised of eighty different species of tree shrubs that grow, many partially submerged, in coastal wetlands within tropical and subtropical latitudes. The soil of these mangrove forests is estimated to hold the equivalent of two years of the entire global emissions of carbon—22 billion tons of carbon. As these coastal wetlands are destroyed, much of that 22 billion tons of carbon will be released into the atmosphere. Coastal wetlands, which retain carbon, also retrieve additional carbon from our atmosphere every day. They also serve as the first line of defense against flooding from hurricanes and tropical storms. Coastal wetlands are nurseries for fish, feeding grounds for migratory birds, and act as nature's filtration system, boosting water quality and recharging aquifers.[51]

Project Drawdown did not model the financial cost of an overall Coastal Wetland Protection Plan because this type of work is not normally done by the private sector. However, this is exactly the type of work that is done by the public sector, and with publicly created money we can pay for the restoration and protection of our coastal wetlands. Project Drawdown concentrates on implementing solutions that are cost beneficial to the private sector. That is all well and good, but many of the solutions required will need to be done by the public sector using publicly created money.

These are just a few examples of the solutions that Project Drawdown endorses in their book *Drawdown*, available for free online at drawdown.org. Now that we know there are ways for us to solve our man-made environmental problems, it's time to take a look at some of them that many of us may not be aware of.

Expert Witness: Johan Rockström of the Stockholm Resilience Centre—9 Planetary Boundaries for a Healthy Planet

By now we have all heard of climate change, but there are other existential environmental crises that *Spaceship Earth* faces on her journey, such as the ability to maintain resilient ecosystems. The Stockholm Resilience Centre (SRC) is "an international research centre on resilience and sustainability science."[52] In 2009, the Stockholm Resilience Center's director, Johan Rockström, led a group of twenty-eight internationally renowned scientists including American climate scientist James Hansen, Director of the Program on Climate Science, Awareness and Solutions of the Earth Institute at Columbia University,[53] which identified and published the nine natural processes that regulate the stability and resilience of the Earth. If humanity chooses to work within these planetary boundaries, *Spaceship Earth* and its passengers have a chance to survive into the future. If not, the future is at best uncertain and at worst, unimaginable.

John Bellamy Foster, Brett Clark, and Richard York wrote a book in 2010 that I read and took to heart: *The Ecological Rift—Capitalism's War on the Earth*, [54] which described the results of research on the nine planetary boundaries that the Stockholm Resilience Centre identified. At the time I was so troubled, moved, and inspired by this knowledge and the challenge confronting us, that I put a chart together on the subject and presented it at the 2012 Annual Participatory Democracy Conference at Indiana University Northwest.

My chart was composed in 2012, using statistics from 2009 or earlier. As such the stats in all categories can be assumed to be getting worse; e.g., the carbon or CO2 in the atmosphere is increasing, accelerating climate change. The CO2 pre-industrial level (before 1750 AD) was 278 ppm (parts per million). In 2009 it was 390 ppm CO2, as referenced in *The Ecological Rift*, and by 2021 it had reached 417 ppm according to the Mauna Loa Observatory in Hawaii.[55]

The nine planetary boundaries represent the point from which the scientists involved determined that the Earth cannot completely recover. Breaching these boundaries or points does not necessarily mean that all is lost, but it does mean that in some ways we will never be able to return the ecosystems of *Spaceship Earth* to their status before breaching.

9 Planetary Boundaries Crucial to a Livable Human Environment on Earth

1. Climate Change: melting of polar ice cap, rise in sea levels, increase in number and severity of severe weather events; e.g., droughts, floods, wildfires, hurricanes, and tornadoes. The boundary of 350 parts per million (ppm) CO2 (carbon dioxide) has been breached, CO2 in the atmosphere reached 419 ppm in 2021.[56]

2. Biodiversity/Species Loss: representing loss of species that are a part of a whole ecosystem. Their loss threatens the entire ecosystem. And this lost ecosystem may very well take with it the very assistance that we will need to combat the next pandemic. The boundary of losing 10 species per million species per year has been breached. Earth is presently losing more than 100 species per million species per year.[57]

3. Nitrogen & Phosphorus Cycles: resulting in ocean dead zones and increased ocean acidity. Boundary of 35 million tons of nitrogen removed from atmosphere has been breached. As of 2010 a total of 121 million tons had been removed. Boundary of 11 million tons of phosphorus put into oceans has almost been breached; as of 2010 a total of 9 million tons had been added to the oceans.

4. Ocean Acidification: resulting in massive shellfish die-down. Boundary of 2.75 aragonite saturation, almost

breached (lower rate being worse); as of 2010 aragonite saturation was 2.90.

5. Freshwater Use: resulting in a collapse of terrestrial and aquatic ecosystems. Boundary of 4,000 cubic kilometers, not yet breached. As of 2010, 2,600 cubic km were being used.

6. Land Used as Cropland: breaching will have catastrophic effects on ecosystems. Boundary of 15% of ice-free land used as cropland, not breached. 2010 rate was 11.7% of ice-free land used as cropland.

7. Chemical Pollution: status uncertain, measurement not yet devised for POPs (persistent organic pollutants; e.g., plastics, endocrine disruptors, heavy metals, nuclear waste).

8. Atmospheric Aerosol Loading (overall particulate concentration in atmosphere): disrupts monsoon seasons, causes health problems, interacts with our climate and freshwater boundaries. No measurement yet devised.

9. Stratospheric Ozone Depletion: now under control, but damage from the sun's increased ultraviolet radiation will continue for decades at the poles.

As we decide what type of monetary/economic system we have moving forward, we would do well to look at the nine planetary boundaries and decide if the monetary/economic system we presently have is geared toward remediating the damage which has already been done, keeping us from further crossing these boundaries in the future, and destroying our planet for human life as we know it.

The World Wildlife Fund in its 2022 Living Planet Report found that in the 48 years from 1970 to 2018, there was an average 69% decline in monitored wildlife populations around the world. It found that land-use change was currently the biggest cause of species and biodiversity loss. But that human induced climate change would soon overtake it as the greatest facilitator of additional loss.[58]

Expert Witness: Bjarke Ingels—Giving The Future Form

The above list certainly highlights the complexity of work to do. Looking at where we want to be in the future, by first looking to the past to see where we have come from, should make it easier to accept the changes that we need to make to get there. One who has used that method of interpretation is world-renowned Danish architect Bjarke Ingels, whose Bjarke Ingels Group (BIG) has gone from one person to a force of 700,[59] providing transformative architecture to the world:

> To feel that we have license to imagine a future different from today, all we have to do is look back ten years, a hundred years, a thousand years, to realize how radically different things were then than they are today. The same will be true if we can look ahead with the same clarity of vision. As we tackle the complexities of everyday life, these six evolutionary trajectories allow us to place a firm gaze on the horizon of time to prevent us from being derailed by the random distractions of today. Since we know from our past that our future is bound to be different from our present, rather than waiting for it to take shape on its own, we have the power to give it form.[60]

If we step outside the box, first looking back at our planet 10 years, 100 years, 1,000 years ago, and then looking at what sort of planet we want *Spaceship Earth* to be in 10 years, 100 years, 1,000 years, we will be able to see what we have to do today to begin to get there.

The Danish word for architecture translates into English as "form-giving." Bjarke Ingels's book *Formgiving* is his look at the past and present. If we want to form the future, we must first determine what sort of future we want to give *Spaceship Earth*: a future with no excess human greenhouse gas emissions in our atmosphere; a future with healthy oceans and marine life; a future in which humanity has chosen to use only materials that are biodegradable and digestible by the planet or that can all be recycled and reused; a future in which we have chosen to accept our roles as being a part of nature, instead of the masters of nature. Once the decision for the future is made, we must institute a plan to achieve it. Naysayers within the bank-created debt-money system will tell us that we cannot afford to do that which, we all know we must do. With the Money Power securely in public hands by enacting an updated NEED Act, we will have the power to publicly create money for the projects necessary to realize our vision for the future.

Do we really want to imagine a future in which *Spaceship Earth* continues to be powered by fossil fuels, paid for with bank-created debt-money, 10 years, 100 years, 1,000 years in the future? How many of our lifeforms that survive today, including us, will survive in the future if nothing changes?

---

1. Britannica, "The Wealth of Nations," https://www.britannica.com/topic/the-Wealth-of-Nations
2. Hayes, Adam, "Adam Smith and 'The Wealth of Nations,'" Investopedia, April 9, 2024, https://www.investopedia.com/updates/adam-smith-wealth-of-nations/
3. Adam Smith Institute, https://www.adamsmith.org/about-the-asi
4. Google search, "bible of economics wealth of nations," AI Overview.
5. Graeber, David, *Debt: The First 5,000 Years*, Melville House, 2011, p. 29.
6. Graeber, David, *Debt—The First 5,000 Years*, Melvillehouse, Brooklyn, NY, 2011.
7. Kumhof, Michael & Benes, Jaromir, "The Chicago Plan Revisited," International Monetary Fund, Working Paper, August 2012, chrome-extension://efaidnbmnnnibpcajpcglclefindmkaj/https://www.imf.org/external/pubs/ft/wp/2012/wp12202.PDF
8. Britannica, "Origins of Agriculture," https://www.britannica.com/topic/agriculture/Earliest-beginnings
9. Forces War Records, "Hitler's Black Book -- information for Doctor Fritz Heichelheim," https://www.forces-war-records.co.uk/hitlers-black-book/person/334/doctor-fritz-heichelheim
10. Heichelheim, Fritz, *An Ancient Economic History*, transl. Joyce Stevens, A.W. Sijtho#s Uitgeversmaatschappij, Leiden, 1958, pgs. 104-5.
11. Kumhof, Michael & Benes, Jaromir, *The Chicago Plan Revisited,* International Monetary Fund, Working Paper, p. 12, https://www.imf.org/external/pubs/ft/wp/2012/wp12202.PDF
12. Heichelheim, Fritz, *An Ancient Economic History*, pgs. 54-55.
13. *Ibid.*

14. Hudson, Michael, *Temples of Enterprise*, Islet, Baskerville, 2024, Back cover.
15. *Ibid,* p. 9.
16. Heichelheim, Fritz, *An Ancient Economic History*, pgs. 104-5
17. Hudson, Michael, *Temples of Enterprise*, p. 20.
18. Ibid, pgs. 250-251.
19. Plutarch, *Parallel Lives*, The Life of Lycurgus, Chapter 9, https://penelope.uchicago.edu/Thayer/E/Roman/Texts/Plutarch/Lives/Lycurgus*.html
20. Zarlenga, Stephen, *The Lost Science of Money,* American Monetary Institute, 2002, Valatie, NY, Chapter 2.
21. Aristotle, *Nicomachean Ethics,* Internet Classics, Translated W. D. Ross, https://classics.mit.edu/Aristotle/nicomachaen.html
22. Egnatz, Nick, *History of Money 101*, Amazon, 2023, p.22.
23. National Geographic, "Rome's Transition from Republic to Empire," Education, Grades 3 – 12, https://education.nationalgeographic.org/resource/romes-transition-republic-empire/#:~:text=The%20Roman%20Republic%20was%20founded,the%20form%20of%20a%20republic.
24. Zarlenga, Stephen, *The Lost Science of Money,* Chapter 2
25. Del Mar, Alexander, *History of Monetary Systems*, Charles H. Kerr & Company, Chicago, 1895, Chapter 1.
26. Egnatz, Nick, *History of Money 101*, Amazon, 2023, Chapter 3.
27. Ibid, Chapter 3.
28. Smith, Adam, The Wealth of Nations, Harriman House, (originally published 1776), 2007, p. 16.
29. Glass, Andrew, "Rep. McDonald dies when Soviets shoot down Boeing 747, Sept 1, 1983," Politico, Sept 1, 2017, https://www.politico.com/story/2017/09/01/rep-mcdonald-dies-when-soviets-shoot-down-boeing-747-sept-1-1983-242130
30. Aksenov, Pavel, "Stanislav Petrov: The man who may have saved the world," BBC News, Sept 26, 2013, https://www.bbc.com/news/world-europe-24280831
31. U.S. Department of Defense, "America's Nuclear Triad," https://www.defense.gov/Experience/Americas-Nuclear-Triad/
32. Statista Research Service, "Estimated number of nuclear warheads in each country from 1945 to 2023," https://www.statista.com/statistics/1071026/nuclear-warheads-per-country-historical-development/
33. Aksenov, Pavel, "Stanislav Petrov: The man who may have saved the world," BBC News.
34. Little, Allan -- Moscow Correspondent, "How I stopped nuclear war," interview Stanislav Petrov, Oct. 21, 1998, http://news.bbc.co.uk/2/hi/europe/198173.stm
35. Leiserowitz, Anthony, et al, "Climate Change in the American Mind, March 2021" Yale Program on Climate Change Communication, https://climatecommunication.yale.edu/publications/climate-change-in-the-american-mind-march-2021/2/
36. *Ibid.*
37. Milman, Oliver & Niranjan, Ajit, "'A wrecking ball': experts warn Trump's win sets back global climate action," The Guardian, Nov 6, 2024, https://www.theguardian.com/us-news/2024/nov/06/trump-climate-change-environment-threat
38. NASA Global Climate Change, "Scientific Consensus: Earth's Climate is Warming," https://climate.nasa.gov/scientific-consensus/
39. NASA Global Climate Change, "The Effects of Climate Change," https://climate.nasa.gov/effects/

40. *Ibid.*
41. U.S. Global Change Research Program 2014, Third Climate Assessment, "Climate Change Impacts in the United States," https://nca2014.globalchange.gov/highlights
42. *Ibid.*
43. Merriam-Webster Online Dictionary, "hegemony", https://www.merriam-webster.com/dictionary/hegemony
44. National Emergency Employment Defense Act (NEED Act), 112th Congress, Sept. 21, 2011, https://www.congress.gov/bill/112th-congress/house-bill/2990/text
45. Hawken, Paul, editor, "Drawdown -- the Most Comprehensive Plan Ever Proposed to Reverse Global Warming" Penguin, New York, 2017, p. x.
46. D'Souza, Deborah, "The Green New Deal Explained," Investopedia, June 23, 2021, https://www.investopedia.com/the-green-new-deal-explained-4588463
47. Hawken, Paul, editor, "Drawdown -- the Most Comprehensive Plan Ever Proposed to Reverse Global Warming," p. xi
48. Project Drawdown, "The World's Leading Resource for Climate Solutions," https://drawdown.org/
49. Project Drawdown, "Abandoned Farmland Restoration," Solutions, https://drawdown.org/solutions/abandoned-farmland-restoration
50. Project Drawdown, "Distributed Energy Storage," Solutions, https://drawdown.org/solutions/distributed-energy-storage
51. Project Drawdown, "Coastal Wetland Protection," Solutions, https://drawdown.org/solutions/coastal-wetland-protection
52. Stockholm Resilience Centre, Stockholm University/Beijer Institute of Ecological Economics, Royal Swedish Academy of Sciences, Founded 2007, https://stockholmresilience.org/about-us.html
53. The Earth Institute Columbia University, Dr. James Hansen, Earth Institute Staff Directory, https://www.earth.columbia.edu/users/profile/james-e-hansen
54. Foster, John Bellamy, Clark, Brett & York, Richard, *The Ecological Rift -- Capitalism's War on the Earth,* Monthly Review Press, New York, 2010.
55. Betts, Richard,--Head of Climate Impacts Research at the Met Office Hadley Centre & University of Exeter, "Met Office: Atmospheric CO2 now hitting 50% higher than pre-industrial levels," March 16, 2021, https://www.carbonbrief.org/met-office-atmospheric-co2-now-hitting-50-higher-than-pre-industrial-levels#:~:text=Atmospheric%20CO2%20has%20been%20rising,over%20the%201750%2D1800%20average.
56. National Oceanic and Atmospheric Research, "Carbon dioxide peaks near 420 parts per million at Mauna Loa Observatory," June 7, 2021, https://research.noaa.gov/article/ArtMID/587/ArticleID/2764/Coronavirus-response-barely-slows-rising-carbon-dioxide
57. Stockholm Resilience Centre, "Human prosperity requires global sustainability," Biodiversity, chrome-extension://efaidnbmnnnibpcajpcglclefindmkaj/https://www.stockholmresilience.org/download/18.416c425f13e06f977b110f4/1459560257140/Human_prosperity_requires_global_sustainability_Schultz.pdf
58. World Wildlife Fund, "Living Planet Report 2022," Building a Nature-Positive Society, chrome-extension://efaidnbmnnnibpcajpcglclefindmkaj/https://wwflpr.awsassets.panda.org/downloads/lpr_2022_full_report.pdf
59. Bjarke Ingels Group, "BIG, https://big.dk/

60. Ingels, Bjarke, *BIG. Formgiving, An Architectural Future History,* Taschen, https://parametric-architecture.com/big-formgiving-an-architectural-future-history/

FOUR

The Plastic Invasion of Oceans and Organs

Geologically Speaking, What Time Is It—Holocene, Anthropocene, or Plasticene?

Spaceship Earth's history is divided into large chunks of time by geologists called eons, eras, periods, epochs, and ages, with eons being the largest time periods and ages the smallest. [Although one expert may call a certain time period an age and another expert may call the same time period an epoch and succeed in completely confusing us.] These time periods are based upon the geological record of fossils in rock layers representing a difference in life forms and climate of that particular age. Officially we currently live in the Holocene epoch, beginning 11,700 years ago and representing the period after the last major ice age, the Pleistocene epoch, which lasted from 2.6 million years ago to 11,700 years ago.[1]

But many scientists have begun to refer to the present age as the Anthropocene, meaning the Age of Man. In the Fertile Crescent this period corresponds almost perfectly to the period in which human activity had begun to affect the planet. Some think that the name Holocene should just be replaced by Anthropocene; others feel that the Anthropocene age should be separate, beginning with the Industrial

Revolution around 1750. Still others suggest that it should begin around 1945 with the invention and use of nuclear weapons. The International Union of Geological Sciences (IUGS) is the organization charged with naming epochs. In 2016 the Anthropocene Working Group within the IUGS agreed that the Anthropocene is different from the Holocene and that, unofficially for now, the Anthropocene epoch began in 1950.[2]

The Anthropocene epoch represents the period in which humans began to release huge amounts of pollutants onto the Earth and into the atmosphere, leaving a geologic record behind in sediment and ice cores consisting of nitrogen, aluminum, lead, plutonium, microplastics, and persistent organic pollutants such as plastic. A Holocene/Anthropocene boundary may be placed mid-twentieth century because this is when industrial pollution dramatically took off.[3] I take it personally that the destructive Anthropocene epoch that threatens *Spaceship Earth* and humanity's future, parallels my own life.

Incredibly, in 2024 by a 12 – 10 vote margin, the Subcommission of Quaternary Stratigraphy (SQS) part of the International Union of Geological Sciences voted no, thus killing the proposal to accept that a new era began in 1950 called Anthropocene. The vote was taken before outstanding recommendations by the OIGS Geoethics Commission were implemented to remove 11 of those who voted (10 of them voting no), because they had exceeded their term limits on the SQS and were ineligible to vote.[4] Those who voted to quash the Anthropocene Era claimed that humans have been changing the environment at least since the beginning of agriculture and the year 1950 isn't a distinct enough time to claim a special designation.[5]

I have made clear that I have no academic standing. Thus, I have no status in an academic debate that makes as much sense to me as arguing how many angels can dance on the head of a pin? I do wonder though why the academics in charge of naming geological eras can have a vigorous debate on whether or not an Anthropocene epoch exists, and the economics academics are allowed to completely ignore (shun) any public debate on whether or not or money should continue to be privately created by banks, or should instead be publicly created by us through our government. While the geologic debate rages on and monetary debate is shunned, all the lifeforms on *Spaceship Earth* move progressively closer to extinction.

Plasticene Era

As a result of the growth of plastics and their resulting pollution, this same 1950-onward time period has also been referred to as the Plasticene era.

A Plasticene Lexicon identifies twelve words that have come into the scientific vocabulary of ecologists, geologists, chemists, and garbologists:

- epiplastic, adj. (2014), organisms that live on floating plastic in the oceans.
- plasticized, adj. (2014), made abstractly plastic by the pollution in the environment.
- plastisphere, noun (2013), the living microbiotic and macrobiotic communities colonizing plastic, usually in the oceans.
- plastivore, noun (2011), any organism that ingests, processes, regurgitates, and defecates plastics.
- plastic cycle, noun (2019), continuous, complex movement of plastic from source, to production, to its use, evolution, and change in properties, interactions, impacts, and sinks in the environment.
- Plasticene, noun & adj. (2011), an era in the Earth's history beginning around 1950 referring to the ubiquitous use of plastic.
- plasticrust, adj. (2019), plastic debris attached to rocky intertidal shores.
- plastiglomerate, noun (2014), a matrix of plastic, rocks, coral, wood, and sand that are cemented together usually by campfires.

- pyroplastic, noun (2019), a mass of plastic melted together that can then float in seawater.
- nurdle, noun (1990s), a small pellet of plastic that is used to manufacture plastic items.
- plastic confetti, noun (2011), multicolored plastic fragments of degraded plastics found in the oceans.
- plastitrash, noun (2011), plastic litter, garbage, debris.[6]

The Plasticene era sounds very similar to the Pleistocene epoch, which lasted from 2.6 million years ago to 11,700 years ago. But they are not related.[a] For now, let's take a closer look at plastics from which the Plasticine era derives its name. Plastics were included under the category of Chemical Pollution, POPs (persistent organic pollutants), a subcategory of one of the 9 Planetary Boundaries Crucial to a Livable Human Environment on Earth.[7] We do not have the space here, nor I the expertise, to go into great detail on the threats posed to all nine planetary boundaries that are currently under assault by human activity. Here we will also discuss plastics and the threats to our oceans.

From One Word in The Graduate to...

You might remember the unforgettable one-word line in the movie *The Graduate*. Your author watched that movie in Seattle, Washington, before getting on a midnight flight to the Vietnam War in 1968. The protagonist, Benjamin, played by a young Dustin Hoffman, had just graduated from college and was searching for his mission in life. His parents had a cocktail party at home in his honor and one particularly inebriated gentleman friend of his parents told Benjamin:

---

[a] Also, the Plasticene era has nothing to do with Plasticine, the trademarked name for a non-drying children's modeling material invented in 1897 and patented two years later by art teacher William Harbutt in Bath, England. Plasticine was manufactured by the Harbutt Company until 1983 when production was moved to Thailand. Plasticine is made of gypsum, petroleum jelly, lanolin, lime, and stearic acid. As such, plasticine is digestible and much friendlier to the planet than the plastic products that have come after it. The Beatles' 1967 song "Lucy in the Sky with Diamonds" mentions Plasticine. This was almost surely taken from their childhood use of Plasticine modeling clay in England.

I want to say one word to you, Benjamin. One word.
Yes sir.
Are you listening?
Yes sir.
Plastics.

Benjamin looked at him, dumbfounded. After a long pause, the gentleman continued:

There is a great future in plastics. Think about it. Will you think about it?[8]

Why that line sticks with me, I don't know. Perhaps because I had a long flight to the opposite end of the globe to think about it. Perhaps because I had a year controlling aircraft in the Vietnam War to think about it. Or perhaps because I think about a lot of things these days in our society that just don't make sense. I grew up in the 1950s when we were just starting to make almost everything out of plastic. There was no one asking the question about what happens to the plastic squirt gun, dinner plate, toy soldier, doll, block, Lego, salad bowl, telephone, laundry hamper, toy kitchen, swimming pool, prescription container, deodorant delivery system, etc., when its present use is over. Who within our economic and political systems is asking that question and asking it not after the item's use is over, but before it is designed and manufactured? If these questions, for every item we use, are not properly asked and then answered in a sustainable manner, the economic/political/monetary system, that we and *Spaceship Earth* are dependent on, is dysfunctional.

The Mouths of Babes

This reminds me of a story. Best guess is it was 10–15 years ago. Chicago has a huge air show on the shore of Lake Michigan every summer. There are military planes, bombers, the Blue Angels, the Thunderbirds, parachute teams, and more besides. It's also a great recruitment vehicle for the armed forces. Since I opposed our wars in Iraq and Afghanistan, I met some friends for a demonstration at the air show (we like to present an alternative to military service to our youth. All done so that they just do not end up in an illegal, immoral war, like I did in Vietnam).

We walked through the throngs of people on the beach with anti-war signs and talked with a variety of people in the crowd. Those we talked with were very supportive. I have a large Veterans for Peace flag on a pole that I carry. I was wearing my straw hat with loads of anti-war and social justice buttons. One button says "F Wall Street." I'm particularly fond of it, but my wife doesn't like me to wear it if I'm with her. She objects to kids seeing it, and her point is well taken. But it is still a crucial part of my activist wardrobe, and she wasn't with me. When I left the air show, I had to catch a bus and then a commuter train home. I started talking with a guy as we were walking toward the bus stop. He had his son with him, maybe seven or eight. His son spoke up, "Dad, I know what that button means." "What button?" said his dad, hoping it would be any button but that button. "'F Wall Street' means Wall Street gets a failing grade," said the young lad. Both his much-relieved father and I loved it – wisdom from the mouth of babes.

We have to give our economic/political/monetary system a failing grade if they cannot implement a system of sustainable plastic manufacture and use. I try to recycle everything I can. Big deal—unfortunately, most plastics are not recyclable. And even if they technically could be recycled, the recyclers don't accept them. They only take plastic bottles, some bags, and maybe a few other things, while we live in a society where almost everything is made out of plastic. During COVID, we were eating our share of takeout food, trying to keep a few of our restaurants in business somehow and every order had multiple plastic containers, plastic utensils, all wrapped in plastic bags. In a more perfect world—and it is up to us to insist that it is more perfect—all plastic things would have to be manufactured so that they could easily be recycled. If that means that manufacturers would then be responsible for recycling, so be it. The manufacturers would have to demonstrate how everything they make of plastic can be recycled and ensure that there is a recycling system up and running, in which it can be done.

Expert Witness: Professor Plastics—Professor Emeritus, American Chemistry Council

Professor Plastics was the cartoon spokesperson of the American Chemistry Council, who explained plastic in such an innocent manner that we could almost forget the ever-present plastic trash littering our towns, cities, and countryside, to say nothing of the plastic choking our landfills, streams, oceans and marine life:

> The chemistry of plastics can be complex, but the basics are straightforward. Think back to your high school science lessons about atoms and molecules (groups of atoms). Plastics are simply chains of like molecules linked together. These chains are called polymers. This is why many plastics begin with "poly," such as polyethylene, polystyrene, and polypropylene. Polymers often are made of carbon and hydrogen and sometimes oxygen, nitrogen, sulfur, chlorine, fluorine, phosphorous, or silicon.[9]

Sadly, Professor Plastics is no longer with us. When I first wrote about him in 2020, Professor Plastics was used to explain plastics to the public through the American Chemical Council's website. As of 2023, I could find no trace of him, and can only surmise that he has retired or expired. I made the decision to give the professor emeritus status in his title above, because I could not bear to think of his future as expired: being neither recyclable nor digestible by the Earth, as just one more discarded plastic item on the roadside, in a landfill, or perhaps floating in the ocean.

Professor Plastics made it all sound innocent enough. Monomers make up the polymers that Professor Plastics so cheerfully informed us about.[10] But almost all of the monomers that are used to make plastics, such as propylene and ethylene, are derived from fossil hydrocarbons.

Almost none of the plastics that we commonly use are biodegradable. Rather than decompose, they accumulate in landfills or the natural environment. If we want to permanently eliminate plastic waste, we must do so by destructive thermal treatment, such as combustion or pyrolysis.

Expert Witness: Professor Noelle Eckley Selin—Institute for Data, Systems and Society & Department of Earth, Atmospheric and Planetary Sciences, MIT

> When plastic is burned, it releases dangerous chemicals such as hydrochloric acid, sulfur dioxide, dioxins, furans and heavy metals, as well as particulates. These emissions are known to cause respiratory ailments and stress human immune systems, and they're potentially carcinogenic.[11]

Pyrolysis Is Not the Solution to Our Plastic Problem

Pyrolysis is the thermal degradation of plastic waste at different temperatures (300–900°C), in the absence of oxygen, to produce liquid oil.[12] The same huge petrochemical corporations that manufacture plastics and cheerfully brought us Professor Plastics representing the American Chemistry Council understand that there is a structural problem within such a system. We presently have unlimited plastic production and use, the vast majority of which is unable to be recycled and almost none of which is able to be naturally digested by the Earth. The solution chosen by petrochemical corporations such as Dow, BASF, Shell, ExxonMobil, Lyondell Basell Industries, Sabic, Ineos, Braskem, and Total Energies is to use pyrolysis to in some manner convert mixed plastic waste into hydrocarbon liquids. Dow and its partner Mura Technology are building plants in England, South Korea, and Japan in which the plastic can be loaded into its ethylene cracker at the site for conversion back into new plastics.[13]

Expert Witness: Matt Casale

Mr. Casale is the former Director of Environment Campaigns, Public Interest Research Group (PIRG). In 2022 Mr. Casale sent a letter to Congress, co-signed by more than 200 environmental organizations sounding the alarm on the danger of pyrolysis as a solution to our plastic problem:

> Plastic contains hundreds of toxic chemicals, including heavy metals, phthalates, flame retardants, bisphenol A and PFAS. The process of burning plastic via pyrolysis and gasification generates even more toxic pollution, including chemicals known to cause cancer, birth defects and other serious health harms. Emissions include dioxins, benzene, cadmium, arsenic, lead, polycyclic aromatic hydrocarbons (PAHs) and mercury. Removing existing Clean Air Act limitations on burning plastic will allow chemical manufacturers to produce and release these toxic chemicals into our communities without limitation.[14]

Casale informed Congress that the Clean Air Act of 1970, 1977, and 1990[15] stands in the way of this pyrolysis non-solution to a very real plastic problem. Pyrolysis and gasification incinerators burn solid waste, making them incinerators under the Clean Air Act. This was recognized by the Environmental Protection Agency (EPA) when it set emission standards under the Clean Air Act. The American Chemistry Council is pushing Congress and the EPA to exempt pyrolysis and gasification incinerators from all the other incinerators that are covered under the Clean Air Act, saying that they are not incinerators. Their next step may very well be to say that plastic waste is not waste under the Resource Conservation and Recovery Act. If the American Chemistry Council is successful, it will leave the incineration of plastic via pyrolysis and gasification completely unregulated under federal law, while twenty states have already been persuaded to relax state-level regulations on the same.[16]

Readers agreeing with Mr. Casale's concerns are invited to forward a copy of the letter to your Congressional Representative and Senators indicating your support for the continuation of strict environmental regulations.

It is encouraging that those who create plastic petrochemicals are struggling, out of absolute necessity, to find a way in which to somehow get rid of plastic. Hopefully, with us pushing them hard, they might start searching for answers that do not send all manner of toxins into our atmosphere. The results at this juncture are far from encouraging—so far just yielding more contamination of *Spaceship Earth* with plastic waste.[17] Or perhaps even worse, transforming plastic waste into hundreds of different toxic chemicals, including those that cause cancer and birth defects, and then pumping this pathogenic concoction into our atmosphere hardly sounds like much of an improvement.[18]

Plastic is ubiquitous; it is in everything and it is everywhere. Yet it is practically impossible to deconstruct once it's made, and today most of it is practically impossible to recycle. Of the 8.3 billion metric tons of plastic that have been produced, only somewhere between 5–9%[19] of it has been recycled, while 79% has accumulated in landfills, is floating in the oceans, or is litter on the side of the road.[20] We can assume that the remaining 12–17% is currently being used, is in inventory somewhere, or perhaps is in my basement or your attic gathering dust.

Plastic in Oceans

Whether or not life on *Spaceship Earth* began in the oceans or on land is now a matter of debate in the scientific community.[21] Not a matter of debate is the all-out frontal assault that humanity has directed against our oceans. Adding to the mix of dead zones, ocean acidity, and massive shellfish die-downs from the man-made, out-of-control nitrogen and phosphorous cycles run amok are the huge garbage patches that have formed in our oceans. Rotating ocean currents called gyres act as huge whirlpools, pulling plastic and other objects in, creating these garbage patches. The oceans currently have five gyres, two in the Pacific, two in the Atlantic, and one in the Indian Ocean.

The Great Pacific Garbage Patch, located in the North Pacific between Hawaii and California, is the largest. While some areas of the garbage patches may look like a dump, most of the plastic has been broken down to smaller microplastic pieces, not seen at first glance by the human eye.[22]

Most of us have seen pictures of dead sharks, whales, and other sea animals who, when cut open and photographed, contain all matter of plastic debris in their stomachs. In 2017, United Nations Secretary-General Antonio Guterres issued a dire warning on the health of our oceans:

> Pollution, overfishing and the effects of climate change are severely damaging the health of our oceans ... According to one recent study, plastic could outweigh fish—if nothing happens—in our seas by 2050.[23]

U.N. General Assembly President Peter Thomson of Fiji gave his own admonishment:

> The time has come for us to correct our wrongful ways. ...We have unleashed a plague of plastic upon the ocean that is defiling nature in so many tragic ways.... It is inexcusable that humanity tips the equivalent of a large garbage truck of plastic into the ocean every minute of every day.[24]

Marine animals are hardly alone; elephants, revered in Sri Lanka, are now dying as a result of eating plastic garbage. Twenty elephants have been found dead with plastic garbage in their stomachs in recent years. They ingest the plastic while eating other garbage. The sharper pieces of plastic damage their digestive systems and they eventually just stop eating, soon to die. [25]

There are 1,440 minutes in a day. Garbage and recycling trucks have a legal weight limit of 51,000 lbs. The trucks weigh about 33,000 lbs. That leaves 18,000 lbs. or 9 tons for their payload. They usually hit their weight limit before completely filling, so we can calculate that the

9-ton payload dumped 1,440 times a day into the ocean equals 10,080 tons of plastic a day. That's 3,679,200 tons of plastic added every year to our oceans.[26]

In 2018 with 7.8 billion people on Earth, we had created 7.6 billion metric tons of plastic that we are unable to get rid of, representing 91% of the 8.3 billion metric tons that had been manufactured and not recycled.[27] More than a ton of plastic for each one of us, this equals 2,148 pounds of plastic for each person on Earth. Plastic, plastic, everywhere, and *Spaceship Earth* is unable to properly digest it.

Expert Witness: ABC News—Trashed: The Secret Life of Plastic Recycling

Contrast our present plastic predicament with a perfectly sustainable world in which plastic products could only be made if there was a complete recycling loop in place that itself did not contribute to the pollution, warming and destruction of the planet. It is our job as citizens to either see that there is such a sustainable recycling loop, or to not allow the production of plastic products. "Trashed: The Secret Life of Plastic Recycling," a 2023 ABC News video report graphically shows the stark reality of plastic recycling today.

In the year 1950, the beginning of the plastic era, worldwide 2 million tons of plastic was produced. In 2017, 348 million tons of plastic was produced worldwide. In 2020, the weight of plastic in the world was greater than the weight of all creatures on the planet.[28] In 2023 the United Nations estimated that plastic production had increased to 430 million tons per year.[29]

Think of the plastics industry as the combination of the fossil fuel industry and the chemical industry. The plastics industry grossed $548 billion in 2022, while employing over one million workers.[30] This money and these workers are not directed at recycling, but rather the endless creation of new plastic. *Spaceship Earth* and our own bodies are left holding the plastic bag, bottle, and everything else that is made of plastic.

ABC News put 46 trackers in plastic bags and then placed them in recycling drop offs at stores such as Wall Mart and Target. The trackers would send a signal or ping back to ABC News so that it could be determined where they were recycled or otherwise disposed of. The results were that 23 last pinged at landfills or trash incinerators (not recycled), 7 were last heard from at transfer stations that do not recycle or sort bags that go to recycling (not recycled), 6 last pinged at the store they were dropped off at and were not heard from again for months (not recycled), and 3 were shipped to Southeast Asia (not recycled). One of these went 9,500 miles from a Wall Mart in Kingston, New Jersey to Batam, Indonesia. Another went more than 9,300 miles from a Wall Mart in Wichita, Kansas to Kuala Lumpur, Malaysia. And the last went more than 10,000 miles from a Wall Mart in Ormand Beach, Florida to Selangor, Malaysia. This dumping of plastic waste in Indonesia and Malaysia, while certainly no solution to our own plastic problem, also creates tremendous environmental and health problems in these countries. ABC News believes that only 4 of the 46 plastic bags containing trackers, less than 9%, ended up being recycled.[31]

The Plastic We Don't See

While the plastic that we can see and can't get rid of is quite scary, the plastic that we cannot see is the scariest. For whatever reason, the list of twelve plastic-derived new words missed a few, perhaps because they have already been used so much by the scientific community. One of those words is microplastics, defined as small pieces of plastic that are 5 mm or smaller (about one-fifth of an inch or smaller). Many of the microplastics come from the degradation of larger plastic debris in the oceans. But plastic can break down into smaller pieces anywhere. What it cannot do is biodegrade and return to nature, leaving *Spaceship Earth* with a severe case of plastic indigestion.[32]

Microbeads are very tiny pieces of polyethylene plastic that have been manufactured to be added as exfoliants to health and beauty products such as cleansers and toothpaste. They are small enough that they easily pass through our water filtration systems and now they are everywhere in our oceans and freshwater. They had been in use for more than 50 years until President Obama signed the Microbead-Free Waters Act in 2015, which banned microbeads from cosmetics and personal care products.[33]

It's not like all these microbeads and other microplastics have been confining themselves to marine life and animals. People have not been spared. Rolf Halden, Director of the Arizona State University (ASU) Biodesign Center for Environmental Health Engineering, is the bearer of bad news: "We have detected these chemicals of plastics in every single [human] organ that we have investigated."[34]

Dianna Cohen, CEO of the non-profit Plastic Pollution Coalition, informs us that we all ingest about 5 grams of plastic each week, the amount of plastic in a credit card. Yikes—it doesn't help to know that, according to Ms. Cohen, it is impossible to protect ourselves from ingesting plastic. It is in our tap water, our bottled water, and the very air that we all breathe.[35]

Nanoplastics

Even smaller than microplastics are nanoplastics. Their size has been debated by the scientific community. Nine scientists have stepped forward with a definition of nanoplastic in the April 2018 issue of *Environmental Pollution*: Julien Gigault, Alexandra ter Halle, Magalie Baudrimont, Pierre-Yves Pascal, Fabienne Gauffre, Thuy-Lin Phi, Hind El Hadri, Bruno Grassl, and Stephanie Reynaud. Nanoplastics are particles resulting from the degradation of plastic objects. They exhibit a colloidal behavior, meaning that they are dispersed throughout another substance. Their size ranges from 1 to 1,000 nanometers, or from 1 billionth to 1 millionth of a meter.[36] They are present in plants and animals, and you can't avoid them by eating organic food. It matters not if you are a vegan, a vegetarian, a fruitarian, or an omnivore, nanoplastics are in our bodies and our blood—everyone's.[37] And we have no idea how harmful they really are.

The simple fact is that plastics, once made, are nearly impossible to deconstruct. My plastic knife, fork, spoon, and salad bowl with lid from a takeout lunch last week will in all probability outlive everyone reading this—all our kids and all their kids too. They will in all probability degrade into smaller pieces, eventually becoming microplastics and even nanoplastics, but they will not break down to their chemical element form and then be able to become something else. Our current political/economic/monetary system has saddled us with an unsustainable future. It is up to us to demand that the things we use in our lives are designed and manufactured to be reused over and over again, and when they are finally obsolete, they can be recycled and reused in another manner. This is nothing more than us, the crew and passengers on *Spaceship Earth*, taking responsibility for our own housekeeping—the maintenance of our planet. And if our political/economic/monetary system is not up to also taking responsibility for our planet, we need to work out a new system that does.

Does Plastic in the Oceans Speed Up Global Warming?

The oceans are *Spaceship Earth's* largest carbon sink (safe resting place for carbon). They keep carbon out of the atmosphere so that it does not contribute to climate change. The biological carbon pump (BCP) of the oceans in 2021 took one-third[38] of the 37 billion metric tons of CO2 pumped into the atmosphere by fossil fuels and industry, safely storing it in deep water and on the ocean floor.[39] Clara Manno, marine ecologist at the British Antarctic Survey, tells us the vital work that it does: "The biological carbon pump helps to keep the planet healthy. It helps the mitigation of climate change."[40]

Here's how the biological carbon pump works. Carbon dioxide from the atmosphere dissolves into the water on the ocean's surface. Through photosynthesis, tiny marine algae called phytoplankton then absorb the carbon into their bodies. Zooplankton eat the phytoplankton and excrete the carbon in fecal pellets that sink down the water column to the ocean floor, where the carbon can either be re-mineralized into rocks or just stay in the deep water, prevented from escaping back into the atmosphere.[41]

The latest research is beginning to show that the tiny nanoplastic particles in the ocean are disrupting this process. It seems the tiny microplastic and nanoplastic particles in the ocean are digested by the plankton and their buoyancy causes the fecal pellets to sink "way, way more slowly," according to Matthew Cole, senior marine ecologist and ecotoxicologist at the Plymouth Marine Laboratory in the U.K.[42] Because they sink much more slowly, more of them are eaten by other marine life, never making it to the bottom at all. Indicating that less carbon makes it way to the ocean's floor to be safely sequestered. But more research has to be done in this area to know for sure.[43]

"A Fundamental Renegotiation of Our Relationship with Polymers" —Expert Witness: Matt Simon—Science Journalist, Wired Magazine

> *A Poison Like No Other—How Microplastics Corrupted Our Planet and Our Bodies*[44]
>
> "Humanity has fallen into a plasticene progress trap: the modern world wouldn't be possible without polymers, but the wundermaterials have locked us into an increasingly dark trajectory. Like the invention of agriculture made our species dependent on crops to survive, and like the industrial revolution hooked civilization on fossil fuels, so too has plastic set humanity down an ostensibly prosperous path that belies the reality of environmental defilement. Without plastic we'd have no modern medicine or gadgets or wire insulation to keep our homes from burning down. But *with* plastic we've contaminated every corner of Earth and our own bodies, the consequences of which scientists are now desperate to understand.
>
> "Extricating humanity from the plastic trap demands an extraordinary—yet feasible—campaign waged across our civilization. There are ways to filter clothing microfibers out of wastewater, to be sure, but technologies are no substitute for what we and the planet really need: a fundamental renegotiation of our relationship with polymers. It wasn't too long ago that humanity got on perfectly fine with cardboard and glass instead of single-use plastic. Plastics *are* fossil fuels, and plastics *are*

> climate change, so in scorning the material we'll tackle both crises—really, we can't fix one without fixing the other…(I)f the (plastic) industry were a country it would be the fifth largest emitter…of greenhouse gases… And as they age in the environment microplastics release greenhouse gases, suggesting that plastic pollution is a significant overlooked contributor to climate change. Failing to act will doom this world to runaway temperatures and runaway microplastic contamination, the degrees and particles piling up into an unbearable burden for the species of Earth."[45]

Mr. Simon's 2020 book is nothing if not a wake-up call to humanity that our continuing use of plastic, at anything even remotely resembling our present rate, is simply unsustainable. That is, if we are to have a planet that we can continue to live on.

Only a morally bankrupt political/economic/monetary system allows the rampant production and use of plastic. It is up to us as citizens to sort out and solve our plastic problem. Before Professor Plastics went into emeritus status, he explained how plastic was made by attaching monomers together in chains to make polymers. He also mentioned that carbon was one of the monomers frequently used. Professor Plastics neglected to mention that almost all carbon used to make the plastic polymers comes from the fossil fuel industry and that recycling only exists for a tiny percentage of the plastic made.

Did the disastrous lack of an all-inclusive recycling feedback loop in plastics come about by happenstance or accident? Or did it come about because our free-market capitalist system rewards those who make the maximum profit—the environment be damned. This, even though all future life on Earth is dependent upon the health of the environment that we have damned. Today in 2024, we are mired in an economic/political/monetary system that is incapable of solving this problem. Outside the box thinking is needed and publicly created money is exactly the type of outside the box thinking that can help solve our plastic problem.

Expert Witness: Professor Iseult Lynch—Professor Environmental Nanoscience, Earth and Environmental Sciences, University of Birmingham, United Kingdom

> When you have done the extraction of the oil and the refining of the oil, all the things that are left over then are basically used as the basis of pretty much all of our synthetic chemicals...So it's actually much, much cheaper just to keep refining virgin plastic than it is to recycle or reuse or recover. And that's the main problem, that if they're extracting it for the oil and gas industry, then these byproducts are always going to just be cheap."[46,47]

Led by ExxonMobil, just twenty companies are responsible for 55% of 'throwaway' plastic waste, according to a study conducted by academics from the London School of Economics, the Stockholm Environment Institute, Wood Mackenzie, and others.[48] In other words, it is good business to pollute *Spaceship Earth* with unrecyclable plastic waste and there is no need for them to cease doing so.

Plasticizers Join Plastics in Our Food and Bodies

As if it wasn't bad enough that we have micro and nano plastic in our bodies, we are now learning that we have plasticizers in our bodies: chemicals used to make the plastic more flexible and durable called bisphenols and phthalates. Consumer Reports found phthalates in almost every food they tested, often at high levels. They were also found in all different types of food packaging. They are endocrine disruptors that can interfere with production and regulation of hormones such as estrogen. This disruption can lead to, "diabetes, obesity, cardiovascular disease, certain cancers, birth defects, premature birth, neurodevelopmental disorders, and infertility."[49] [50]

A Different Kind of Plastic

Bioplastics, or biodegradable plastics, are basically plant-based instead of petroleum-based plastics that can be digested naturally by the earth. Ironically, the modern use of plastic actually began with a bioplastic. In 1862, English artisan and chemist Alexander Parkes patented a process using cotton fibers, vegetable oil, and nitric and sulfuric acid under the name Parkesine. It was the first man-made plastic, a bioplastic at that could serve as a cheap replacement for ivory and tortoiseshell, used to make items ranging from combs to billiard balls.[51] Parkesine also provided some degree of relief to the diminishing number of elephants and tortoises across the globe that were being killed for their ivory and shells.

In the 1920s, French researcher Maurice Lemoigne developed the biodegradable plastic polyhydroxy butyrate (PHB) using the bacterium Bacillus megaterium. His work was overlooked for three decades until 1957–58 when microbiologists working independently in the U.S. and the U.K. rediscovered PHB. With cheap oil prices, there had been little interest in PHB until the 1970s when, ironically, the Organization of Petroleum Exporting Countries (OPEC) resurrected it again by instigating an oil crisis. But as the developed capitalist countries worked their way through this economic shock, concern for an alternative to non-biodegradable petroleum-based plastics waned.

In the 1990s, interest in an alternative again peaked, this time from the biomedical industry.[52] This appears to be the first effort to look at plastic from a health and safety aspect instead of just from the cost and availability outlook used by the economic/political/monetary system. Finally, people were beginning to be concerned with the safety of using potentially toxic petroleum-based plastic within the human body, although they were doing so only for medical implants. Little did they know that thirty years later we would all have microplastics throughout our bodies, and they didn't get there from medical devices. Despite the concern for human safety, feigned or otherwise, our economic/political/monetary system continued to ignore the harm plastic was doing to our planet.

Expert Witness: Andrew Falcon—CEO Full Cycle Bioplastics

PHA (polyhydroxyalkanoate) is a type of bioplastic made by microorganisms, sometimes genetically engineered, that produce plastic from organic materials. Since PHA is biodegradable and does not harm living tissue, it can be used for all sorts of medical applications and for single-use food packaging. Full Cycle Bioplastics in California produces PHA from all types of organic waste, including food waste and crop residue, as well as paper and cardboard that have not been recycled. Currently being used to make containers, bags, bottles and cutlery, it is compostable and marine degradable. If it finds its way into the ocean or fresh water, the fish and bacteria will eventually eat and digest it. And if not consumed by nature, it can be reprocessed at the end of its life into virgin bioplastic to be used again.[53]

Full Cycle Bioplastics CEO Andrew Falcon is heartened by the enthusiasm shown by consumers and companies for the circular materials loop his company has developed for organic waste and plastics:

> But this is a new material technology that is expensive to demonstrate, and to scale. We have a much deeper and wider 'valley of death' than a typical startup focused on software or the next big app. Access to capital and partners to showcase successful operation of our system is essential, as is a better understanding of the long-term need.[54]

A perfect example of what publicly created money can do—fund the expansion of this bioplastic technology across the country and across the globe.

Project Drawdown provides a positive note on what we can do now to begin to control plastic. Among the 100 solutions for reducing the carbon and harmful greenhouse gases in our atmosphere is the use of bioplastics. Drawdown states that switching over to bioplastics for just 46% of the estimated plastic market by 2050 will result in keeping 3.8 gigatons of CO2 from going into the atmosphere.[55] That's great.

However, it would seem that by 2050 we had better be making most, if not all, of our plastic as bioplastics.

Can the Insect World Save Us from Our Plastic Addiction?

Scientists have discovered more than 50 known species of microorganisms, mostly bacteria and fungi, called plastivores, which will eat some of the most common plastics, turning the plastics into energy. Insects that eat plastic, such as the greater wax moth, also offer a degree of hope in completing the plastic loop to sustainability. These wax worms presently exist in nature as bee pests that invade beehives and live off the honeycomb. To the wax worm, a plastic bag is the nutritional equivalent of a bee honeycomb. The structure of honeycomb wax is made of long chains of carbon and hydrogen molecules called hydrocarbons, very similar to Professor Plastics' cheerful description of polymers. To the wax worm and the gut bacteria which does its digestion, these hydrocarbon chains of the honeycomb and plastic are equally enticing. Some of the wax worms' gut bacteria even seem to get better results with plastic than with bee honeycombs.[56]

Expert Witnesses: Federica Bertocchini, Developmental Biologist, University of Cantabria, Spain and Bryan Cassone, Associate Professor of Biology, Brandon University, Manitoba, Canada

Dr. Bertocchini made the discovery accidentally in 2015 while cleaning out her backyard beehives. She took some wax worms (*Galleria mellonella*) out of the hive they were living in and put them in an old plastic bag. An hour later when she looked at the bag, she discovered small holes in the part of the bag with the larvae. Although Bertocchini wasn't an entomologist, she guessed immediately what was happening. The wax worms were eating the plastic bag.[57]

Unknown is how the large-scale commercial consumption of plastic by wax worms would impact their health. Also, a very real concern is how the commercial use of wax worms on plastic would affect bee populations, which are already under great stress from climate change, habitat destruction, and mites. Dr. Cassone describes using the gut bacteria of the wax worm to break down plastic:

> We envision harnessing the waxworm and its microbiome [community of microorganisms that exists in a particular environment] to develop approaches that do not require whole organisms – rather the products or by-products produced from their interactions that make their ability to breakdown plastic so efficient.[58]

Can the digestive bacteria inside the wax worm, and perhaps other insects, ultimately save humanity from its plastic addiction? Hopefully, they can be part of the solution. But it seems that we need to concentrate on a massive shift to biodegradable plastics, a revamping of recycling systems, and to focus on manufacturing non-biodegradable plastic products that can be recycled and for which there are the recycling facilities available to do so.

Can our present system of private bank-created debt-money provide the public funds necessary to fund such a monumental undertaking as safely ridding *Spaceship Earth* of its plastic problem without putting us deeper into debt and toxic exposure from pyrolysis? Thus far, no. Our job is to spread the news that publicly created money can provide the funding to take the necessary steps to cure our plastic addiction.

---

1. Zimmerman, Kim Ann, "Pleistocene Epoch: Facts About the Last Ice Age," LiveScience, Aug 29, 2017, https://www.livescience.com/40311-pleistocene-epoch.html
2. Myers, Joe, "What is the Anthropocene? And why does it matter?" World Economic Forum, Nature and Biodiversity, Aug 31, 2016, https://www.weforum.org/stories/2016/08/what-is-the-anthropocene-and-why-does-it-matter/
3. Encyclopedia of the Anthropocene, "Geologic History and Energy," A. Galuska & Z.M. Migaszewski, 2018, https://www.sciencedirect.com/topics/earth-and-planetary-sciences/anthropocene
4. Barnosky, Anthony & Hannibal, Mary Ellen, "Despite Official Vote, the Evidence of the Anthropocene Is Clear," Yale Environment 360, Yale School of the Environment, April 2, 2024, https://e360.yale.edu/features/anthropocene-denied
5. *Ibid.*

6. Haram, Linsey E.; Carlton, James T.; Ruiz, Gregory M.; Maximenko, Nikolai A, "A Plasticene Lexicon," Marine Pollution Bulletin, Jan. 2020, https://www.sciencedirect.com/science/article/pii/S0025326X19308707
7. Foster, John Bellamy, Clark, Brett & York, Richard, *The Ecological Rift -- Capitalism's War on the Earth,* Monthly Review Press, New York, 2010.
8. Rotten Tomatoes, "The Graduate Quotes," https://www.rottentomatoes.com/m/graduate/quotes/#:~:text=Mr.-,Maguire%3A%20Plastics.,that%2C%20I%20find%20you%20desirable
9. Professor Plastics, "What Are Plastics?" PlasticsMakeItPossible.com, https://www.plasticsmakeitpossible.com/about-plastics/types-of-plastics/what-are-plastics/
10. Helmenstine, Anne Marie, Ph.D., "Monomers and Polymers in Chemistry," ThoughtCo.com, https://www.thoughtco.com/monomers-and-polymers-intro-608928#:~:text=Monomers%20are%20small%20molecules%20which,through%20a%20process%20called%20polymerization
11. Biemiller, Amy, "Can we safely burn used plastic objects in a domestic fireplace?" MIT School of Engineering, https://engineering.mit.edu/engage/ask-an-engineer/can-we-safely-burn-used-plastic-objects-in-a-domestic-fireplace/
12. Miandad, Rashid, et al, "Catalytic Pyrolysis of Plastic Waste: Moving Toward Pyrolysis Based Biorefineries," Frontiers in Energy Research, Mar 19, 2019, https://www.frontiersin.org/articles/10.3389/fenrg.2019.00027/full
13. Tullo, Alexander H., "Amid controversy industry goes all in on plastics pyrolysis," Chemical & Engineering News, Oct 10, 2022, https://cen.acs.org/articles/100/i36/Amid-controversy-industry-goes-plastics-pyrolysis.html
14. *Ibid.*
15. United States Environmental Protection Agency, "Evolution of the Clean Air Act," https://www.epa.gov/clean-air-act-overview/evolution-clean-air-act#:~:text=The%20enactment%20of%20the%20Clean,industrial)%20sources%20and%20mobile%20sources
16. Casale, Matt, "Letter: Reject Burning Plastic," Public Interest Research Group, Sept 19, 2022, https://publicinterestnetwork.org/wp-content/uploads/2022/09/House-Letter-Concerning-Federal-Plastic-Burning-_-Chemical-Recycling-Bill.pdf
17. Geyer, Roland, Jambeck, Jenna R. & Law, Karen Lavender, "Production, use and fate of all plastics ever made," Science Advances, July 19, 2017, American Association for the Advancement in Science, https://advances.sciencemag.org/content/3/7/e1700782.full
18. Casale, Matt, "Letter: Reject Burning Plastic," Public Interest Research Group, Sept 19, 2022.
19. Kummer, Frank, "Only about 5% of plastic waste gets recycled in US, new report says," Phys.Org, May 5, 2022, https://phys.org/news/2022-05-plastic-recycled.html
20. Parker, Laura, "A whopping 91% of plastic isn't recycled," National Geographic, Dec 20, 2018, https://www.nationalgeographic.com/news/2017/07/plastic-produced-recycling-waste-ocean-trash-debris-environment/#:~:text=Of%20the%208.3%20billion%20metric,the%20natural%20environment%20as%20litter
21. Brazil, Rachel, "Life's Origins by Land or Sea? Debate Gets Hot," *Scientific American, Chemistry World*, May 15, 2017, https://www.scientificamerican.com/article/lifes-origins-by-land-or-sea-debate-gets-hot/

22. Marine Debris Program, "Garbage Patches," U.S. Department of Commerce, National Oceanic Atmospheric Administration, National Ocean Service, https://marinedebris.noaa.gov/info/patch.html
23. Wright, Pam, "UN Ocean Conference: Plastics Dumped In Oceans Could Outweigh Fish by 2050, Secretary-General Says," The Weather Channel, June 6, 2017, https://weather.com/science/environment/news/united-nations-ocean-conference-antonio-guterres-plastics
24. Thomson, Peter, "The Ocean Conference: A Game Changer," United Nations, https://www.un.org/en/chronicle/article/ocean-conference-game-changer
25. Pussalla, Achala, "Elephants dying from eating plastic waste in Sri Lanka dump," AP News, Jan 14, 2022, https://apnews.com/article/elephants-dying-plastic-waste-sri-lanka-af9c9e843c518bcbc02af760fb84ee33
26. Miller, Chaz, "How Green Was My Garbage Truck?" Waste360.com, May 1, 2011, https://www.waste360.com/blog/how-green-was-my-garbage-truck
27. Parker, Laura, "A whopping 91% of plastic isn't recycled."
28. *Ibid.*
29. United Nations, "What Is Plastic Pollution," Sustainable Development Goals, https://www.un.org/sustainabledevelopment/blog/2023/08/explainer-what-is-plastic-pollution/
30. Plastics Industry Association, "2023 Size and Impact," https://www.plasticsindustry.org/data-report/size-and-impact-2023/
31. ABC News, "Trashed: The Secret Life of Plastic Recycling," May 24, 2023, YouTube, "Trashed: The Secret Life of Plastic Recycling."
32. Cho, Renee, "The Truth about Bioplastics," Columbia Climate School, State of the Planet, Dec 13, 2017, https://news.climate.columbia.edu/2017/12/13/the-truth-about-bioplastics/
33. National Oceanic and Atmospheric Administration, "What are microplastics?" U.S. Department of Commerce, https://oceanservice.noaa.gov/facts/microplastics.html
34. Thompson, Dennis, "Autopsies Show Microplastics in All Major Human Organs," U.S. News & World Report, Aug 17, 2020, https://www.usnews.com/news/health-news/articles/2020-08-17/autopsies-show-microplastics-in-all-major-human-organs
35. Nash, Sam, "Our Bodies Consume a Credit Card's Worth of Plastic Every Week," Medium.com Being Well, Aug 19, 2020, https://medium.com/beingwell/our-bodies-consume-a-credit-cards-worth-of-plastic-every-week-a402fe95a092
36. Gigault, Julien, et al, "Current Opinion: What is a nanoplastic?" Environmental Pollution Volume 235, April 2018, pp. 1030-34, https://www.sciencedirect.com/science/article/abs/pii/S0269749117337247
37. Nash, Sam, "Our Bodies Consume a Credit Card's Worth of Plastic Every Week," Medium.com Being Well, Aug 19, 2020.
38. Winters, Joseph, "All that plastic in the ocean is a climate change problem, too," Grist, Oct 17, 2022, https://grist.org/science/all-that-plastic-in-the-ocean-is-a-climate-change-problem-too/
39. Global Climate Change Data Lab, "Our World in Data—Annual CO2 emissions," Oxford Martin School, University of Oxford, https://ourworldindata.org/grapher/annual-co2-emissions-per-country?country=~OWID_WRL
40. Winters, Joseph, "All that plastic in the ocean is a climate change problem, too," Grist, Oct 17, 2022,
41. *Ibid.*

42. *Ibid.*
43. Shen, Maocai; Ye, Shujing; Zeng, Guangming; Zhang, Yaxin; Xing, Lang; Tang, Wangwang; Wen, Xiaofe ng & Liu, Shaoheng, "Can microplastics pose a threat to ocean carbon sequestration?" Marine Pollution Bulletin, Volume 150, January 2020, https://www.sciencedirect.com/science/article/abs/pii/S0025326X19308689?via%3Dihub
44. Simon, Matt, *A Poison Like No Other—How Microplastics Corrupted Our Planet and Our Bodies*, Island Press, 2022, Washington, D.C., https://islandpress.org/books/poison-no-other
45. Simon, Matt, *A Poison Like No Other—How Microplastics Corrupted Our Planet and Our Bodies*, Island Press, 2022, Washington, D.C., pp. 8-9.
46. Lynch, Iseult, University of Birmingham, U.K., https://research.birmingham.ac.uk/en/persons/iseult-lynch
47. Lynch, Iseult, quoted in, Simon, Matt, *A Poison Like No Other—How Microplastics Corrupted Our Planet and Our Bodies*, Island Press, 2022, Washington, D.C., p. 17
48. Meredith, Sam, "Led by ExxonMobil, 20 companies are responsible for over half of 'throwaway' plastic waste." CNBC, May 18, 2021, https://www.cnbc.com/2021/05/18/20-companies-responsible-for-55percent-of-single-use-plastic-waste-study.html#:~:text%3DThe%20study%20says%20100%20companies,glob-al%20banks%2C%20the%20study%20said.
49. Friedman Lauren F., "The Plastic Chemicals Hiding in Your Food," Consumer Reports, Jan 4, 2024, https://www.consumerreports.org/health/food-contaminants/the-plastic-chemicals-hiding-in-your-food-a7358224781/
50. Wang, Yufei & Qian, Haifeng, "Phthalates and Their Impacts on Human Health," National Library of Medicine, May 18, 2021, https://www.ncbi.nlm.nih.gov/pmc/articles/PMC8157593/
51. Science Museum, "The Age of Plastic: from Parkensine to Pollution," Oct 11, 2019, London, England, https://www.sciencemuseum.org.uk/objects-and-stories/chemistry/age-plastic-parkesine-pollution
52. Flint, Kristen L., "Biodegradable Plastics: Its Promises and Consequences," Dartmouth Undergraduate School of Science, March 2, 2013, https://sites.dartmouth.edu/dujs/2013/03/02/biodegradable-plastic-its-promises-and-consequences/
53. Cho, Renee, "The Truth about Bioplastics"
54. Musings Magazine, "Full Cycle Bioplastics Turns Bacteria Waste into 'Nature's Plastic,'" July 11, 2019, https://www.musingsmag.com/full-cycle-bioplastics-turns-bacteria-waste-into-natures-plastic/
55. Project Drawdown, "Bioplastics," Solution, https://drawdown.org/solutions/bioplastics
56. Betz, Eric, "Scientists Found a Caterpillar that Eats Plastic. Could It Help Solve Our Plastic Crisis?" Discover Magazine, Mar 4, 2020,https://www.discovermagazine.com/environment/scientists-found-a-caterpillar-that-eats-plastic-could-it-help-solveour
57. Arnold, Carrie, "This Bug Can Eat Plastic. But Can It Clean Up Our Mess?", National Geographic, April 24, 2017, https://www.nationalgeographic.com/science/article/wax-worms-eat-plastic-polyethylene-trash-pollution-cleanup
58. Bote, Joshua, "These tiny plastic-munching caterpillars can clean up our world—but there's a catch," USA Today, March 6, 2020, https://www.usatoday.com/story/

news/nation/2020/03/06/waxworms-caterpillars-eat-plastic-pollution-but-could-also-hurt-bees/4952495002/

FIVE

Heat Waves, Droughts, Wildfires & Floods, Oh My!

Not forgetting the ever-increasing number and intensity of hurricanes and tornadoes to add to those mentioned above. This is the new normal as the climate warms and simply ignoring the problem will not make it go away. Just as Dorothy and her companions in *The Wizard of Oz* skipped along the yellow brick road singing to keep up their courage, "Lions and tigers and bears, oh my!" we need to steel ourselves for the task ahead. Publicly created money, the one thing the economics establishment absolutely shuns today, is the only way forward to create, debt-free, the tremendous amounts of money needed to properly address the crises that confront us. Let us not forget that millions of good-paying jobs will also be created when we begin real climate action to draw down the greenhouse gasses in our atmosphere, responsibly clean up our plastic pollution and tackle our other environmental crises.

The COVID-19 pandemic and the inflation that followed it present a whole host of issues that our present bank-created debt-money system is simply not capable of resolving without piling up mountains of debt. History tells us that this is not the last pandemic or economic crisis we will face. And common sense tells us that our destruction of the environment will continue to add crises to the mix, fast and furious. The future of *Spaceship Earth* rests in how we proceed.

Reexamining Our Zeitgeist

'Zeitgeist' is the German word for the general beliefs, ideas, and spirit that predominate a time and place. Earlier in 2020, when the COVID pandemic was first raging in the Northeast and we were in lockdown in the Midwest, I heard someone say that COVID could be Earth's response to the human assault on the environment. Nature was fighting back because man is destroying nature. At first, I chuckled thinking that it was kind of a clever proposition to make. But the more I thought about it, the more sense it made. We exist within the zeitgeist of a capitalist-heavy economic system, combined with a democracy-light political system and a debt-slavery money system, the combination of which have put *Spaceship Earth's* life forms on a death spiral. Why wouldn't our Mother Earth fire a COVID warning shot across humanity's bow to get our attention?

Is it just possible that humanity has made some serious errors in judgment, and that it is now up to us to do some course correcting? Author of *Spillover: Animal Infections and the Next Pandemic*, David Quammen:

> We invade tropical forests and other wild landscapes, which harbor so many species of animals and plants—and within those creatures, so many unknown viruses. We cut the trees, we kill the animals or cage them and send them to markets. We disrupt ecosystems, and we shake viruses loose from their natural hosts. When that happens, they need a new host. Often, we are it.[1]

Enacting a system of publicly created money would solve the funding problem so that we could get our act together and develop a sustainable manner of living in relationship to the other life forms and ecosystems on our planet. Continuing on with the fraudulent, dysfunctional, bank-created debt-money system, on the other hand, will yield more debt and similar results to what we are currently getting. In *Money Creation 101*: Chapter 7 we presented the NEED Act which was put into Congress in 2011. This system of publicly created money was promptly shunned by Congress, the Federal Reserve, the vast majority of the economics profession, and the mainstream media. If one wonders why we continue to use the bank-created debt-money system, it is precisely because the economics profession refuses to debate the merits of publicly created money. If there is no honest debate, there is no chance that the American people will ever get the opportunity to choose between the crisis-prone, bank-created debt-money system or a Constitutional and democratic system of publicly created money.

When the heat waves, droughts, wildfires, floods, tornadoes and hurricanes hit close to home, even the most adamant climate change deniers are slowly beginning to realize that something must be done. As it also becomes apparent that the bank-created debt-money system is not structurally equipped to properly fund these crises, with each potentially costing trillions of dollars, that is precisely the time to begin an open discussion of publicly creating our money.

Climate Change Rears Its Head

The Pacific Northwest states of Washington and Oregon, along with neighboring British Columbia, Canada, are known for mild weather, largely as a result of their proximity to the Pacific Ocean. Yet for the three days of June 26–28, 2021, they experienced one of the most severe heat waves in our two countries' history. What is so extraordinary about this heat wave was not only its intensity but also the fact that it occurred in a geographic area that is characterized by its moderate weather. The average daytime high temperature in Portland, Oregon, is 74 degrees Fahrenheit in June and 81 degrees Fahrenheit in July. In Seattle, Washington, it is 70 degrees in June and 76 degrees in July.[2] During the three-day June 2021 heat wave, Portland experienced temperatures up to 116 degrees (35–42 degrees above normal),[3] while

Seattle had temperatures up to 108 degrees (32–38 degrees above normal).[4] If what happened in the Pacific Northwest in 2021 is the harbinger of things to come, we need to immediately do whatever is necessary to stop climate change in its tracks.

On June 27, 2021, the tiny town of Lytton, British Columbia, recorded a temperature of 116 degrees Fahrenheit, the warmest temperature ever recorded anywhere in Canada. It broke the record the next day June 28 with a temperature of 118 degrees, and then again, the following day June 29 with a temperature of 121 degrees.[5] The only warmer recorded temperatures in the U.S. and Canada have been recorded in places like the Mojave and Sonoran Deserts in the American Southwest. Lytton is 1,200 miles north of these American deserts.

A year earlier the Furnace Creek Visitor Center at Death Valley National Park in California set its own records for recorded hot temperatures. On August 16, 2020, temperatures were recorded at 129.9 degrees, and then the new record was set on July 9, 2021, of 130.0 degrees.[a] [6]

During the late summer of 2021, the majority of California, Oregon, Washington, Nevada, Idaho, Montana, Utah, Arizona, North Dakota, South Dakota, and Minnesota experienced extreme to exceptional drought, while significant areas of New Mexico, Colorado, Wyoming, Iowa, Maine, Vermont, Wisconsin, Illinois, Nebraska, Kansas, West Virginia, and Virginia had moderate to severe drought, as reported by CNN and the U.S. Drought Monitor.[7] [8] The True North Fire, Weather & Avalanche Center showed more than 100 active wildfires in the U.S. on September 2, 2021.[9]

On August 29, 2021, Hurricane Ida slammed into the Louisiana

---

[a] Although the official world record from the World Meteorological Organization (WMO) is 134% recorded at Furnace Creek in 1913, this reading and others from Africa of above 130 degrees have been widely disputed by climatologists Christopher Burt, William Reid and Maximiliano Herrera. "The old Death Valley record from July 1913 is 100% bogus (not just 99.9% such), as are all other temperature readings of 130 degrees Fahrenheit or higher from Africa in the past," Burt said. But decertifying the WMO record would require forming an investigative committee and a multi-year process of review for which there is now no motivation.

Gulf Coast near New Orleans as one of the five largest hurricanes to ever hit the U.S. As the remnants of the storm moved up the Eastern Atlantic states it delivered unmatched flash flooding, killing nearly 50 people in New York, New Jersey, Pennsylvania, and Connecticut. Ida delivered this death and destruction 1,100 miles from where it had made landfall in Louisiana, leaving more than one million people without water and power. Many of these people had little hope of getting either water or power restored for a month or more, at the same time as a heat wave put temperatures in the nineties and the heat index over 100 degrees in Louisiana.[10] The United States Geological Survey states that we can expect more intense storms, droughts, and wildfires as a result of mankind's climate change–induced global warming.[11]

Expert Witness: National Oceanic and Atmospheric Administration–Annual 2023 Global Climate Report:

> The year 2023 was the warmest year since global records began in 1850 at 1.18°C (2.12°F) above the 20th century average of 13.9°C (57.0°F) ... The 10 warmest years in the 174-year record have been the last ten years (2014–2023).[12] [13]

Last year 2023 was the warmest on record and the last ten individual years have been the warmest ten individual years in the 174-years we have been keeping temperature records. Yikes!

As these storms increase in frequency and intensity, we may decide as a society that some of our population centers need to be relocated to higher ground away from the storm-frequented areas. Within the structure of the debt-money system, the billions and trillions of dollars needed to deal with the weather caused destruction and the relocation of people in flood prone areas, all exacerbated by climate change, must be created by private banks and then loaned to us and our government, at interest, to spend on the crises. The people themselves, through our federal government, will be responsible for repaying the loans plus interest. As long as our money continues to be created as debt by private banks, we will never have enough money available to properly tackle climate change and help our people cope with the destruction it causes. We have a choice. We can either reclaim the ancient lost power of publicly created money, enabling us to proceed confidently into the future aboard *Spaceship Earth*, or we can timidly continue under the bank-created debt-money system, terrified of what new disasters tomorrow may bring.

The 16 U.S. Weather Disasters of 2022 Exceeding $1 Billion in Damage

Located within the National Oceanic and Atmospheric Administration (NOAA), the National Centers for Environmental Administration are tasked with charting weather disasters and computing their damage. A total of 90 declared disasters were listed in 2022,[14] 15 of which exceeded $1 billion.[15] Winter Storm Elliott occurred late in December 2022 and was not yet on the website, but already has a $5.4 billion estimated cost by catastrophe modeler Karen Clark & Co,[16] became our sixteenth billion-dollar-plus weather disaster of the year 2022.

The 16 U.S. Billion-Dollar-Plus Weather Disasters of 2022 in Chronological Order[17]

1. Southern Tornado Outbreak, March 30, 2022: An outbreak of 83 tornadoes focused across the Gulf Coast states of Louisiana, Mississippi, Alabama, and Florida. One of the EF-3 tornadoes in Washington County, Arkansas, damaged an elementary school, homes, businesses, and buildings at the Springdale Municipal Airport. Cost $1.3 billion. Deaths 2.

2. Southeastern Tornado Outbreak, April 4–6: A tornado outbreak with 100 preliminary tornadoes occurred across Texas, Louisiana, Mississippi, Alabama, Georgia, Florida, and South Carolina. An EF-4 tornado in Pembroke, Georgia, on April 5 with winds up to 185 mph destroyed

several neighborhoods. Many of the other tornadoes across the South caused considerable damage to homes, businesses, vehicles, and other infrastructure. Cost $1.4 billion. Deaths 3.

3. Southern Severe Weather, April 11–13, 2022: Over three days severe weather, including high winds and tornadoes, occurred across Arkansas, Louisiana, Mississippi, Alabama, Texas, Tennessee, and Kentucky, damaging homes, businesses, farms, outbuildings, and other infrastructure. There was also considerable hail damage across Wisconsin and Minnesota. Cost $2.7 billion. Deaths 1.

4. Southern Central Severe Weather, May 1–3, 2022: Southern and Central states including Texas, Oklahoma, Ohio, and Pennsylvania experienced high winds and large hail damaging homes, businesses, vehicles, and agriculture assets. Cost $1.1 billion. Deaths 1.

5. North Central Hailstorms, May 9, 2022: Hailstorms across south-central Minnesota and into western Wisconsin, some with golf ball–to baseball-sized hail, caused extensive damage to homes, vehicles, businesses, and other infrastructure. Cost $1.9 billion. No deaths reported.

6. North Central Severe Weather, May 11–12, 2022: Severe weather caused tornado, hail, and high wind damage across several states including South Dakota, Nebraska, Minnesota, and Wisconsin. Eastern Nebraska and Southern Minnesota, including St. Cloud and the Minneapolis metro area, experienced hail and high winds. South Dakota and central Minnesota had more than two dozen tornadoes which caused damage to homes, vehicles, businesses, agriculture, and other infrastructure. Cost $2.6 billion. Deaths 1.

7. North Central Hailstorms, May 19, 2022: Numerous golf ball–sized hailstorms caused damage across southeastern Minnesota and western Wisconsin. These hailstorms were south of the hailstorms that had occurred just 10 days earlier on May 9. Cost $1.8 billion. No deaths reported.

8. Central Severe Weather, June 7–8, 2022: Damaging hail, high winds, and more than two dozen tornadoes across numerous states, including Colorado, Nebraska, Kansas, Missouri, Oklahoma, Texas, Iowa, and Ohio, caused widespread damage to homes, businesses, vehicles, farms, and agriculture and other infrastructure. Cost $1.8 billion. No deaths reported.

9. Central Derecho,[b] June 13, 2022: A powerful storm with high winds that hit Michigan, Illinois, Indiana, and Ohio. Thousands of trees were lost, uprooted by the winds, causing damage to homes, businesses, vehicles, power lines, and infrastructure. Cost $2.9 billion. Deaths 1.

10. North Central and Eastern Severe Weather, July 22–24, 2022: Severe weather with high winds and 19 tornadoes hit numerous states including North Dakota, Minnesota, Wisconsin, Michigan, Illinois, Indiana, Ohio, Pennsylvania, Virginia, Maryland, and New York. Homes, businesses, vehicles, agriculture, and other infrastructure were damaged. Cost $1.3 billion. Deaths 1.

11. Kentucky and Missouri Flooding, July 2022: Stalled frontal system delivered 9–12 inches of rainfall in the St. Louis

---

[b] A derecho is a wide, powerful storm that moves through extremely fast, bringing strong wind, rain, and hail. They are frightening to experience, both as they are seen approaching and then as they are endured. Just a few years ago in NW Indiana we experienced 3 or 4 of them within a month. Previously in seventy-some years on Earth I had never even seen one or heard the word *derecho* before.

metro area and 5–10+ inches across eastern Kentucky, producing deadly flash flooding. More than 600 helicopter and numerous swift water rescues by boat were needed to save people trapped by the quickly rising flood waters. Cost $1.2 billion. Deaths 42.

12. Hurricane Fiona, Sept 17–18, 2022: Category 1 hurricane in Puerto Rico with 12–18 inches of rain caused widespread flooding, mudslides, and significant damage to regional power grids, homes, businesses, vehicles, and infrastructure. Cost to be determined. Deaths 15.

13. Western/Southern Plains Drought & Heat Wave, Jan–Sept 2022: Western and Southern Plains states under extreme drought conditions. Lake Mead, Lake Powell, Lake Oroville, Shasta Lake, and other large reservoirs continue to be depleted. The nation's largest reservoir, Lake Mead, is nearing dead pool status and is at the lowest level since it was filled in the 1930s. The Great Salt Lake is also near record-low levels. [The heavy snows in 2024 have finally somewhat alleviated this drought, specifically in Lake Mead and Lake Powell.[18]] The drought has severely affected agricultural crops and feed costs for livestock. Drought conditions exacerbate wildfire risk. Extreme heat developed for many days across Western and Central states and caused more than one hundred heat-related fatalities across Arizona, Nevada, California, Oregon, and Texas. Cost $9.3 billion. Deaths 117.

14. Western Wildfires, spring–fall 2022: Severe drought and extreme heat provided conditions favorable for another damaging western wildfire season most focused across New Mexico, California, Oregon, Washington, Idaho, Montana, and Alaska. More than 6.9 million acres burned in the Calf Canyon and Hermits Peak Fires (New Mexico), the Double

Creek Fire (Oregon), the Moose Fire (Idaho), the Mosquito Fire (California), the Trail Creek Fire (Montana), the Lime Complex Fire (Alaska), and many others. Cost $2.5 billion. Deaths 17.

15. Hurricane Ian, Sept 28–30, 2022: Hurricane Ian slammed into the Florida Gulf Coast at Cayo Costa on September 28, 2022, as a category 4 hurricane with maximum sustained winds of 155 mph, tying the record for the fifth-strongest hurricane on record to strike the United States. It carried a storm surge of 15 to 18 feet and dumped 10–20 inches of rain across the central part of Florida.[19] The estimated cost is yet to be determined by the National Oceanic and Atmospheric Administration. Dr. Adam Rose estimates cost at $42–$258 billion. Deaths 131. [Updated cost is $112 billion, 156 dead.[20]]

16. Winter Storm Elliott, Dec 21–31: Huge swath of U.S., the most affected states were Georgia, New York, North Carolina, Tennessee, and Texas. Buffalo, N.Y., had 70 mph winds and 49 inches of snow.[21] Estimated cost $8.6 billion. Deaths were at least 39 in Erie County, New York, where Buffalo is located.[22] Many who died were people trapped in their cars, as rescue workers were unable to get to them in time because of the severity of the storm. A total of 87 people died.[23]

Billion-Dollar Weather and Climate Disasters Increase from 16 to 28 in 2023

The National Centers for Environmental Information reports that the number of Billion-Dollar Weather and Climate Disasters, adjusted for inflation, increased from the record of 16 in 2022 to a new record of 28 in 2023. There is no reason to believe that these increases will not continue unless we find a way to create and spend the massive amounts of money, that will be necessary to stop pumping carbon and other dangerous greenhouse gasses into *Spaceship Earth's* atmosphere. National Centers for Environmental Information reported:

> In 2023, there were 28 confirmed weather/climate disaster events with losses exceeding $1 billion each to affect United States. These events included 1 drought event, 4 flooding events, 19 severe storm events, 2 tropical cyclone events, 1 wildfire event, and 1 winter storm event. Overall, these events resulted in the deaths of 492 people and had significant economic effects on the areas impacted.[24]

Adjusted for inflation, from 1980-1984 we had only 5 individual Billion-Dollar Weather and Climate Disasters in the U.S., or an average of 1 per year.[25] In one-year 2023, we had 28 in a single year, also adjusted for inflation. In the span of just four decades, we are now 28 times more likely to have a major climate disaster.

On September 26, 2024, Hurricane Helene made landfall on the Big Bend area of the Florida Panhandle, wreaking havoc across Florida, Georgia, the Carolinas, Tennessee and Kentucky. The federal website to provide us information is down: "National Center for Environmental Information in Asheville, North Carolina has been significantly impacted by Hurricane Helene. We are working to resolve these issues as soon as possible. We apologize for any inconvenience."[26] Asheville, North Carolina is 539 miles from Horseshoe Beach, Florida where Helene made landfall and it has been hit the hardest by the flooding in this peaceful mountain town of 94,000 people. North Carolina has reported 77 deaths from Helene, with Buncombe County, home to Asheville, reporting 40 deaths. More are expected. Early estimates are that Hurricane Helene damage will be $225-250 billion.[27]

Hurricane Milton is scheduled to make landfall in Central Florida near Tampa on the evening of October 10, 2024, two weeks after Hurricane Helene made landfall.[28]

Why We Are Experiencing Increased Disasters & What We Should Do

Adam Rose, Professor of Public Policy at the University of Southern California, had pegged the cost of 2022's Hurricane Ian at somewhere between $42 and $258 billion, with the cost likely somewhere in the middle.[29] In August 2023 the cost is estimated at $112.9 billion and 152 people dead.[30] Very costly and deadly, but trailing 2006 Hurricane Katrina at $186 billion, with 1,833 lost lives.[31]

Expert Witness: Dr. Adam Rose

Professor of Public Policy University of Southern California

Professor Rose on why we are experiencing an increase in climate and environmental disasters. What should have been done in the past and what should be done in the future to lessen these disasters:

> The U.S. would have benefited from better land-use planning in the mid-20th century. And it would have also helped if Americans had started decades ago to take action to mitigate climate change in the first place by reducing greenhouse gas emissions and slowing the pace of deforestation.
>
> What could make future disasters less costly?
>
> Natural disasters occur due to a combination of physical events, like hurricanes and earthquakes, and the vulnerability of homes, businesses and all the structures people rely on. Storms are getting stronger and human settlement systems are expanding, thereby increasing their vulnerability.
>
> More people are moving closer to the coastlines as others who lost homes in disasters are rebuilding in floodplains—perpetuating losses.
>
> In 2005, I led a report to Congress known as the Natural Hazard Mitigation Saves study, for which our team examined 10 years of FEMA Hazard Mitigation Assistance Grants.[32] This money flows to state and local governments, Indian tribal

> organizations and nonprofits for projects designed to rebuild and lower the risk of future property damage and business interruption losses after a presidential disaster declaration.
>
> We found that one of the most effective tactics to reduce disaster losses was to buy out properties from homeowners residing in flood-prone areas to eliminate the need to help them rebuild again and again.[33]

Professor Rose's conclusion that one of the most effective things we could do is buy out properties from homeowners that live in flood-prone areas, so that we don't have to keep helping them "rebuild again and again" in the future, exposes the structural flaw in the bank-created debt-money system. Within this convoluted system, this huge investment in our country's people and their future could only be done through a massive increase in public debt. Yet the Republican political party has no appetite to massively increase debt for what most of us know must be done. While some in the Democratic political party might be willing to take the plunge and massively increase debt to save Earth, this is hardly a unanimous position. What is unanimous among both of our political parties is their almost absolute ignorance of the concept of publicly created money that could solve the funding issue, without increasing debt or raising taxes.

The Bank-Created Debt-Money System Unclothed

As we demonstrated throughout *Money Creation 101*, there is an alternative to the dreadful bank-created debt-money system. Despite the revelations by the Bank of England,[34] Dr. Joseph Huber,[35] Drs. Michael Kumhof & Jaromir Benes,[36] Dr. Richard Werner,[37] Dr. Kaoru Yamaguchi,[38] Stephen Zarlenga,[39] and others, the economics profession in general has ignored their work. The concept of a system of just, sovereign, publicly created money continues to be kept in the shadows by economics professionals, who refuse to recognize its past historical successes (documented in *History of Money 101*) and future promise. Many of these economists inadvertently carry the water for the bank-created debt-money system. Perhaps, they do so because they have been taught nothing about the concept of publicly created money in their own education. Or perhaps, they are simply not willing to risk their own careers by pointing out that the bank-created debt-money system stands fraudulent and dysfunctional before us, completely unable to heal our people or our planet—as naked as was the emperor in Hans Christian Andersen's nineteenth-century Danish fairy tale *The Emperor's New Clothes*.[40]

Hurricane Ian v. Babcock Ranch, Florida

Fort Myers Beach, Florida took a direct hit in 2022 from Hurricane Ian's eighteen-foot storm surge that damaged or completely destroyed 97% of its structures.[41] Ian proceeded through Fort Myers on an east-northeast course across the state. Babcock Ranch, just 14 miles north-east of Fort Myers, took a major lashing from Ian, yet sustained minimal damage with no loss of power to any of the 2,000 homes in the Charlotte County community. Meanwhile, Ian had taken out the power to 2.6 million homes in the state, including 90% of the homes in Charlotte County in which Babcock Ranch is located.[42] What is different about Babcock Ranch?

Babcock Ranch calls itself "America's first solar-powered town." It has a solar grid of 700,000 individual panels that is enough to power the town now and into the future. All the town's utilities are underground. The town's streets are not built up to discourage flooding; rather, they are built slightly below ground level to guide storm-water to run off into lower natural areas and keep the homes from flooding. As Hurricane Ian pounded southwest Florida, Babcock did see some huge trees uprooted and some homes lost a few shingles; otherwise, things were perfectly normal when the residents stepped outside their homes. After the storm had passed, the school field house was used to take in residents from other nearby communities whose homes had been destroyed.[43] In 2024, Hurricane Milton hit Central Florida's Gulf Coast, and again, Babcock Ranch had minimal damage and was able to take in evacuees from other towns into its school, 40,000-square-foot sports facility and private homes.[44]

Counting the Cost 2022: A Year of Climate Breakdown

This report was released by Christian Aid on December 27, 2022. It lists 2022's ten costliest climate events across the globe, each costing at least $3 billion. Also included is another list that includes ten other climate events in the poorer Global South, many of which caused much more massive suffering than those in the developed world without the corresponding monetary damage because their infrastructure is much simpler and less expensive than ours. [45]

Most Expensive Climate Events of 2022 in Chronological Order[46]

- Storm Eunice, Feb 14–19, Extra-tropical Cyclone, Belgium, Germany, Ireland, Poland & UK, Deaths 16, Displaced unreported, Cost $4.3 billion
- East Australia Floods, Feb 23–Mar 31, Deaths 27, Displaced 60,000+, Cost $7.5 billion
- KwaZulu Natal & Eastern Cape Floods, South Africa, April 8–15, Deaths 459, Displaced 40,000+, Cost $3 billion
- Pakistan Floods, June–Sept, Deaths 1,739, Displaced 7 million, Cost $5.6 billion
- China Floods, June–Sept, Deaths 0, Displaced 239, Cost $12.3 billion
- European Drought, June–Sept, All Europe, Deaths & Displaced unreported, Cost $20 billion
- Hurricane Fiona, Sept 14–28, Caribbean, Canada, Deaths 25+, Displaced 13,000, Cost $3 billion
- Hurricane Ian, Sept 23–Oct 2, Tropical Cyclone, Cuba, U.S., Deaths 130, Displaced 40,000+, Cost $100 billion
- Brazil Drought, all year, Deaths & Displaced unreported, Cost $4 billion

- China Drought, all year, Deaths & Displaced unreported, Cost $8.4 billion

Other 2022 Noteworthy Events [Cost Unknown] in the Global South:[47]

- Malaysian Floods, Dec 16, 2021–Jan 19, 2022, tropical depression, Deaths 54, Displaced 70,000, Cost Unknown
- Back-to-back Storms in Southeast Africa, Jan 22–Feb 5, tropical storms & cyclones, Madagascar, Mozambique & Malawi, Deaths 366, Displaced Unknown, Cost Unknown
- Tierra del Fuego Wildfire, Jan 20–Mar 16, Chile, Deaths, Displaced & Cost Unknown
- Petropolis Floods, Feb 15, Brazil, Deaths 231, Displaced 1,400, Cost Unknown
- Arctic & Antarctic Heat Waves, March 18, Heat Wave, Deaths, Displaced & Cost Unknown [The ultimate cost of these polar heat waves which melt glacier and sea ice will eventually be felt by the entire planet.]
- India & Pakistan Heat Wave, March & April, Reported Deaths 90 (the real figure is probably orders of magnitude higher), Displaced & Cost Unknown
- West Africa Floods, October, Mali, Cameroon, Nigeria & Niger, Deaths 600+, Displaced 1.3 million, Cost Unknown
- Cyclone Sitrang, October, Bangladesh, Deaths 35, Displaced 1 million, Cost Unknown
- Tropical Storm Nalgae, October, Philippines, Deaths 162, Displaced 850,000, Cost Unknown
- Horn of Africa Drought, All Year, Somalia, Ethiopia & Kenya, 36 million people affected, Deaths, Displaced & Cost Unknown

When assessing these climate disasters across the globe, it is important to remember that the monetary cost experienced is always many times greater in the U.S. and the rest of the developed world than for the Global South. This for the simple reason that we in the developed world have much more expensive physical buildings and infrastructure that can be damaged than the much simpler huts and other buildings in the undeveloped world. In addition to their smaller price tag, their lives lost and displaced are often not even counted, while their suffering is often greater than ours because they have less ability to pay to rebuild.

American Monetary Institute Conference Statements to COP26 and COP28

Linking the climate crisis to our deeply flawed bank-created money system, the American Monetary Institute's 17th and 19th Annual Conferences on Monetary Reform issued statements to the participants of the UN Climate Conferences COP26 in 2021 and COP28 in 2023.

The American Monetary Institute 2023 Conference Statement to COP 28:

> To: The participants of the UN Climate Conference's COP28
> Re: The Monetary Dimension of Environmental Degradation
> From: The American Monetary Institute, other civic organizations, and concerned individuals
> Date: November 6, 2023
>
> Dear participants,
>
> This is a timely and urgent message to all of you who are concerned about the causes and solutions of climate change.
>
> We are a group of concerned citizens–including academics, experts and activists–who have delved into the current, global monetary system and its problematic impact on society and the environment.
>
> We were gathered at the 19th Monetary Reform Conference organized by the American Monetary Institute in which context we have formulated this letter…
>
> Our concise statement with ample background references is the following:

We acknowledge there exists a strong correlation between the current, debt-based monetary system [i, ii] and environmental degradation, including climate change. It acts through multiple paths of transmission [iii, iv, v, vi], which have to be taken into account to find just and sustainable solutions.

The current monetary system is a debt-based system, because most of the money used for economic transactions, both in the real economy and the Finance, Insurance and Real Estate (FIRE) sector [vii], is generated through the creation of debt when banks extend loans [vii, ix]. This system is also a major cause of destructive economic boom and bust cycles, and creates socioeconomic inequality and political polarisation between and within creditor and a debtor classes [x].

Furthermore, we strongly believe that sovereign monetary reform (SMR) [xi, xi, xii, xiii] will allow substantial public investments, which are required [xiv, xv] to steer global civilization [xvi] from our brown, carbon-based age to a green, equitable, post- fossil fuel age [xvii] with a balanced carbon cycle [xviii].

In the case of the USA, SMR would entail the three following inter-connected changes to its current design:

- Requires Congress to be the sole creator of all U.S. money debt-free, as authorized in the U.S. Constitution [xix];
- Ends the privilege of commercial banks to create money; and
- Makes all remaining operations of the Federal Reserve System accountable to the public [xx].

At an international level parallel institutions and regulations should be developed including: 1) a supranational reserve currency; 2) an international clearing system [xxi]; 3) a monetary authority of currency issuance [xxii]; and 4) an advisory Intergovernmental Panel on Economic and Social Issues (IPESI) to assess progress and detect problems [xxiii].

Given the promising nature of SMR, we, the undersigned, therefore call for a UN Monetary Commission to investigate the strengths and weaknesses of the current monetary system, and to evaluate alternate proposals, especially SMR, to improve it [xiv, xxv, xxvi].

We invite you to become familiar with this line of analysis and, based on it, our policy proposal, to which we hope you will give due attention.[48]

Author's Note: The statement is then signed by more than 30 organizations and 80 individuals, both in the US and worldwide that support a system of sovereign money [publicly created money]. The footnotes in the report provide the academic explanations for publicly creating money to combat climate change and reduce inequality, in both the US and across the globe. The easiest way to access the footnotes is to use the link in the endnote above and go to the American Monetary Institute website for the AMI Conference Statement to COP28 and access the footnotes online that offer concise statements for each author.

These are academic arguments being made for an academic audience at COP28. The goal of the entire three books of the *People, Planet & Power of Money Project* has been to present information in an easily understandable manner. Yet, we also must be able to refute the automatic, academic consensus acceptance of the bank-created debt-money system. This requires occasional forays into academic discussions, some of which may be difficult for newcomers to understand. Please remember, we are refuting a money system that was not designed to be understood.

---

1. Vidal, John, "Destroyed Habitat Creates the Perfect Conditions for Coronavirus to Emerge," Scientific American, March 18, 2020, https://www.scientificamerican.com/article/destroyed-habitat-creates-the-perfect-conditions-for-coronavirus-to-emerge/
2. Sperling's Best Places, "2021 Compare Climate & Weather: Portland, OR vs. Seattle, WA," https://www.bestplaces.net/climate/?c1=54159000&c2=55363000

3. Di Liberto, Tom, "Astounding heat obliterates all-time records across the Pacific Northwest and Western Canada in June 2021," Climate.gov, June 30, 2021, https://www.climate.gov/news-features/event-tracker/astounding-heat-obliterates-all-time-records-across-pacific-northwest
4. Wu, Daniel, "3 of Seattle's 4 hottest days on record just happened," June 29, 2021, Seattle Times, https://www.seattletimes.com/seattle-news/3-of-seattles-4-hottest-days-on-record-just-happened/
5. Mack Eric, "Canada Has Never Been this Hot; We're Talking Death Valley Hot," Forbes, June 29, 2021, https://www.forbes.com/sites/ericmack/2021/06/29/canada-has-never-been-this-hot-were-talking-death-valley-hot/
6. Masters, Jeff, "Death Valley, California breaks the all-time world heat record for the second year in a row," Yale Climate Connections, July 12, 2021, https://yaleclimate connections.org/2021/07/death-valley-california-breaks-the-all-time-world-heat-record-for-the-second-year-in-a-row/
7. Gray, Jennifer, "This above-average wildfire season is predicted to continue through September -- or maybe longer," CNN Weather, Aug 2, 2021, https://www.cnn.com/2021/08/02/weather/us-wildfires-2021-forecast/index.html
8. U.S. Drought Monitor, "Map Released: Sept 2, 2021," https://droughtmonitor.unl.edu/CurrentMap.aspx
9. Fire, Weather & Avalanche Center, True North, https://www.fireweatheravalanche.org/fire/
10. Osborn, Mark, et al, "Ida updates: Almost 50 dead in the Northeast after flooding as death toll continues to rise," ABC News, Sept 3, 2021, https://abcnews.go.com/US/idas-remnants-deluge-york-jersey-flooding-rain-tornadoes/story?id=79780365
11. USGS, "Climate and Land Use Change," Frequently Asked Questions, https://www.usgs.gov/faqs/will-global-warming-produce-more-frequent-and-more-intense-wild fires?qt-news_science_products=0#qt-news_science_products
12. National Centers for Environmental Information, "Annual 2023 Global Climate Report," National Oceanic and Atmospheric Administration, https://www.ncei.noaa.gov/access/monitoring/monthly-report/global/202313
13. National Centers for Environmental Information, "Annual 2022 Global Climate Report," National Oceanic and Atmospheric Administration, https://www.ncei.noaa.gov/access/monitoring/monthly-report/global/202213/supplemental/page-1#:~:text=This%20graphic%20depicts%20the%20ten,to%2Ddate%20average%20tempera-ture%20anomaly.
14. FEMA, "Disasters," 2022, https://www.fema.gov/disaster/declarations?field_dv2_state_territory_tribal_value=All&field_year_value%5B2022%5D=2022&field_dv2_declaration_type_value=All&field_dv2_incident_type_target_id_selective=All&page=2
15. National Centers for Environmental Information, "Billion-Dollar Weather and Climate Disasters," Events, National Oceanic and Atmospheric Administration, https://www.ncei.noaa.gov/access/billions/events
16. Souter, Gavin, "Winter storm could cost insurers $5.4 billion: KCC," Business Insurance, December 29, 2022,
17. National Centers for Environmental Information, "Billion-Dollar Weather and Climate Disasters," Events, National Oceanic and Atmospheric Administration, https://www.ncei.noaa.gov/access/billions/events

18. "Lake Mead outlook improves in latest water projections," 8News Now, Las Vegas, May 16, 2024, https://www.8newsnow.com/news/local-news/lake-mead-outlook-improves-in-latest-water-projections/
19. National Environmental Satellite Data and Information Service, "Hurricane Ian's Path of Destruction," Oct 4, 2022, Department of Commerce, https://www.nesdis.noaa.gov/news/hurricane-ians-path-of-destruction
20. "Hurricane Ian," National Hurricane Center Tropical Cyclone Report, April 3, 2023, chrome-extension://efaidnbmnnnibpcajpcglclefindmkaj/https://www.nhc.noaa.gov/data/tcr/AL092022_Ian.pdf
21. Souter, Gavin, "Winter storm could cost insurers $5.4 billion: KCC," Business Insurance, December 29, 2022,
22. Childs, Jan Wesner, "Winter Storm Elliott Leaves Dozens Dead," Weather Underground, Dec 29, 2022, https://www.wunderground.com/article/news/news/2022-12-26-winter-storm-elliott-buffalo-blizzard-erie-county
23. National Centers for Environmental Information, "Billion-Dollar Weather and Climate Disasters," Events, Central and Eastern Winter Storm and Cold Wave, Dec 21-26, 2022, National Oceanic and Atmospheric Administration, https://www.ncei.noaa.gov/access/billions/events
24. National Centers for Environmental Information, "Billion-Dollar Weather and Climate Disasters," Overview: 2023 in Summary…, https://www.ncei.noaa.gov/access/billions/
25. Smith, Adam B, Katz, Richard W, "U.S. Billion-Dollar Weather and Climate Disasters: Data Sources, Trends, Accuracy and Biases," chrome-extension://efaidnbmnnnibpcajpcglclefindmkaj/https://www.ncei.noaa.gov/monitoring-content/billions/docs/smith-and-katz-2013.pdf
26. National Centers for Environmental Information, "NCEI Asheville Hurricane Outage," https://www.ncei.noaa.gov/node/6696
27. Chernikoff, Sara; Borresen, Jennifer; Leva, Diana, "Hurricane Helene ravaged Asheville, echoing another disaster 100 years ago," USA Today, Oct 8, 2024, https://www.usatoday.com/story/graphics/2024/10/07/hurricane-helene-great-flood-asheville/75456390007/
28. Belles, Jonathan; Dolce, Chris; Kaiser, Caitlin; Tonks, Sara, "Hurricane Milton to Make Landfall in Florida Tonight With Life-Threatening Storm Surge, Winds, Flooding," Weather Channel, Oct 9, 2024, https://weather.com/storms/hurricane/news/2024-10-09-hurricane-milton-forecast-landfall-florida-storm-surge-wind
29. Rose, Adam, "How the cost of disasters like Hurricane Ian are calculated—and why it takes so long to add them up," The Conversation, Oct 14, 2022, https://theconversation.com/how-the-costs-of-disasters-like-hurricane-ian-are-calculated-and-why-it-takes-so-long-to-add-them-up-191736
30. National Oceanic and Atmospheric Agency, "2022 U.S. billion-dollar weather and climate disasters in historical context," Notable U.S. billion-dollar disasters of 2022, https://www.climate.gov/news-features/blogs/beyond-data/2022-us-billion-dollar-weather-and-climate-disasters-historical#:~:text=Damages%20from%20the%202022%20disasters,Heat%20Wave%20(%2422.1%20billion).
31. Muhlbaum, David, "The Most Expensive Natural Disasters in U.S. History," Kiplinger Media Company, Oct 11, 2022, https://www.kiplinger.com/slideshow/business/t019-s001-most-expensive-natural-disasters-in-u-s-history/index.html

32. FEMA, "Hazard Mitigation Assistance Grants," Federal Emergency Management Agency, https://www.fema.gov/grants/mitigation
33. Rose, Adam, "How the cost of disasters like Hurricane Ian are calculated—and why it takes so long to add them up," The Conversation, Oct 14, 2022.
34. McLeay, Michael; Radia, Amara; Thomas, Ryland; of the Bank's Monetary Analysis Directorate, Bank of England, Quarterly Bulletin 2014 Q1, "Money creation in the modern economy," p. 14, https://www.bankofengland.co.uk/-/media/boe/files/quarterly-bulletin/2014/money-creation-in-the-modern-economy
35. Huber, Joseph, "Split-circuit reserve banking – functioning, dysfunctions and future Perspectives," Real-World Economic Review, #80, 2017, http://www.paecon.net/PAEReview/issue80/Huber80.pdf
36. Kumhof, Michael, & Benes, Jaromir, *The Chicago Plan Revisited,* International Monetary Fund, Working Paper, p. 10-11, https://www.imf.org/external/pubs/ft/wp/2012/wp12202.pdf
37. Werner, Richard A, International Review of Financial Analysis, Sept 8, 2015, "A lost century in economics: Three theories of banking and the conclusive evidence," https://www.sciencedirect.com/science/article/pii/S1057521915001477
38. Yamaguchi, Kaoru, *Workings of A Public Money System of Open Macroeconomies – Modeling the American Monetary Act Completed – (A Revised Version),* 2011, Doshisha University, http://www.muratopia.org/Yamaguchi/doc/DesignOpenMacro.pdf
39. Zarlenga. Stephen, *The Lost Science of Money,* American Monetary Institute, 2002, Valatie, N.Y., Chapter 11, https://www.monetary.org/buy-the-book
40. Andersen, Hans Christian, "The Emperor's New Clothes," The Hans Christian Andersen Centre, University of Southern Denmark, https://andersen.sdu.dk/vaerk/hersholt/TheEmperorsNewClothes_e.html
41. Ramirez, Rachel, "This 100% solar community endured Hurricane Ian with no loss of power and minimal damage," CNN, Oct 2, 2022, https://www.cnn.com/2022/10/02/us/solar-babcock-ranch-florida-hurricane-ian-climate/
42. *Ibid.*
43. Hanes, Stephanie, "The Florida Town that challenged Hurricane Ian and won," Christian Science Monitor, Nov 30, 2022, https://www.csmonitor.com/Environment/2022/1130/The-Florida-town-that-challenged-Hurricane-Ian-and-won
44. Gaffney, Austyn, "A Climate Resistant Community Passed Two Hurricane Tests," New York Times, Oct 15, 2024, https://www.nytimes.com/2024/10/15/climate/florida-climate-resilience-babcock-ranch.html
45. King, Jamilah, "Kamala Harris for the People: Veep Vows to Defeat 'Deeply Unserious' Trump," Mother Jones, Aug 22, 2024, https://www.motherjones.com/politics/2024/08/kamala-harris-for-the-people-veep-vows-to-defeat-deeply-unserious-trump/
46. *Ibid.*
47. *Ibid.*
48. American Monetary Institute 19th Annual Conference on Monetary Reform, "American Monetary Institute Statement to COP28," Nov 6, 2023, https://monetary.org/conference/ami-conference-statement-to-cop28/

SIX

Publicly Created Money, For the People

Money Is Our Lifeblood

Just as Kamala Harris, when San Francisco District Attorney and later as California Attorney General, would introduce herself beginning a trial, "Kamala Harris, for the people,"[1] we now introduce, *Publicly Created Money, for the people.* Ms. Harris and other district attorneys across our country introduce themselves as such to show that they represent the people as an extension of the Rule of Law. In a similar vein, the act of publicly creating the nation's money is a representation of the people's need for a system of public money, as an extension of the Rule of Law.

Money is a nation's very lifeblood, who creates it and how it is created is of the utmost importance to the people. It is the one thing we all need to simply survive in modern society. It can be created privately by banks as debt when they make loans, as it is now. Or it can be created publicly by our government, debt-free, as an asset based upon the Rule of Law that we have chosen to live by. The choice is ours to make, with *Spaceship Earth's* survival dependent upon the choice we make.

Expert Witness: Bank of England on Money Creation

Perhaps, you have not read *Money Creation 101* and are a little bit skeptical that banks really create our money basically out of thin air. I get it, I couldn't believe it either when I first discovered this shocking and almost unknown fact about how our money is created, fifteen or so years ago. The Bank of England is one of the world's oldest central banks. It was chartered in 1694 and was a model for the Federal Reserve System that became law in 1913 in America. The Bank of England's 2014 paper, *Money Creation in the Modern Economy* begins:

> This article explains how the majority of money in the modern economy is created by commercial banks making loans....
>
> In the modern economy, most money takes the form of bank deposits. But how those bank deposits are created is often misunderstood: the principal way is through commercial banks making loans. **Whenever a bank makes a loan, it simultaneously creates a matching deposit in the borrower's bank account, thereby creating new money**. (Emphasis Bank of England)
>
> The reality of how money is created today differs from the description found in some economics textbooks:
>
> - Rather than banks receiving deposits when households save and then lending them out, bank lending creates deposits.
> - In normal times, the central bank does not fix the amount of money in circulation, nor is central bank money 'multiplied up' into more loans and deposits.[2]

(Michael McLeay, Amar Radia and Ryland Thomas of the Bank of England's Monetary Analysis Directorate.)

Publicly Created Money Ignored in Both the Great Depression and the Great Recession/Global Financial Crisis

The American Monetary Act was originally written in 2006 by Stephen Zarlenga and his colleagues at the American Monetary Institute. Five years later in 2011, it was introduced to Congress in legislative form as the National Emergency Employment Defense Act (NEED Act) by U.S. Representatives Dennis Kucinich and John Conyers.[3] In 2011, the NEED Act was completely ignored by Congress, the Federal Reserve's 348 estimated macroeconomists, and almost the entirety of our nation's university economics professors. This somewhat echoed the treatment that an earlier plan for publicly created money known as the Chicago Plan received from Congress and the Federal Reserve, when first proposed in the depths of the Great Depression in 1933 by University of Chicago Economics Professor Henry Simons and Yale University Economics Professor Irving Fischer.

As related in *Money Creation 101*, Chapter 7, "Publicly Created Money in Action—The NEED Act": during the Great Depression the Chicago Plan was resubmitted in July 1939 by economics professors Paul H. Douglas of the University of Chicago, Irving Fisher of Yale University, Frank D. Graham of Princeton University, Earl J. Hamilton of Duke University, Willford I. King of New York University, and Charles R. Whittlesey of Princeton University, officially titled "A Program for Monetary Reform."[4]

In 1939, ten years after it had begun, America remained mired in the Great Depression. President Franklin Delano Roosevelt's legislative program of relief, recovery, and reform, called the New Deal, had provided some degree of relief, recovery, and reform, yet the Great Depression continued. When the Chicago Plan was resubmitted in 1939, Congress and the Federal Reserve again ignored it. Instead of considering a system of publicly created money, President Roosevelt (FDR) and his New Deal had addressed the banking system earlier in the Great Depression in 1932 and 1933 with the twin reforms of the Glass-Steagall Act: federal banking deposit insurance, Federal Deposit Insurance Corporation (FDIC), and with legislation separating commercial and investment banking. While these were great programs and would continue under a future publicly created money system, they did nothing to change, either the character of or the results generated by, the bank-created debt-money system. Thus, the Great Depression continued until we entered World War II in 1941 and began the tremendous mobilization needed to fight the War.

A major difference between the Great Depression in 1939, when the Chicago Plan was submitted, and 2011, when the NEED Act was submitted to Congress and ignored, was that in 1939, the vast majority of economics professors agreed with the proposal to change our money to the system of just, sovereign, publicly created money called for in the Chicago Plan. The proposal was sent to the mailing list of the American Economic Association university economists. Of the 318 university economists that responded, a whopping 85% were in either general approval or approval with some reservations of the publicly created money, Chicago Plan. Two hundred thirty-five university economists (74%) gave their general approval and another forty (12.5%) gave their approval with some reservations. Only forty-three university economists (13.5%) expressed disapproval with the call for publicly created money in the 1939 Chicago Plan. [5]

Shunning Publicly Created Money Is Abuse

Contrast this overwhelming support in 1939 for the publicly created money in the Chicago Plan by the nation's university economics professors, with the reception the NEED Act received when it was proposed in 2011. It was ignored by Congress, ignored by Federal Reserve economists, and ignored by the vast majority of university economics professors. It was shunned and continues to be shunned; this is commonly called the silent treatment, and is a form of abuse. Purdue University psychologist Kipling Williams in his book *Ostracism: The Power of Silence* relates that shunning and ostracism are particularly prevalent in the workplace when a worker has reported wrongdoing. Why? Because it is much more difficult to prove that those doing the shunning are the aggressors, as their aggressive acts are non-acts.[6]

Shunning is prevalent when someone in the workplace reports wrongdoing, both the Chicago Plan during the Great Depression and the NEED Act during the Global Financial Crisis reported wrongdoing. What was the wrongdoing that the Money Power (those who benefit from creating our money) did not want revealed? Simply that our nation's very lifeblood, our money, was created as debt by private banks and only existed as debt. The vast majority of professional economists today continue to do the dirty work of the Money Power by quietly ignoring the potential of publicly created money, whenever it has been written about or proposed in Congress.

Money Creation 101 provides evidence that many economists do not understand the truth about how our money is created. Testimony was provided from two university economists at top ranked economics programs that did not understand what the Bank of England plainly said in 2014:

> This article explains how the majority of money in the modern economy is created by commercial banks making loans....[7]

A Federal Reserve macroeconomist would not answer the question, *who creates our money?* Instead, directing me to the Federal Reserve Public Relations Department. This Fed economist also revealed that this was a subject often discussed privately at the Fed. Many years later and I still haven't received a response from the Fed Public Relations Department revealing who creates our money.

Stephen Zarlenga and the American Monetary Institute

In spite of this shunning on how our money is created, the truth of money creation is starting to break through. *Money Creation 101* covers this material in greater detail. My mentor in monetary reform was the late Stephen Zarlenga, Director of the American Monetary Institute. Stephen was a businessman who was involved in trading gold futures. He knew that something was wrong with the money system. In 1991 he founded the American Monetary Institute and began his deep dive into monetary history, culminating in 2002 with the publication of his tour de force, *The Lost Science of Money*.[8] Zarlenga called it "The Mythology of Money—The Story of Power." Who was I to disagree with my mentor? I had been hesitant to read it, as an anti-war/social justice/environmental activist I thought his book was for economists. Boy was I wrong. After just getting started, I called Stephen and asked him, "Why didn't you tell me that *The Lost Science of Money* was about social justice?" He laughed and told me that monetary reform is social justice. Stephen died in 2017; I wish I could hear him laugh one more time.

In 2024 the American Monetary Institute (AMI) is now led by Steven Walsh. Instead of director, Steven refers to his position as Lead-Steward of AMI. Steven is a retired Chicago school teacher and a wonderful man. His studies in anthropology as a young man led him to living with the native Eskimo people in Alaska for a couple of years and he loves to give us occasional salutations in Eskimo dialects during our meetings and conferences.

The American Monetary Institute in September, 2024 recently concluded its 20th Annual AMI Conference on Monetary Reform. Originally the conferences were held in Chicago and brought in people from across the globe. After Stephen's death, AMI switched to online ZOOM conferences beginning in 2018. We were a little bit on our heels without our mentor Stephen Zarlenga, monetary reformer Robert Poteat took over the reins, but only for a year before he too died. Then it was New Zealand civil engineer Jamie Walton who took over for a couple of years, travelling back and forth between New Zealand, Europe and the U.S. in the cause of monetary reform. Fortuitously, Steven Walsh who had been with AMI since it became located in Chicago, has been our leader for the last few years. The AMI conferences have grown in recent years with more economists and academics of all persuasions taking part.

Alliance For Just Money

After recovering from the shock of AMI Director Zarlenga's death, monetary reformers began a new sister organization to AMI: the Alliance For Just Money (AFJM).[9] While AMI is an educational research group of ordinary people committed to fixing our money system, the Alliance For Just Money's mission is to research, educate, and organize for real monetary reform. In May 2024, AFJM led an action, *Mayday for Money!* at the Chicago Federal Reserve in which we simply asked Federal Reserve officials to take a look at an alternative to the Federal Reserve led bank-created debt-money system. The president of the Chicago Fed was politely sent a letter well in advance, requesting that a few members of our group be allowed a few minutes time to present materials to Fed officials about the alternative to the present crisis-prone debt-money system. We were told no. We asked if we could present the material to staff. Again, the Fed said no. Is this shunning? You be the judge. We mailed the material to them and have not received a reply.

Expert Witness: Dr. Kaoru Yamaguchi—University of California, Berkeley; Doshisha University, Japan; Ankara University, Turkey

The American Monetary Institute, led by Zarlenga, wrote the American Monetary Act. Japanese economist Kaoru Yamaguchi in 2010 published "Workings of a Public Money System of Open Macroeconomies — Modeling the American Monetary Act Completed." Dr. Yamaguchi, used the Systems Dynamics method of modeling developed by American computer engineer and Systems Dynamics Theorist at MIT Jay W. Forrester. Dr. Yamaguchi concluded:

> The system of money as debt…is demonstrated, very costly, triggering economic recessions and business cycles…
>
> The alternative system… of debt-free money, in which only the government can issue money, and the government debt, it is

> shown, can be gradually eliminated. Moreover, it turns out that higher economic growth is simultaneously attained.
>
> In this sense, the alternative macroeconomic system, from a viewpoint of system design, seems to be worth being implemented if we wish to avoid accumulating government debt, unfair income distribution, repeated financial crises, war and environmental destruction.[10]

The question is what do we want? Debt and business cycles of economic recessions. Or a non-accumulation of government debt, and an avoidance of unfair income distribution, repeated financial crises, war and environmental destruction. The choice is clear: bank-created debt-money or publicly created money. Pick one.

The NEED Act

In 2011, The NEED Act (National Emergency Employment Defense Act), based on the American Monetary Act was put into Congress by Dennis Kucinich and John Conyers. It was completely ignored by Congress and the hundreds of Federal Reserve System macroeconomists. Rather than telling us how bad or good the concept of publicly created money in the NEED Act was, it was so much easier and more effective for them to just ignore it.

Expert Witnesses: German Economist Dr. Michael Kumhof & Brazilian Economist Jaromir Benes

Dr. Kumhof was Deputy Division Chief, Economic Modeling Division, International Monetary Fund, in 2012 when he and Dr. Benes, published The Chicago Plan Revisited, an International Monetary Fund Working Paper. They used a DSGE model of the U.S. economy (dynamic stochastic general equilibrium, the same type of modeling the Federal Reserve System uses). Kumhof and Benes concluded that a system of public money such as that proposed by the Chicago Plan during the Great Depression would:

1. Be a much better control of a major source of business cycle fluctuations, sudden increases and contractions of bank credit and of the supply of bank-created money.
2. Complete elimination of bank runs.
3. Dramatic reduction of the (net) public debt.
4. Dramatic reduction of private debt, as money creation no longer requires simultaneous debt creation. [Also concluding that "output gains (for the economy would) approach 10 percent and steady state inflation can drop to zero without posing problems for the conduct of monetary policy."][11]

Expert Witness: Jonathan Adair Turner—Baron of Ecchinswell & Member of the U.K. House of Lords, Former chairmen of the U.K. Pensions Commission & the Committee on Climate Change

Former Director-General of the Confederation of British Industry, with lofty positions at BP, Chase Manhattan Bank, Merrill Lynch Europe, while also lecturing part-time at the London School of Economics. Dr. Turner has referred to himself as a 'technocrat' and he checks all the boxes as an inside member of the financial elite.

In September, 2013 Turner gave a guest lecture to the prestigious Stockholm School of Economics: "Credit, Money and Leverage: What Wicksell, Hayek and Fisher Knew and Modern Macroeconomics Forgot." It was done via video, since his schedule prevented him from appearing in person. The entire lecture is on YouTube and the elapsed time in the lecture is noted before each statement. Technocrat Turner's remarkable 2013 observations:

> *7:00* The flip side of creating purchasing power with credit and money creation is that you create a set of ongoing debt contracts thereafter.

> *8:35* Investment funding has become a small part of what the bank or shadow bank system does.

> *14:00* "I think it is reasonable to say that both in undergraduate textbooks today and in advanced economics and in central bank orthodoxy we have tended to work on a way of thinking about the credit creation process which is simply not true.
>
> *14:30* Modern textbook assumptions. I think it's fair to say that they make 3 assumptions which are dramatic and wrong over the best simplifications. They tend to assume that what banks do is take deposits from household depositors and lend it to borrowers. That misses the insight that banks create credit and money and purchasing power. They tend still and I have read back through several economic textbooks over the last several months to check this. They tend to say that what banks do with that money is that they lend it to businesses in order to fund those projects that have a higher return than the interest rate. That ignores almost entirely the fact that most credit extension is no longer funding business capital projects.[12] [13]

If bank credit is no longer funding capital projects in the real economy, what is it funding? One doesn't have to be a genius or a member of the economic establishment to know that bank credit (money creation) is funding wars, bubbles and speculation for the wealthy and debt for the rest of us. And let's not forget Dr. Turner's stark admission that our economic textbooks have been lying to us about the money creation process and doing so in a dramatically wrong way.

Shortly thereafter in 2014, the final big domino fell revealing the bank-created debt-money system, when the Bank of England's Monetary Analysis Directorate issued their paper *Money Creation in the Modern Economy,* which we began the chapter with.

Open Letter: Rethinking the Role of Banks in Economics Education

"Rethinking Economics is a global network of students and organisers fighting for a new way of teaching and practising economics so that it truly helps us deal with the real-world challenges we all face today like climate collapse and inequality."[14] Currently they list 120 plus student groups in 40 countries with active Rethinking Economics groups.[15] The two in the U.S. are Duke University and Connecticut College. From their Open Letter:

> Dear Economics Professors and Teaching Staff,
>
> … As those with the power to influence the next generation of economists, it is essential that you review the teaching of the role of banks in economics courses and bring it in line with up-to-date research…
>
> Economics textbooks across the world, some of them first published in the 1960s, continue to teach students a model of the monetary system in which commercial banks act as intermediaries, that only move existing money around the system, like lubricant in a machine…
>
> As research from the Bank of England, Bundesbank and numerous academics has shown, banks are not intermediaries channeling pre-existing funds from savers to borrowers. Commercial banks create the vast majority of money in circulation. Unlike other financial institutions, they create money when they extend loans to borrowers…
>
> Commercial banks also determine where money is directed in the economy. Around 80% of new money created in countries like the US and UK currently goes towards existing property and financial markets, rather than the 'real' or productive economy, leading to soaring house and land prices, and housing crises. In the Global South, 33 major global banks poured $1.9 trillion into fossil fuels since the 2015 Paris Climate Agreement, directly influencing the trajectory of economies that will be hit first and hardest by climate change. The power of banks to create money therefore has enormous implications for the shape and stability of our economy. Yet, in an overwhelming number of cases, economics textbooks and courses do not teach this to the economists of tomorrow.[16]

The students' open letter, printed in its entirety in *Money Creation 101*, Chapter 11, goes on to beseech their universities to simply teach them the truth about how our money is created as debt by private banks. The letter states that these economics students will become leaders of the future world and "must have a real-world understanding of banks and money creation"[17] to solve these problems. Rethinking Economics Open Letter: Rethinking the Role of Banks in Economics Education is signed by 26 student groups, 12 civil society organizations and more than 50 individuals, many at the doctorate level.[18]

Expert Witness: Professor Richard A. Werner

Dr. Werner holds an undergraduate degree from the London School of Economics and a doctorate degree from Oxford University, both in economics. He has made video presentations to American Monetary Institute Annual Conferences on Monetary Reform which I have attended. German economist Richard A. Werner's shocking 2014 statement:

> One reason for the neglect of the institutional and operational details of banks in the research literature in the past decades is likely the fact that no law, statute or bank regulation explicitly grants banks the right (usually considered a sovereign prerogative) to create and allocate the money supply. As a result, many economists, finance researchers, lawyers, accountants, even bankers, let alone the general public, have not been aware of the role of banks as creators and allocators of the money supply.[19]

There are no laws that explicitly give the banks the right to create our money. Since the banks have not been granted the right to create our money, the rest of us, including many economists and even bankers are unaware that is how our money is created. Since this lack of basic knowledge on how our money is created is unknown to many economists, it is no wonder that they are reluctant to challenge the system.

A democracy can only function if its citizens are well-informed about the most essential thing in our society—money. The economics profession has a duty to examine and debate an alternative system of just, sovereign, publicly created money as was originally proposed in the NEED Act, modeled by Drs. Yamaguchi, Kumhof and Benes, and further exposed by Drs. Turner and Werner. The failure to critically analyze publicly created money, represents an unconscionable lapse in the profession's duty as researchers and educators. This failure to critique and write about publicly created money is primarily directed at the Federal Reserve System. They dominate the monetary profession in America and they must lead the discussion of publicly created money, instead of shunning it. *Money Creation 101*: Chapter 10, A Plea to the Economics Profession examines this subject in much greater detail.

There are three ways to get to publicly created money. One way is via a Supreme Court ruling finding that our present Federal Reserve-led, bank-created debt-money system is unconstitutional. We have made this argument in *History of Money 101*: Chapter 6, "The U.S. Constitution and Money Creation." The second way is through the Constitutional Amendment process, which is long and arduous, and many would say impossible in today's political climate. The third most direct and likely way to get publicly created money is through Congressional legislation.

Fulfilling Our Monetary Destiny with The American Monetary Reform Act of 2024

Throughout the *People, Planet & the Power of Money Project*, we have referred to an update of the NEED Act as The NEED Act Revisited. The American Monetary Reform Act of 2024 is an update of the NEED Act written by colleagues at the Alliance for Just Money and is based on the NEED Act put into Congress by Dennis Kucinich in 2011 and co-sponsored by John Conyers.

I can think of no issue that would improve the lives of poor and working-class people today more than publicly created money would. Environmental organizations, climate action groups, the NAACP, unions, the Poor People's Campaign, Feeding America, mortgage relief organizations, student debt relief organizations, living wage organizations, Medicare for All proponents and supporters of universal basic income should all be looking to publicly created money as a way to fund and realize their important goals. We can also add to the mix of interested parties all Americans who are concerned about individual debt and governmental debt. While advocating for a legislative fix, we should also try to amend the Constitution and appeal to the Supreme Court to declare the Federal Reserve bank-created debt-money system unconstitutional, if for no other reason than doing so will be helpful in educating the public about publicly created money.

In *Money Creation 101*, we began our discussion of *who creates our money?* by putting out the premise that most people have an understanding that the following are true:

1. Our federal government creates our money.
2. Banks loan us money that has already been created by our federal government.
3. The Federal Reserve is a part of our government.

We were then forced to be the bearer of bad news, as we informed our readers that although we intuitively believe all three of the above statements should be true, they are all false within our present bank-created debt-money system:

1. Our federal government creates only a tiny sliver of our money.
2. Banks create almost all of our money, as debt when they make loans.
3. The Federal Reserve Banks are all owned by the private banks in their districts. Our government does appoint some of the Federal Reserve decision makers and Congress has the power to direct its actions. But a Congress composed of members that do not understand how the banks create money and that receives financial donations from the banks,

is in desperate need of citizens telling it to change the system.

Enacting the NEED Act in 2011 would have made all three of our present misconceptions about our money a reality. The American Monetary Reform Act of 2024, or a form of what we have referred to as The NEED Act Revisited, would make these same misconceptions reality today. Of course, just because we intuitively think our government should make our money, doesn't necessarily mean that our government making our money is the best system. *History of Money 101* did provide three examples of American publicly created money systems though. Without these three systems of publicly created money, our country might very well be quite different than it is today:

- Publicly created bills of credit enabled the colonies, starved for a system of money, to build infrastructure, grow and prosper.
- The publicly created Continental Currency financed our Revolution, without it our country would not exist, and we would still be colonies of England.
- The publicly created Greenbacks were used to fight and win the Civil War, free our enslaved people and save our nation.

Today if we make the decision to base our money not upon debt, but rather the industry of the people it will allow us to fulfill our destiny of liberty, equality, and democracy, not just for the elite but for all Americans.

Strategizing Monetary Reform

When the NEED Act was originally written and put into Congress in 2011, a decision was reached to keep it focused on specifically changing to a system of publicly created money, something that could and should be supported by both sides of the political spectrum. The NEED Act called for implementing the American Society of Civil

Engineers (ASCE) Infrastructure Report Card[20] as a guide to rebuilding our country's crumbling infrastructure, which would have created an estimated 7.2 million new, good-paying jobs.[21] [a] It also was generally committed to funding education, people with underwater mortgages and a Citizens' Dividend of an unspecified amount, which would have to be spelled out in separate legislation. The NEED Act received no support outside of its two sponsors, Dennis Kucinich and John Conyers.

I believe that in 2011, when the NEED Act was introduced to Congress, it was ignored because there was no grassroots support, so politicians in both parties simply ignored it. To be successful today, we need to start at the grassroots level. Hopefully with the help of our readers, the message of the *People, Planet & the Power of Money Project* will help our fellow citizens better understand the benefits of publicly created money. Only then will we begin to see the way out of the morass of debt, ignorance, and inaction that is the bank-created debt-money system.

Other areas that either can be included in the monetary reform legislation, or proposed and be considered as separate legislation, and that can be funded partially or wholly with publicly created money:

- Expanded Medicare for All—an all-inclusive real national health care system.

- Legislation to keep us within all nine planetary boundaries (Climate Change, Biodiversity Loss, Nitrogen/Phosphorous Cycle, Ocean Acidification, Freshwater Use, Land Use, Chemical Pollution, Atmospheric Aerosol Loading, and Stratospheric Ozone Depletion).

---

[a] Every 4 years the American Society of Civil Engineers grades the 18 categories of our nation's infrastructure, with a letter grade based upon its condition. The ASCE 2021 Report Card gave our infrastructure an overall grade of C–.

- Legislation that all plastics made must be either naturally biodegradable or part of an environmentally sustainable recycling feedback loop. This means that those corporations that insist on making the things that we need out of plastic, and then packaging them in even more plastic, must be required to either use a biodegradable plastic or put in place an easily accessible and environmentally sustainable recycling system for all things made from plastic.

- Enact the American Society of Civil Engineers' sustainable Infrastructure Report Card, creating 7–10 million good-paying jobs. A much smaller part of the ASCE Report Card was covered in the bipartisan infrastructure legislation signed into law by President Biden on November 15, 2021.

- Enact a universal basic income, Citizens Freedom Dividend starting at $300/week, with automatic increases for inflation, for each adult American citizen 18 years or older. This is an automatic pay raise for all American adults. This brings all adults up to a basic living standard of $15/hour (assuming a 40-hour work week).

- The federal minimum wage is $7.25/hour and has not been raised since July 2009, more than 15 years ago. Raise the federal minimum wage to $13.50 combined with the Citizens Freedom Dividend of $300/week would give our essential workers at the bottom of our system what would amount to a $21.00/hour income, based on a 40-hour workweek.

- SOS for Small Businesses: small businesses with less than 50 employees account for 27% of US businesses, and those with less than 250 employees around 44% of our entire workforce.[22] Allow small businesses that show through their financial statements and tax returns that they cannot pay the increased minimum wage, to have the federal government make up the difference until such time as their financial situation improves, so that they can pay the entire amount themselves.

- To address the student debt crisis, all student debt accrued with money created out of thin air could be forgiven and simply erased off the computers that created it. Any student debt in which actual money was lent could be repaid by our government with publicly created money.

- Climate change is the defining issue of our time, and the monetary reform legislation in my opinion should specifically contain language that new U.S. Money will be created and spent in whatever amounts are needed until the greenhouse gases in the atmosphere recede and begin to drawdown below the planetary boundary of 350 parts per million carbon-dioxide.

Reclaiming the ancient lost power of publicly created money will allow us to accomplish all this by creating and spending debt-free money. Anything else we need to address can be included in the legislation or accomplished through subsequent separate legislation. The money that we will be able to publicly create can cover any funding gaps that taxes are unable to cover.

The *People, Planet & the Power of Money Project* has used the term The NEED Act Revisited to describe a redo of the NEED Act. The Alliance for Just Money drafted their revisions to the original American Monetary Act as the American Monetary Reform Act of 2024. I have proposed certain things that I would like included in any legislation. I acknowledge that monetary reform will have to be made through our democratic process and that I may not get the inclusion of all the social spending projects that I would like. I am of the belief that, if necessary, achieving a system of publicly created money is so important that removal of all the spending on people and planet parts of the proposed legislation is better than not passing the legislation and keeping the present fraudulent, dysfunctional bank-created debt-money we now are saddled with. If such a stripped-down monetary reform bill was made the law of the land, people would soon learn that we can create and spend the money necessary to save all the lifeforms on *Spaceship Earth*, without increasing either debt or inflation.

With a system of publicly created money. The seigniorage (difference between the cost of making and distributing the money and the value given to the money) belongs to the people through their government. Since it is spent into existence for the needs of the people as determined by Congress, it has the ability to do great things. Since it is not a loan, it is not destroyed like bank-created debt-money is when it is repaid. It stays in the economy. Some of it will go back to the government via various taxes and will be available to be spent again by the government for the programs we deem necessary. Some of it will stay with the people who work for it, allowing ordinary people to build up wealth and economic security. Some of it will be invested by these people with banks to lend to the public and share in the profits with the bank. If inflation begins, we may have to cut back on the new money being created and/or increase taxes (preferably on the wealthy) to make up the difference. More on inflation soon.

Expert Witness: Alliance For Just Money

"The Alliance for Just Money is a nonpartisan network of individuals, chapters, and organizational members from all walks of life who are working together to achieve a just, transparent, democratic, and sustainable money system that is accountable to the people."[23]

Explaining the American Monetary Reform Act of 2024:

"Change Our Money, Change Our World"[24]

The American Monetary Reform Act of 2024 (AMRA) is in need of sponsors and co-sponsors in Congress and endorsements from civil society organizations and units of local government from all 50 states. AMRA is an update of the 2011-2012 National Emergency Employment Defense Act (H.R.2990, the NEED Act).

What does the American Monetary Reform Act of 2024 (AMRA) do?

In order to enable government to correct inherent flaws in our monetary system, fund the public good as Congress over time defines it, gradually retire the federal debt, and reduce the flow of wealth from the real economy into the financial sector, the American Monetary Reform Act (AMRA):

1. Transfers creation of money from banks to the federal government, ending money creation by banks through fractional reserve lending or any other means, thereby transferring authority for, modulation of, and seigniorage[b] from creating the nation's money supply (including coin, paper, digital and account-based United States money) from private banks to the public sector as provided for in Section 1, Article 8 of the US Constitution.

2. Establishes within the US Department of Treasury:
   a. an independent Monetary Authority to establish appropriate rates of new US money creation by government in order to avoid inflation or deflation;

---

[b] Seigniorage is the gain that accrues from the creation and first use of money. It arises from the difference between the cost of producing and the face value—or purchasing power—of new money.

   b. Bank Transition Assistance Fund for lending to banks in case such lending is necessary to maintain the liquidity for bank lending of pre-existing US money, especially during the transition to the new system;
   c. a Monetary Bureau to incorporate into the Treasury the needed functions of the Federal Reserve system while ending the existence of the Federal Reserve as an entity owned by private banks.

3. Specifies that banks shall offer two kinds of customer accounts:
   a. transaction accounts, for use as a payment system, to be kept in bailment,[c] separate from bank balance sheets and, thus, protected from possible bank failure;
   b. saving and investment accounts to be used by banks for investing on behalf of customers, returning interest to customers who deposit money in these accounts.

4. Provides for an orderly transition from the present debt-based bank money system to a 100% public money system.

The Alliance For Just Money explains Why We Need AMRA Now:

- We have a dire NEED and unprecedented opportunity to change our money system, once and for all, from a private debt-based money system to a public asset money system.

---

[c] Bailment refers to a legal relationship between two parties in common law, where assets or property are transferred from a bailor to a bailee. In this relationship, the bailor transfers physical possession of a piece of personal property to the bailee for a certain period of time but retains ownership. Under the present bank-created debt-money system your money deposited in bank savings and checking accounts no longer belongs to you. It belongs to the bank and you have a claim for it, but your claim is not first-in-line. [Explained in detail in *Book One: Money Creation 101*: Chapter 8, "Financial Shenanigans & the Cultural Hegemony of Debt-Money."] Under the publicly created money system of AMRA, the bank that holds your money in a transaction account is holding it for you in bailment and is unable to use it for any purpose or give it to anyone else.

- Most people don't even know the vast majority of our means of payment today is privately created through account entries by commercial banks when borrowers sign loan contracts. The problem with this money system is NOT its "fiat" [creation of our legal system] nature, but that it is created out of private debt.

- As such, it is inherently unstable, unjust, and unsustainable. It imposes a growth imperative on our and—due to the global dominance of the US dollar—other economies. The only way to keep paying the interest that debt-money bears is to exploit people and planet and to borrow more money into circulation. The role of money in politics to keep this system going, further undermines democracy.

- While money is necessary in a market economy, money does not have to be credit-and-debt-based. Modern money simply is. But we can change it, and we must if we care about tomorrow's children and the survival of human life on this planet and the lives of other species with which we share it.

- Why is the opportunity for AMRA today unprecedented? Because, whether we like it or not, some shift to new digital money is coming. Central bankers, commercial bankers, owners of non-financial multinational corporations like Facebook and Amazon, cryptocurrency and so-called "stablecoin" providers, and governments all see the writing on the wall, and are struggling to figure out the future of money. If We, the People, do not understand money, none of these other players can be expected to work for the public and private good of us all.

- But if We, the People, do understand money and why and how to reform it, we can and will achieve a public money

> system that serves the public good and the sustainable commerce of ALL Americans to make a living and a life for ourselves and our loved ones within communities across the US, within a global community of peaceful and trading nations whose people are doing similarly.[25]

The entire American Monetary Reform Act of 2024 is available online at the Alliance for Just Money.[26]

Publicly Created Money vs. Inflation

Anyone would have to be either blind or rich to not notice that inflation has reared its head since we began to come out of the COVID Pandemic in 2021. Much of the inflation was due to supply chain issues as economic activity increased post Pandemic. Adding to that was Vladimir Putin's invasion of Ukraine that began on February, 24, 2022, causing major worldwide disruptions in grain and energy supplies. Additionally, some good old fashioned price gouging that has been referred to as "greedflation" by economists at the Kansas City Federal Reserve Bank, "firms are capitalizing on their market power by raising their prices higher and faster than the growth in their production costs."[27]

Also, some of the inflation after the Pandemic is because of a shortage of workers who want to do much of our essential work, their wages have gone up even without a federal increase in the minimum wage. That is not a bad thing. A bad thing is workers at essential jobs, providing services that make our lives better, who are not being paid a living wage.

The first rejoinder I hear from skeptics when proposing publicly created money is that it will be inflationary. This despite the fact that the 3 previous examples of publicly created money in our nation's history were not, in and of themselves, particularly inflationary:

- The colonial scrip bills of credit that were issued by the American colonies, beginning with Massachusetts in 1690 were by and large judiciously issued and were responsible for building prosperity and colonial infrastructure.

- The Continental Currency, paper fiat currency issued by the Continental Congress to finance what would be the Revolution was successful in taking us to within 5 months of the final victory before they were abandoned by the Continental Congress. Termed "the Revolution itself," by monetary historian Alexander Del Mar, the Continental Currency lost much of its face value as a result of massive British and local criminal counterfeiting. Also, because our Founders failed to grasp that the Continental Currency was money in and of itself. Instead, our Continental Congress promised to redeem them for specie currency (gold and silver coins) that we did not have and had no way of getting, thus causing the American people to lose confidence in them.

- The Greenbacks were fiat paper money, created by President Lincoln and Congress to fight and win the Civil War, saving our union and nation. They held their value just fine and the people liked them so much that most had no desire to turn them in for specie currency when later given the chance.

Inflation under Federal Reserve System of bank-created debt-money, since 1914 when the Federal Reserve System began operating until 2024, is a cumulative rate of 3,053%.[28] This is mentioned so as to provide perspective when we hear the pot calling the kettle black. The pot being the bank-created debt-money system and the kettle the ignored concept of publicly created money. We have 3 examples of publicly created money: the first built prosperity and infrastructure, the second fought and won the Revolution and the third fought the Confederacy, saved the Union and freed the enslaved people. Contrast this with the Federal Reserve-led bank-created debt-money system which has given us a cumulative 3,053% worth of inflation from its inception 110 years ago, along with a country in which we have 801 billionaires and roughly one-half of our people (170,000,000) with no net worth.[29] [30]

Yes, We Can, Afford to Care for People & Planet with Publicly Created Money

In *Money Creation 101*, Chapter 5, we showed that the recovery from the Great Recession/Global Financial Crisis was equal to $166,000 per person in the country over a 10.5-year period—$15,800 per person per year. This $54.6 trillion increase in U.S. wealth was not divided equally among the people and has been referred to as K-shaped recovery. The wealthiest profited tremendously, the next tier generally did okay to quite well, while more than half of our people got little to nothing.

The recovery from the Global Financial Crisis demonstrates that a tremendous creation of wealth does not have to be inflationary. It was successful in creating wealth for the wealthy but had no actual benefits to society at large. Simply shoveling wealth to the wealthy is comparable to putting carbon into a carbon sink. Wealth goes in but it doesn't come out. But while carbon sinks are necessary and good for our environment, simply shoveling wealth to the wealthy is not necessary and is, in fact, bad for our people. Certainly, nothing tangible was achieved on the order of health care for all, rebuilding our country's infrastructure, transitioning to clean renewable energy, or paying a universal basic income, investments which would transform the lives of at least half of our people for the better.

So, I believe that yes, on *Spaceship Earth* we can do a universal basic income, an infrastructure plan, an all-inclusive national health care plan, and immediately attack climate change and the other ecological disasters our society has been creating, putting millions of our people to work at good-paying jobs. Now is exactly the time for us to reclaim the ancient lost power of publicly created money to heal our planet and ourselves. Our job is to work to educate our friends and families to join in our quest. In the next chapters, we take a closer look at our political and economic systems to see if just perhaps they need a tweak or two, so as to make them a part of the solution rather than the problem itself.

---

1. King, Jamilah, "Kamala Harris for the People: Veep Vows to Defeat 'Deeply Unserious' Trump," Mother Jones, Aug 22, 2024, https://www.motherjones.com/politics/2024/08/kamala-harris-for-the-people-veep-vows-to-defeat-deeply-unserious-trump/
2. McLeay, Michael; Radia, Amar & Thomas, Ryland of the Bank's Monetary Analysis Directorate, "Money creation in the modern economy," Bank of England, Quarterly Bulletin, 2014, Q1, chrome-extension://efaidnbmnnnibpcajpcglclefindmkaj/https://www.bankofengland.co.uk/-/media/boe/files/quarterly-bulletin/2014/money-creation-in-the-modern-economy.pdf
3. National Emergency Employment Defense Act (NEED Act), 112th Congress, Sept. 21, 2011, https://www.congress.gov/bill/112th-congress/house-bill/2990/text
4. Paul H. Douglas, University of Chicago; Irving Fisher, Yale University; Frank D. Graham, Princeton University; Earl J. Hamilton, Duke University; Willford I. King, New York University; Charles R. Whittlesey, Princeton University, "A Program for Monetary Reform," July, 1939, https://faculty.chicagobooth.edu/amir.sufi/research/monetaryreform_1939.
5. *Ibid.*
6. Harper, Janice Ph.D., "The Silence of Shunning: A Conversation With Kipling Williams," *Psychology Today*, Sept 4, 2015, https://www.psychologytoday.com/us/blog/beyond-bullying/201309/the-silence-shunning-conversation-kipling-william
7. Ibid. McLeay, Michael; Radia, Amar & Thomas, Ryland of the Bank's Monetary Analysis Directorate, "Money creation in the modern economy," Bank of England.
8. Zarlenga, Stephen, *The Lost Science of Money*, American Monetary Institute, 2002, Valatie, N.Y., https://monetary.org/misc/buy-the-book/
9. Alliance For Just Money, https://www.monetaryalliance.org/
10. Yamaguchi, Kaoru, "On the Liquidation of Government Debt under A Debt-Free Money System—Modeling the American Monetary Act," Doshisha University, Japan, Presented at 28th International Conference of the System Dynamics Society, Seoul, Korea, July 26, 2010, chrome-extension://efaidnbmnnnibpcajpcglclefindmkaj/https://monetary.org/images/pdfs/yamaguchipaper-latest.pdf
11. Kumhof, Michael, & Benes, Jaromir, *The Chicago Plan Revisited,* International Monetary Fund, Working Paper, p. 10-11, https://www.imf.org/external/pubs/ft/wp/2012/wp12202.pdf
12. YouTube, "Adair Turner Part 3," https://www.youtube.com/watch?v=XoHs7vCdl3E
13. Turner, Johnathan Adair, "Credit, Money and Leverage: What Wicksell, Hayek, Fischer Knew and Mainstream Economics Forgot," Stockholm School of Economics, Sept 12, 2013, https://www.scribd.com/document/172514424/What-Wicksell-Hayek-Fischer-Knew-and-Mainstream-Forgot-Adair-Turner-Stockholm-School-of-Economics-September-12, also available on YouTube.
14. Rethinking Economics, https://www.rethinkeconomics.org/

15. *Ibid.*
16. Rethinking Economics, "Open Letter: Rethinking the Role of Banks in Economics Education," https://www.rethinkeconomics.org/journal/open-letter-rrob/
17. *Ibid.*
18. *Ibid.*
19. Werner, Richard A., "How do banks create money, and why can other firms not do the same? An explanation for the coexistence of lending and and deposit-taking," International Review of Financial Analysis, December 2014, https://www.sciencedirect.com/science/article/pii/S1057521914001434
20. American Society of Civil Engineers, "2021 America's Infrastructure Scores a C–," https://infrastructurereportcard.org/
21. American Monetary Institute, "Fact Sheet Infrastructure Job Numbers," https://www.monetary.org/wp-content/uploads/2011/10/revised-Fact-Sheet-plus-Job-Numbers-for-NEED1.pdf
22. U.S. Department of the Treasury, "Small Business and Entrepreneurship in the Post-COVID Expansion," Sept 3, 2024, https://home.treasury.gov/news/featured-stories/small-business-and-entrepreneurship-in-the-post-covid-expansion
23. Alliance For Just Money, "Who We Are?" https://www.monetaryalliance.org/
24. Alliance For Just Money, "What does the American Monetary Reform Act (AMRA) do?" https://www.monetaryalliance.org/wp-content/uploads/AMRA-Fact-Sheet.pdf
25. *Ibid.*
26. Alliance For Just Money, "American Monetary Reform Act of 2024," chrome-extension://efaidnbmnnnibpcajpcglclefindmkaj/https://www.monetaryalliance.org/wp-content/uploads/AMRA2024.pdf
27. Glover, Andrew; Mustre-del-Rio & Von Ende-Becker, Alice, "How Much Have Record Corporate Profits Contributed to Recent Inflation?" Economic Review, First Quarter 2023, Federal Reserve Bank of Kansas City,
28. Coin News Media Group, "Inflation Calculator," https://www.usinflationcalculator.com/
29. Warren, Katie, "One brutal sentence captures what a disaster money in America has become," Business Insider, May 23, 2019, https://www.businessinsider.com/bottom-half-of-americans-negative-net-worth-2019-5
30. Steverman, Ben, "The Wealth Detective Who Finds the Hidden Money of the Super Rich," Bloomberg Businessweek, May 23, 2019, https://www.bloomberg.com/news/features/2019-05-23/the-wealth-detective-who-finds-the-hidden-money-of-the-super-rich

SEVEN

Avoiding the Capitalist/Socialist Divide

Divided by Two Words

Capitalism and socialism are terms hurled back and forth in our political discourse, often used with the sole intent to lay additional bricks on the wall that already divides our people into a right and a left. Our collective future requires that we change our money system so that we have the money necessary to drawdown the greenhouse gasses warming *Spaceship Earth.* Reaching drawdown is impossible if we remain divided into separate capitalist and socialist camps. Imagine *Spaceship Earth* with a pilot flying us in one direction, assisted by a co-pilot intent upon taking us all in the exact opposite direction; a recipe for disaster.

The reality is that one side of the divide does blindly support capitalism. The other side is somewhat supportive of capitalism too, yet also looking for ways that it can achieve better results. Rather than allowing ourselves to be divided by the labels and terms, a more pragmatic alternative is to see how we can use the better aspects of each to get optimum results. The first draft of *People, Planet & the Power of Money* was sent to seven test readers to get their thoughts and suggestions. An almost unanimous request from these readers was for me to expand the discussion of capitalism and socialism, with emphasis on further explaining socialism. Every year Merriam-Webster Dictionary proclaims the word that is most looked up in their online dictionary as the word of the year. As a result of the Occupy Movement, Merriam-Webster's had to announce two words for the year 2012—capitalism and socialism.[1]

> Capitalism: "an economic system characterized by private or corporate ownership of capital goods, by investments that are determined by private decision, and by prices, production, and the distribution of goods that are determined mainly by competition in a free market."
>
> Socialism: "any of various economic and political theories advocating collective or governmental ownership and administration of the means of production and distribution of goods."

Capitalism Replaces Mercantilism

Capitalism has been defined as an economic system in which private individuals or businesses own the means of production such as natural resources, factories, and agricultural fields. Goods and services are produced in what capitalists term a free market based on the principle of supply and demand. Capitalism offers up the planet and its resources to individual and corporate ownership, allowing them to do whatever they want with them, even if the majority of society would take issue with a particular action. An example would be a capitalist factory that has been polluting the air and water of those downwind and downstream of the factory for years. Even if the majority of people that are subject to the pollution want it to stop, under capitalism it is the capitalist's right to continue to do what he sees fit to compete and win in the free market. *Laissez-faire* capitalism, from the French for "leave alone," also called free market capitalism, considers any sort of regulation to be a violation of this fundamental right.

Capitalists have shown a great propensity toward fighting any and all regulations proposed upon themselves throughout history. A modern consequence of this *laissez-faire* capitalism is the indiscriminate production of plastic without a recycling feedback loop. Whether it is the plastic encasing your take-out lunch, deodorant, lip balm, toothpaste, fresh broccoli, salad mix, dry dog food, topsoil, mulch, fertilizer, shower nozzle replacement, or generic item of almost any description, most of it is also now packaged in layers of unrecyclable plastic. Incased within the unrecyclable packaging nightmare is the reality that most items we purchase, such as our precious children's toys, are also made of non-recyclable plastic.

Capitalism replaced mercantilism; the European economic system prevalent in the sixteenth to eighteenth centuries. Under mercantilism each individual nation had the absolute power to regulate their own individual nation's economy, thereby boosting their national power. Mercantilism was the economic counterpart to political absolutism with the sovereign ruler of the nation as monarch. All this was based on the mindset that money was precious metal—gold and silver. These were to be valued above all else and hoarded by the nation's monarch. The precious metals were largely retrieved from the Earth by the enslavement of other people.

As the gold and silver in their own nations became more difficult to find, the mercantilist European nations then reached out across the globe to find new sources of these precious metals. After first stealing the gold and silver from the existing civilizations in these new worlds, the Europeans began to establish colonies and enslave the people to further extract resources and grow crops for profit. The colonies provided the Mother Country with raw materials to manufacture goods, while those in the colonies were denied the right to manufacture their own goods. This developed into a favorable balance of trade for the Mother Country with the goal to accumulate gold and silver to be hoarded by the sovereign king and queen. Slavery and colonialism fit hand and glove with both the mercantilist and the capitalist system that replaced it.

A New Definition and Way to Look at Capitalism

Another definition of capitalism has emerged more recently. The other parts of capitalism are present in this newer way to look at capitalism. Individual ownership of the Earth and a market economy put in place by the Rule of Law are prerequisites, but the emphasis on what differentiates capitalism from the earlier definition is quite compelling.

Expert Witness: Jonathan McMillan

> "Hence, we define *capitalism* as an economic order in which most capital is managed by corporations."[2]

The above definition is from Jonathan McMillan's 2024 book, *Capitalism and the Market Economy.* McMillan makes the point that what differentiates capitalism from its predecessor is that as capitalism began to take hold:

> With the rise of capitalism, most means of production were no longer in individual private ownership. Instead, the means of production have been increasingly owned collectively via corporations.[3]

What is the big deal about corporations owning the means of production in place of individual people? Corporations are legal entities that have protections under the Rule of Law. The protections being not so much for the corporations, but rather those who own the corporations, the stockholders. If the corporation engages in reckless behavior, becomes insolvent and ends up owing creditors and or real people it has done harm to, the corporation may have to dissolve and be liquidated. But the corporate owners and the stockholders are protected from any liability. McMillan believes this is the foundation of capitalism — capitalists can engage in risky financial behavior through their corporations that he calls insolvency, without risking their own private wealth. We will hear more from McMillan in Chapter 9.

Monopoly: Board Game or Life Sentence?

Neither capitalism nor socialism has ever existed for any length of time in its pure form. Capitalism is too rapacious to do so. Because it is literally an economic system of the strong eating the weak, it requires regulation or it will devour itself. Perhaps the best way to understand the true nature of capitalism is through the board game Monopoly, which uses the basics of capitalism. The game ends when only one player is left standing. This one player has everything, all property and money, while the rest of the players are left bankrupt and in debt with nothing. Hardly the system a sane people would choose as the basis of their society.

The board game Monopoly has largely been presented as a rags-to-riches Depression-era story. Charles Darrow, a struggling, unemployed salesman during the Great Depression, invented the game, marketed it himself, and then sold it to Parker Brothers in 1935, eventually making both Mr. Darrow and Parker Brothers millions.[4] Although the game has become a global symbol of capitalism, ironically it was conceived as quite the opposite.

The truth is that the game was not invented by Darrow in the 1930s, but by a progressive woman named Elizabeth Magie, also known as Elizabeth Phillips. She had applied for a patent for what she called The Landlord Game almost three decades earlier in 1903 and the patent was granted in 1904.[5] Her game had two sets of rules, one a capitalist set to create monopolies and dominate opponents, and another a progressive set or anti-monopolist set demonstrating how all could be rewarded instead of having just one winner. It was meant to be a teaching tool showing the moral bankruptcy of capitalism. "It is a practical demonstration of the present system of land-grabbing with all its usual outcomes and consequences," Elizabeth Magie explained.[6]

Ms. Magie's father was a newspaper editor and abolitionist who had covered the Abraham Lincoln/Stephen Douglas debates across

Illinois in Lincoln's failed bid for the Senate. In addition to inventing what would become the world's most popular board game and being in the anti-monopoly movement, Elizabeth Magie was also an activist for women's rights. She had gained national attention by putting an ad in the newspaper in which she offered herself for sale to the highest bidder as a "young woman American slave," saying she was "not beautiful, but very attractive," having "features full of character and strength, yet truly feminine."[7] Magie told reporters that her ad was meant as a statement about the dismal position of women in society: "We are not machines.... Girls have minds, desires, hopes and ambition."[8]

The Landlord Game was individually reproduced and played for decades by progressives in the Northeast, including the Ivy League college campuses of Harvard, Columbia, and the Wharton School of Finance. It also was played by the Quaker community in Atlantic City, which is where Mr. Darrow is first said to have played the game.[9] After Darrow did so, he made some changes, such as changing the names from the likes of Easy Street and Poverty Place to Park Place and Boardwalk. As a child, Darrow had vacationed in Atlantic City, so he used names from his boyhood vacation site. When he originally submitted it to Parker Brothers, he was turned down. Darrow then made some graphic changes and marketed it on his own. He had success selling it to Philadelphia department stores who sold out of the game during the busy Christmas season. Parker Brothers took note and bought the rights.[10] After Monopoly took off, Parker Bothers later paid Elizabeth Magie the grand total of $500 for the rights to her Landlord Game and two other games she had invented.[11]

The Real Get Out of Jail Card

By 2010 more than 250 million Monopoly games had been sold worldwide, but perhaps the most important Monopoly games were those that were not sold but given away. During World War II, British manufacturing company John Waddington Ltd. was the licensed manufacturer of Monopoly outside the United States. Waddington had also perfected the process of printing on silk. They used this process to print silk escape maps which were smuggled into the troops held in German POW camps. Silk does not deteriorate when wet like paper and is silent while paper escape maps were much easier to detect. Waddington set up a top-secret room in their plant to make Monopoly games that included—secreted away within the game and its pieces—silk escape maps, a metal file, and a magnetic compass; even actual German, Italian, and French money was mixed in with the game money. Allied soldiers who were headed to the front lines, along with pilots, were told to look for the game if captured. The identifying mark of the games that held the escape goodies was a tiny red dot in the corner of the Free Parking space. An estimated 35,000 Allied POWs escaped from German prison camps during the war, many of them assisted by these special Monopoly games.[12] At the end of the war this entire operation was broken down and kept secret, the reasoning being that it might be necessary to do it all again during the next war.

Early Seeds of Socialism—Sparta and Early Christians

Long before the word *socialism* was even conceived, Sparta in the 8th century BC, under King Lycurgus, is considered an early example of a socialist state by some scholars.[13] In *History of Money 101* we related that Spartans under King Lycurgus eschewed personal luxuries, dined at collective meals, abolished private wealth accumulation by designing a money system of fiat iron bars called Pelanors (which were almost too heavy and cumbersome to be used at all), and divided the land in equal parcels amongst its citizens. This certainly gave Sparta the attributes of a socialist state. The Spartans were able to have this proto-socialist state because they also had slaves and a servant class under them. But that was the ancient world they resided in; societies developed with slaves and servants. Eight centuries later, the early Christians offer another example of people renouncing the material world and living together in a proto-communist/socialist community.[14] And yes, many of the early Christians also continued to hold slaves.[15]

Although Sparta and early Christian societies embraced many of the hallmarks of what would later be called socialism, they were not called socialist, because the word *socialism* did not exist. It only came into existence as a theoretical answer to capitalism, which did not exist in ancient times. The term *socialism* was first used in 1832 in the French newspaper, *Le Globe*, owned by Pierre Leroux.[16] It was popularized by Karl Marx and Friedrich Engels as they constructed their theoretical answer to what they had determined to be the predatory nature of capitalism in the 1848 pamphlet *The Communist Manifesto* and later in the three volumes of *Das Kapital*, published from 1867–83. Marx and Engels were responding to a developing *laissez-faire* capitalist system in which factory-owning industrialists were becoming fabulously wealthy while their workers remained paupers.

Many of us think that socialism is a system in which everything is divided equally. While it certainly could be such, it is not so by definition. Socialism is an economic system in which either the workers or the state owns and controls the means of production (factories, agriculture, and businesses), in contrast to individuals and corporations owning and controlling the means of production in a capitalist system. Socialism is nothing more than a series of attempts to create a more equal and level playing field. But Marx and Engels were not the only ones who had grappled with the problem of unregulated capitalism.

Sir Thomas More's Utopia

Sir Thomas More was an English social philosopher and statesman and later was canonized as a saint by the Catholic Church. His 1516 book *Utopia* depicts fictional life on an island in which everything is communally owned except personal items such as clothing. As such, it depicted a life similar to that of a monastery. Since socialism was conceived as an answer to capitalism, and Thomas More wrote in the early mercantile period before the capitalist period, he is not thought of as a socialist. But he did conceive of a life without private property, save personal items. On his imaginary island of Utopia, people would switch houses every 10 years. Money would have been abolished on the island and since they lived simply, people only needed to work a few hours every day. The rest of the time was left for leisure.

Thomas More was undoubtedly influenced by early Christians who practiced a simple form of socialism by sharing their labor and goods. He himself lived in a monastery for four years before deciding against the priesthood and instead pursuing a career in public service. In 1521, More was knighted by King Henry VIII and in 1523, became Henry's closest advisor when he became speaker of the House of Commons. But when Speaker More refused to accept Henry's divorce from Catherine of Aragon and upcoming marriage to Anne Boleyn, Henry had him convicted as a traitor and beheaded in 1535.[17] The Roman Catholic Church canonized him as a saint four hundred years later in 1935.[18]

The Diggers of the Protestant Reformation

In the seventeenth century, a movement called the Diggers emerged from the Protestant Reformation in England. They believed that the world was created by God to share and not divide. Following this philosophy, they dug and planted crops on land that they did not own. After Charles I lost the English Civil War and was beheaded, the Diggers believed that the nobility's former lands should be open to their use. Those with claims on the land took them to court for their attempts at squatting, while others went outside the court system and formed violent mobs against them. After years of harassment, they had had enough and disbanded around 1650. Their belief that the Earth belonged to all and could not be divided into private property owned by individuals (a basic tenet of capitalism) qualified them as early socialists even though capitalism had not yet taken hold.[19]

Before mercantilism and capitalism, feudalism was the dominant social system in Europe from the ninth century through the fifteenth century. All power emanated from the king or queen. The nobility was allowed to hold the Crown's lands in their own names and govern them locally under the overall rule of the king or queen. In return for this privilege, the nobility owed allegiance to the Crown, including the military service of themselves and all their serfs and vassals. The serfs or peasants were bound to the land and owed allegiance to their local lord and ultimately the king or queen. The peasants worked the land and were required to provide the nobility with a share of all they produced.

Claude Henri De Saint-Simon's Nouveau Christianisme

Claude Henri De Saint-Simon was born to an impoverished aristocratic family in France. He fought as a captain with the French forces that aided the American Revolution. Later during the French Revolution, using funds advanced by a friend, he speculated and bought up newly nationalized lands. He was imprisoned during the French Revolution's Reign of Terror and, when released in 1794, he found himself wealthy from his land speculation. He proceeded to spend away most of his money.

De Saint-Simon then turned to a life of science, advocating for public control of property through central planning instead of public ownership. In opposition to feudalism and militarism, he supported businessmen and industrial leaders controlling society, with the spiritual direction of society coming from scientists and engineers instead of the Catholic Church. He was considered one of the chief founders of Christian socialism. His major work was *Nouveau Christianisme* (1825), in which he proclaimed that a brotherhood of man must accompany the scientific organization of industry and society. Much of his thought is attributed to the bloody excesses he witnessed during the French Revolution. He foresaw scientists and engineers replacing the Catholic Church in society. He was an advocate for the poor, but he did not take sides in the struggle between capitalism and labor that Marx and Engels would later coalesce around.[20]

Robert Owen's New Harmony

Robert Owen was a Scot industrialist who owned profitable textile mills in Scotland. These were considered humane by the day's standards since no children under the age of ten were employed to work in them. Owen felt human nature was formed by the environment. If social conditions were to improve, people would develop a better nature. To test this idea, in 1825 he established the town of New Harmony on the Wabash River in the southwest corner of Indiana. Wanting to create a socialist paradise, he appealed to the public for settlers. 1,000 people volunteered, but they did not turn out to be the most harmonious fit for the settlement or perhaps any other settlement, since they did little work. Anarchy reigned before New Harmony was eventually disbanded. However, five of Owen's children stayed on with a few teachers and scientists, developing a notable cultural center and a laboratory that later became the U.S. Geological Survey.[21]

Étienne Cabet's Incaria

Philosopher Francois Marie Charles Fourier looked at society and determined that the repetitive nature of labor was responsible for many of society's ills. He imagined a community called a "phalanstery" in which people work cooperatively together if that work engaged their interests and talents. In 1840, French socialist Étienne Cabet wrote a novel about such a community, the utopian fiction *Travels in Incaria.* In the 1850s, Cabet founded a model of Incaria in Illinois. Just as New Harmony in neighboring Indiana was unsuccessful, so also was Incaria in Illinois. Cabet left his experiment behind in 1856.[22]

While the above thinkers had grappled with how to balance the advance of science, industrialization, and capitalism with the type of unequal society capitalism was creating, none of their efforts took hold.

Karl Marx and Friedrich Engels

Karl Marx and Friedrich Engels would follow these early thinkers on socialism. Although their ideas did not take hold during their own lives, they would have a profound impact on history.

While Marx and Engels were born in Germany, they both eventually made their way to Paris where they met and banded together after meeting at the Café de la Régence in 1844. Engels's 1845 book *The Condition of the Working Class in England in 1844* was all Marx needed to latch onto the working class as the instrument for the final revolution to defeat capitalism.

Both Marx and Engels were students of the German philosopher Georg Wilhelm Friedrich Hegel and his dialectic or dialectical method, derived in part from Plato's *Dialogues*, in which Socrates discussed subjects with supposed experts. From the conversation prompted by Socrates' questions to the expert, a conclusion was reached. This conclusion was usually far from the expert's original thinking at the start of the dialogue. Later German philosopher Immanuel Kant also used the dialectic: first proposing a thesis, countered with an antithesis and eventually reaching a synthesis or conclusion. Hegel found both Plato's and Kant's dialectics wanting and proposed his own dialectic: first the Abstract, then Negation of the Abstract, before finally arriving at the Concrete. Kant's dialectic example: the abstract of being or existence is negated by the negative of death. Whatever lives must eventually die. Hegel's concrete solution to his philosophical dilemma was becoming. Life or being is always becoming, even when it is becoming death.[23]

I am hardly a Marxist scholar. As a young man, I attempted to read his work without success. Later in life, reading what others have said to explain his thinking has certainly helped my understanding. I have talked with self-professed Marxists, and what has come through loud and clear is that Marxists interpret all human events through the dialectic. I remember one conversation after an anti-war march in Chicago. I was with a couple of friends, and we stopped at a bodega to get a bite to eat. A gentleman who had also marched, joined our group and proceeded to explain Marx to us. This was Marx defined not from a university professorial viewpoint, which I have also heard, but from the working-class background of one who had read Marx backwards and forwards. My one takeaway from the conversation, in addition to a great deal of respect for the zeal of our guest, was that everything about Marx must be interpreted through the dialectic.

The Revolutions of 1848

Karl Marx is on every list of the world's most influential people. Yet it was both Marx and Engels who together wrote *The Communist Manifesto* in 1847. It was published just before much of Europe erupted in the Revolutions of 1848 that spread from France to Austria, Prussia, Bohemia, Hungary, and parts of Italy. Retrospectively, it might appear to us that *The Communist Manifesto* was behind the Revolutions of 1848, but the *Manifesto* had nothing to do with them. The causes of the revolutions, which hit most of Europe with the two notable exceptions of Britain and Russia, were generally understood to be bad harvests and poor economic conditions. *The Communist Manifesto* was largely written for a group of twenty or so radicals in London and only a couple hundred copies of the pamphlet were originally printed. Those who fought in the Revolutions of 1848 were primarily nationalists and liberals who sought to overthrow old monarchies and establish republics with constitutions to bring unity to their nations. Those who participated in these revolutions had no knowledge of *The Communist Manifesto*, and conversely, those who did have knowledge of it had nothing to do with the 1848 revolutions.[24]

While the revolutionaries were ultimately defeated, they succeeded in changing much of the system. In Germany and the lands under the Habsburg Monarchy, the feudal system, a system in which the lord of the manor owned the land, and the peasants or serfs were bound to the land and the lord, was abolished. The revolutions began in Paris with reform initiatives that provided workshops for universal employment. When the National Assembly, dominated by the professional middle class, voted to shut them down, protests broke out. Four days of fighting resulted in 1,500 workers and 1,000 troops dead. Thousands more workers were arrested and exiled to overseas colonies. However, the right to vote and democracy were secured even though the French then elected a nephew of Napoleon Bonaparte as their new leader. He then promptly established a new empire claiming the title of Napoleon III.[25] Both socialism and feminism came to be looked at as more of a possibility as a result of the revolutions of 1848.[26]

Differentiating Socialism and Communism

The test readers who read the first draft of the *People, Planet & Power of Money Project* had many questions about the difference between socialism and communism. They were hardly alone; your author was also confused by Marx's own words. Marx professed that the trajectory of history would result in capitalism being replaced initially by socialism, and eventually by the perfection of socialism as communism. All history is the history of class struggles, and socialism will eventually take us to communism.[27]

Marx died in 1883 and Engels in 1895, both missing the Russian Revolution of 1917 and the communist Russian/Soviet state that became a reality based on their own historical interpretation of class struggle. Using the dialectic of Marx, it would seem that history would go from capitalism to socialism, then to communism. Except that is not what happened after the Russia Revolution in 1917. Under Vladimir Lenin and the Bolsheviks, the Russian Revolution took Russia from a feudal monarchy under the tsar to a socialist autocracy under first Lenin and then Joseph Stalin. No socialist-lite, so to speak. Instead, the world was treated to a form of communism which immediately became an authoritarian system, and certainly never transformed into a worker's paradise.

Marx and Engels had approached the problems of a capitalist society in what they considered a scientific manner. But forget model communities and a democratic process, they believed socialism would come about through the clash of the classes led by a revolutionary vanguard (the Bolsheviks). Other than describing socialism as a transitory stage to communism, Marx had also failed to provide a clear description of how "communism" actually worked.[28] What we were presented with in the Soviet Union, China, and North Korea was autocratic socialism which according to communist doctrine eventually would lead to a system in which government was no longer needed. That hardly seems likely, since government controlled every aspect of their society.

Expert Witness: Peter Hudis

Peter Hudis, Professor of Humanities and Philosophy at Oakton Community College, has written extensively on Karl Marx. He clears up the misconceptions:

> Marx used many terms to refer to a post-capitalist society—positive humanism, socialism, Communism, realm of free individuality, free association of producers, etc. He used these terms completely interchangeably. The notion that 'socialism' and 'Communism' are distinct historical stages is alien to his work and only entered the lexicon of Marxism after his death.[29]

Using Professor Hudis' interpretation, Marx's dialectic could then explain the process as the abstract of capitalism, the negation of the abstract in revolution, and finally the concrete in socialism/communism (both meaning the exact same thing to Marx).

Professor Hudis also clears up the seeming contradiction within Marx's concept of private property. In *The Communist Manifesto*, Marx says that "the abolition of existing property relations is not at all a distinctive feature of Communism...." Later Marx follows this statement with what appears to be a contradiction: "In this sense, the theory of the Communists may be summed up in the single sentence: Abolition of private property." It would appear that Marx is talking out of both sides of his mouth. Yes, to existing property relations and yes to the abolition of private property. Professor Hudis interprets Marx as saying that individual ownership of private property is okay as long as it remains within the working class.[30] Ownership of private property outside the working class is not allowed. Marx's rationale for this is that those outside the working class would then use the labor of the working class to procure their own private property. Therefore, if they want private property, they should join the working class and work for it like everyone else does.

While Marx did not offer a distinction between communism and socialism, Marx did call for the working class (proletariat) to use violence to take power from the capitalist (bourgeoisie) class. The United States also came to power with a violent revolution. But to our credit, the U.S. did put in place the U.S. Constitution and a legal system that peacefully transferred power between governments. The U.S. system has worked reasonably well with all sides accepting this peaceful transfer of power, sometimes begrudgingly but still accepting it.

The Two Notable Exceptions in the U.S. to the Peaceful Transfer of Power

The two major exceptions to the peaceful transfer of power were the secession of the Confederacy which resulted in the Civil War (1861–65), after the seceding slaveholder states refused to accept President Abraham Lincoln's election. The second was when Donald Trump refused to accept the results of the 2020 presidential election, and turned a mob on the Capitol.[31]

I concluded *Money Creation 101* with an observation that occurred to me as I was researching and rewriting *History of Money 101*, while at the same time watching Donald Trump's efforts to overthrow our constitutional republic with lies and brute force: "If the South had been allowed to peacefully secede or had been militarily successful in defeating the massive effort by the North to keep the Union intact, there is absolutely no reason to believe that the South would not continue to be a slaveholding society today."[32] Yes, if President Lincoln had not mobilized the North to fight and win the Civil War, there is no reason to expect the Confederate States would not have continued to be a slaveholding entity today. I remember being taught in school in the fifties and sixties that the North's industrialization would have soon seeped into the South and slavery would have disappeared, magically on its own. Baloney! The racism of our historical past is exactly the type of latent feeling that Trump has awakened with his base today, as he tries to take us back to the 1860s.

Socialism Unacceptable to U.S. Capitalism: Iran, Chile and Venezuela

Professor Hudis has told his students and us that Marx used the terms socialism and communism interchangeably. Yet, nearly a century and a half after his death, there is a desire to understand the difference between the two concepts. The major difference that I can find in the way the two words have evolved, is that socialism represents coming into power through the democratic electoral process, while communism represents coming into power through the violent revolution as espoused by Marx and Engels.

Three examples of socialists coming to power peacefully were Mohammad Mosaddegh in Iran (1951), Salvador Allende in Chile (1970), and Hugo Chávez in Venezuela (1998). After coming to power peacefully, Premier Mosaddegh in Iran[33] and President Allende in Chile[34] were soon deposed not by the electoral process, but by violent military coups which were supported by the U.S. government. In 2002 President Chávez was also arrested in a military coup[35] that our government also supported.[36] The people of Venezuela then took to the streets in mass support of President Chávez against the military coup. Chávez was released and the coup failed.

Today the U.S. continues to try and overthrow the socialist Venezuelan government led by President Nicolás Maduro, who succeeded Chávez after his death in 2013. The Venezuelan effort at a form of socialism is simply unacceptable to policy makers from both U.S. political parties. Venezuela has been presented to the American people through the lens of our political parties and media as a failed socialist state, although the poor had made huge strides before the U.S. economic sanctions came crushing down on them.

Both major American political parties share the idea that that socialist countries should not exist. And when they do pop-up, we must play whack-a-mole and smash them down. We put in place economic sanctions against Venezuela that have devastated their people and their lopsided oil-based economy.[37] Why? Our official reason is that their elections were not viewed as democratic enough for us. That simply means that the socialists won. First it was Chávez and we tried to get rid of him. Then it was his successor, President Nicolás Maduro. From 2015-2022 the U.S. took the position that the president of the National Assembly President Juan Guaidó was and should be the interim president of Venezuela, even though Maduro was the duly elected president.[38] In January 2023, we stopped backing Guaidó's claim to the presidency and supported the National Assembly as the governing authority, again over Maduro's presidency.[39] We don't want anyone dictating to us how to run our own country, so why can't we just let the Venezuelans make their own political decisions? Is U.S. capitalism really that afraid of a little competition from a mildly socialist Venezuela?

Venezuela: U.S. Overview of U.S. Sanctions

The Congressional Research reported on U.S. sanctions of Venezuela in November 1, 2023. This is a synopsis of that report, which I can no longer find on their website:

The United States since 2005, has imposed sanctions on Venezuelan individuals and entities that have engaged in criminal, anti-democratic, and/or corrupt actions. The Trump Administration expanded the scope of U.S. sanctions, moving beyond individually targeted sanctions to include broader financial sanctions, sectoral sanctions, and sanctions on the government of Nicolás Maduro. Despite those sanctions, which were associated with an economic collapse that has led 7.7 million Venezuelans to flee the country, Maduro consolidated power. The failure of international pressure to dislodge Maduro has led Venezuela's Unity Platform of opposition parties to shift strategies and compete in presidential elections due by October 2024.

The Biden Administration has sought to leverage sanctions relief to incentivize Maduro to negotiate a path toward freer, fairer elections. After the October 17, 2023, signing of a partial electoral roadmap between Maduro and the Unity Platform, the Biden Administration issued licenses easing some sanctions on Venezuela through April 2024. U.S. officials warned, however, that if the Maduro government did not define an expedited process that allows all candidates to run for president and begin to release political prisoners and wrongfully detained U.S. citizens by late November 2023, the licenses would be revoked. Maria Corina Machado won the October 2022 opposition primary with 93% of the vote but is barred from running in the 2024 contest.[40]

Is it possible that ending the U.S. economic sanctions against Venezuela and recognizing the Maduro government would be a better strategy than the continuation of the failed U.S. policy of the last two decades that has led to an economic disaster wreaked upon the Venezuelan people? I freely admit to not being a Venezuelan expert, yet it seems obvious to me that ending the sanctions and working with the current Maduro government would improve the economic conditions on the ground in Venezuela. This should slow down, if not stop, the flow of Venezuelans fleeing their country. These economic refugees from Venezuela and other Latin American countries are the same ones that have been making the arduous trek of thousands of miles to our southern border in Texas. Recognizing their government and working with them, we might actually bring about a migration of Venezuelans returning to their country.

Venezuela 2024 Presidential Election

On July 28, 2024 Venezuela held their presidential election between President Nicolás Maduro and Edmundo González, after ruling that opposition leader Maria Corina Machado was not able to run as a candidate. Venezuela declared President Maduro the winner, yet certainly appears to have failed to openly show the results of the election. The opposition is screaming bloody murder about the claim of victory, especially the millions of people who have left Venezuela in the last decade or so. I can't tell you if Maduro cheated or not. It is quite possible that Maduro, existentially threatened by the U.S., is doing whatever it takes to remain in power, similar to what we will see the Bolsheviks did in Russia a century ago.

Honduras

Many of the refugees who show up at our Southern border are from Honduras. Why? In 2009 Manuel Zelaya was the democratically elected president of Honduras and crime of all crimes, he happened to be a socialist who wanted to redistribute land to somewhat level the uneven playing field for his people. When he proposed a plan to change the constitution to do so, President Zelaya was arrested in the early morning hours in his pajamas by military special forces troops loyal to the country's elite landowners.[41]

U.S. military leaders had advance knowledge of the coup and did nothing to stop it.

> A retired U.S. military intelligence officer, who helped with the lobbying and the Honduran colonels' trip, told me on condition of anonymity that the coup supporters debated "how to manage the U.S." One group, he said, decided to "start using the true and trusted method and say, 'Here is the bogeyman, it's communism.' And who are their [coup plotters] allies? The Republicans."
>
> A network of former Cold Warriors and Republicans in Congress loudly encouraged Honduras's de facto regime and criticized the newly elected Obama administration's handling of the crisis. Zelaya, so his critics alleged, was simply an acolyte of Venezuelan President Hugo Chávez, public enemy No. 1 of the U.S. in the hemisphere.[42]

President Obama's Administration did little to nothing to return President Zelaya to office. The coup succeeded, and conditions on the ground rapidly deteriorated for the Honduran people. Physicians for Human Rights reports:

> According to statistics released by the Center for the Prevention, Treatment and Rehabilitation of Victims of Torture (CPTRT), in the four months following the coup there

> was more than a 4,000 percent spike in human rights violations. The violations included torture, mass arrests, military force used against protesters, violence towards women, minority groups, and the media, sexual violence, and other cruel and degrading treatment. There is also widespread evidence from local Honduran human rights organizations that the majority of the cases have been ignored by the government institutions which examine and assess these victims. Human rights organizations doubt the impartiality of the government institutions as well.[43]

Meanwhile in the U.S., we wonder why we have a migrant crisis at our Southern border; masses of people trekking thousands of miles to find sanctuary in America, the Land of the Free. Many of whom have left countries such as Venezuela, Honduras and Cuba that have tried various forms of socialism, only to see America basically say no to any form of socialism in our hemisphere. Evidently, our capitalist system that espouses free market competition is not interested in competition from socialism.

Communism

In a pure communist country, the state owns and controls the economy and to some extent provides people with life's basic necessities such as food, housing, education, health care, and employment. Although the Communist Party controls the economic and political systems in the communist countries listed, none of them have done away with money or personal property as prescribed by communist doctrine.[44]

Pure communism would entirely reject the concept of private ownership of the Earth and its resources, at least by those in the capitalist class. Within the Soviet Union, people could own small plots of ground on which to grow crops, in addition to furniture, refrigerators, and personal items such as clothes. However, the reality was that ownership of many of these items was absolutely infinitesimal when compared to Western capitalist democracies. However, in the Soviet

Union, they could not save their money and start a business, employing others to work for them.[45] While some concepts of pure socialism might do the same, attempts at state socialism usually have allowed some individual ownership of both real estate and personal property along with individual ownership of stores and businesses.

Social Safety Net or Entitlement Programs?

PoliticalDictionary.com offers the following definition for safety net or social safety net: "refers to the welfare programs that are designed to provide benefits to low-income or elderly Americans." It then provides the very astute observation that reflects the chasm of the Capitalist/Socialist Divide: "Safety net is generally a positive term—people who are opposed to welfare programs usually refer to them as entitlement programs."[46] Social Security, Medicare, Medicaid, unemployment insurance, and Supplemental Nutritional Assistance Program (SNAP, formerly called food stamps)[47] are some of the major parts of our present—take your pick—social safety net or entitlement programs.

The Free Market vs. Democratic Socialism/Capitalism

The Scandinavian countries of Sweden, Denmark, and Norway are often considered to be socialist states, but a better way to look at them is as capitalist countries that have a larger social safety net than we do in America. Democratic socialism is a term popularized by U.S. Senator Bernie Sanders that might better describe the Scandinavian countries, a term meant to describe a capitalist society that is carefully regulated by a representative government that in turn provides a livable social safety net for all its citizens.

Expert Witness: Robert Reich—Secretary of Labor under President Bill Clinton, Professor Emeritus Public Policy, University of California, Berkeley

Dr. Reich co-founded Inequality Media with Emmy-award-winning filmmaker Jacob Kornbluth. Dr. Reich uses the term *democratic capitalism* to describe almost precisely the same thing that Senator Sanders calls democratic socialism, with perhaps just a slight bit more capitalism in the mixture than Sanders would prefer. In his description Secretary Reich is quite critical of the concept of the "free market" that Adam Smith, capitalists, and the mainstream economics community have taken as an accepted article of faith:

> The Great Crash of 1929 followed by the Great Depression taught the nation a crucial lesson that we forgot after Ronald Reagan's presidency: that the so-called "free market" does not exist. It's a fiction. Markets are always and inevitably human creations. They reflect decisions by judges, legislators, and government agencies as to how the market should be organized and enforced — and *for whom.*[48]

Reich describes how the Great Depression was brought on by the market working for a:

> "Monied elite—allowing nearly unlimited borrowing, encouraging people to gamble on Wall Street, suppressing labor unions, holding down wages, and permitting the Street to take huge risks with other people's money."[49]

U.S. President Franklin Delano Roosevelt reorganized the market to serve public purposes. His New Deal stopped Wall Street's excessive borrowing and gambling, encouraged labor unions, established Social Security, and created unemployment insurance, disability insurance, and the 40-hour workweek. Government spending created jobs and put almost all Americans to work. Both Democratic and

Republican administrations that followed extended and grew this democratic capitalism. Wall Street, TV networks, airlines, railroads, and other common carriers were all regulated. Executive pay was modest. Public investments in higher education, a national highway system, and other infrastructure were paid for by taxing the wealthy.

Then along came President Ronald Reagan (1981–1989) with his all-out support of the free market and his war on democratic capitalism. Dr. Reich describes:

> From 1981 onward, a new bipartisan orthodoxy emerged that the so-called 'free market' functioned well only if the government got out of the way (conveniently forgetting that the market required government). The goal of economic policy thereby shifted from public welfare to economic growth. And the means shifted from public oversight of the market to deregulation, free trade, privatization, 'trickle-down' tax cuts, and deficit reduction — all of which helped the monied interests make more money. [neoliberalism]
>
> What happened next? For 40 years, the economy grew, but median wages stagnated. Inequalities of income and wealth ballooned. Wall Street reverted to the betting parlor it had been in the 1920s. Finance once again ruled the economy. Spurred by hostile takeovers, corporations began focusing solely on maximizing shareholder returns — which led them to fight unions, suppress wages, abandon their communities, and outsource abroad. [Move factories to the slave wages paid in the Global South.]
>
> Corporations and the super-rich used their increasing wealth to corrupt politics with campaign donations — buying tax cuts, tax loopholes, government subsidies, bailouts, loan guarantees, non-bid government contracts, and government forbearance from antitrust enforcement, allowing them to monopolize markets.
>
> Democratic capitalism, organized to serve public purposes,

all but disappeared. It was replaced by corporate capitalism, organized to serve the monied interests.[50]

Capitalism Does Not Stand for Competition

We have all been taught to believe that capitalism is a wonderful system built on competition in the free market. Yet this isn't the case. Years ago, when I began to publicly critique the U.S. Iraq War in newspaper letters to the editor, I was viciously attacked in many of the responses to my letters.

My local newspaper, *The Times of Northwest Indiana*, used to allow comments to letters to the editor which were posted online below the letters. Comments to my letters often surpassed one hundred. Putting it mildly, the majority of those commenting did not agree with me. Any critique of foreign or social policy of our government was seen by those commenting as some sort of existential threat to their way of life. They assumed that I was a socialist/communist who hated America. Nothing could be further from the truth, although I readily admit to wanting to change and improve America.

The number one rejoinder they would send my way was that if I did not like it here, I should move to Russia. Pure irony is that many of these same people who a decade or two ago invited me to move to Russia now support Putin's invasion of their peaceful neighbor, Ukraine. They do so because their cult leader Trump is all-in with Putin and they are all-in with Trump. Those who wrote inviting me to move to Russia were evidently not aware that Russia had capitulated to an authoritarian form of gangster capitalism in the early 1990s. The following chapter will explain how this happened.

Capitalism's War on Socialism

Capitalism is an economic system whose supporters proudly boast that it is entirely based on competition in the free market, yet those in power within the capitalist system have used all measures necessary to destroy competing economic systems ("socialism" in particular) from simply existing in other countries. Earlier in the chapter we talked a little about Iran, Chile, Venezuela and Honduras as examples. Successful socialist countries do not exist for the simple reason that capitalism has waged war on socialism from day one.

American capitalists have deployed the US Army, National Guard, police, and private security firms such as the Pinkerton National Detective Agency against striking workers since the 1870s. Some of the more famous actions in which strikers were killed include the 1892 Homestead Steel Strike near Pittsburgh, Pennsylvania, the 1894 Pullman Railway Strike originating in Chicago, Illinois, and the 1903 Colorado Labor War strikes against Colorado mines.[51] The International Workers of the World Union (Wobblies), founded in Chicago in 1905 and opposed to capitalism, were attacked by the First Red Scare and the Palmer Raids in which leftist, socialist, and communist union members were attacked, jailed, and deported.[52]

Child labor laws, minimum wage laws, overtime pay, 40-hour workweek, Social Security, Medicare, and Medicaid were all opposed by the capitalist class when originally proposed. The 1938 Fair Labor Standards Act banned oppressive child labor, set a 25-cents-per-hour minimum wage and 44-hour workweek.[53] The National Association of Manufacturers promptly labeled those 1938 reforms as more than just socialism by saying—that the Fair Labor Standards Act "constitutes a step in the direction of communism, bolshevism, fascism, and Nazism."[54]

Social Security, which lifts more than 26 million Americans out of poverty,[55] is still attacked as "80 years of socialism"[56] by people like Laurence M. Vance, columnist and policy advisor of the Future of Freedom Foundation and associate of the Ludwig von Mises Institute.

The Capitalist War on National Healthcare

Hollywood actor Ronald Reagan, who later became president, got his start in politics by being the spokesperson in the campaign against Medicare and Medicaid:

> Write those letters now. Call your friends and tell them to write. If you don't, this program [Medicare & Medicaid], I promise you, will pass just as surely as the sun will come up tomorrow.... Until, one day ... we will awake to find that we have socialism.[57]

This was included in Ronald Reagan's record album which scornfully attacked the proposed Medicare and Medicaid programs before they were enacted by Congress. The album's name: *Ronald Reagan speaks out against SOCIALIZED MEDICINE* [58] (emphasis from the original).

Ronald Reagan's 1961 record album, done on behalf of the American Medical Association (AMA), was an integral part of the AMA's Operation Coffee Cup: a vicious attack on the programs that eventually became known as Medicare and Medicaid by contemptuously labeling it "SOCIALIZED MEDICINE." Two years later, President John F. Kennedy supported the proposed Medicare and Medicaid legislation but was assassinated in 1963 before he could get it into Congress. After Kennedy was assassinated, Congress went on to pass Medicare and Medicaid. President Lyndon Johnson signed them into law in 1965.[59]

Medicare had its roots in the Wagner-Murray-Dingle Bill, introduced in Congress in 1945, which would have provided much more inclusive coverage than Medicare does today, with universal medical, dental, and nursing home care to be paid for through a dedicated income tax. President Franklin Delano Roosevelt was ill and supportive of the bill but died on April 12, 1945, before it was brought up in Congress. Roosevelt's successor, President Harry Truman, also supported Wagner-Murray-Dingle after winning re-election in 1948.

In 1949, the AMA hired public relations firm Whitaker & Baxter to run a $4.5 million ($59 million in 2024 dollars) public relations campaign featuring an entirely made-up quote from the brutal, revolutionary founding head of Soviet Russia and the Soviet Union, Vladimir Lenin: "Socialized medicine is the keystone to the arch of a socialized state." Since the Soviet Union had just exploded their first nuclear bomb on August 29, 1949,[60] the fake quote attributed to Lenin successfully scared enough people to torpedo national healthcare, the Wagner-Murray-Dingle Bill. It took another 16 years before President Lyndon Johnson was finally able to get the less comprehensive and less progressive Medicare and Medicaid legislation through Congress.[61]

Medpage Today's managing editor John Gever's article, "The AMA's Bogus Lenin Scare Tactic Quote," detailed how the Lenin quote first appeared in Lawrence Sullivan's 54-page book published in 1949, *The Case Against Socialized Medicine*. Mr. Sullivan gave no attribution for the quote in his book. The Lenin quote was then used in a *New Yorker* magazine article, again without attribution and without even mentioning Mr. Sullivan's short book. Mr. Gever's searches through the Library of Congress found nothing even similar to this quote documented to Lenin.[62] No reputable attribution to Lenin has ever been given, yet this falsehood was successful in keeping our country from getting an all-inclusive national health care program, so that even today, 75 years later, we have no comprehensive national health care program. And thirty-two years after this lie initially surfaced, Ronald Reagan's original embrace of it led to his becoming the 40th President of the United States in 1981.

Antonio Gramsci's Theory of Cultural Hegemony

These reactionary, knee-jerk reactions against child labor laws, minimum wage laws, overtime pay, 40-hour workweek, Social Security, Medicare, and Medicaid exemplify the realization in America of Antonio Gramsci's theory of cultural hegemony, presented earlier in *Money Creation 101,* Chapter 8: "Financial Shenanigans & the Cultural Hegemony of Debt-Money." The state and the ruling capitalist class use cultural institutions to maintain power. The dominant class maintains its dominance primarily through the unquestioned acceptance over time of its culture, ideology, and institutions by the subordinated classes.[63]

Today this is evident within the U.S. by its citizens' blind acceptance of the Western capitalist system, regardless of the outcomes it generates. Just as evident is the derision the word *socialist* receives as a U.S. president delivers a State of the Union speech before the nation.[64]Also, every bit as evident in a U.S. system of money that almost none of us understand or even bother to question. And when well-reasoned legislation put into our Congress, like the NEED Act is proposed to replace our pathetic bank-created debt-money system, it is completely ignored. No discussion—end of subject by the media, press, politicians, university professors, and Federal Reserve economists alike. These are perfect examples of Antonio Gramsci's theory of cultural hegemony in action.

Gramsci tells us what to expect: "Not only does the people have no precise consciousness of its own historical identity, it is not even conscious of the historical identity or the exact limits of its adversary."[65] While Gramsci was talking about capitalism and fascism here, what he said almost a century ago pertains equally to our almost complete lack of knowledge of our own monetary history and the pernicious bank-created debt-money system that we are currently saddled with.

We should all be thankful for all those who fought so hard for child labor laws, minimum wage laws, overtime pay, a 40-hour workweek, Social Security, Medicare, and Medicaid. None of these were a slam dunk at the time, not even close to that. They were long and drawn-out struggles. Yet I would venture to say that most Americans would now agree that they are all worthy programs offering vital protections for all American people and that they did not make America a socialized country.

"Tonight, we renew our resolve that America will never be a socialist country."[66] Former President Donald Trump stated this in his 2019 State of the Union speech, which was received with a standing ovation. I believe even a few Democrats stood and applauded. If we were to turn the calendar back, it's easy to imagine Trump and the cheering Congress opposing as socialism: child labor laws, the 40-hour workweek, minimum wage laws, overtime pay, Social Security, Medicare, and Medicaid.

As mentioned earlier, America has used military force, military coups, propaganda, repressive economic sanctions, and blockades on socialist and socialist-leaning countries.[67] Space limitations preclude documenting the huge record of the U.S. violations of the sovereignty of socialist-leaning countries.[68]

The Polar Bear Expedition

Consider the U.S. response to the 1917 Russian Revolution. As World War I was wrapping up in 1918, President Woodrow Wilson sent troops into Russia to undo the 1917 Russian Revolution.[69] Known as the Polar Bear Expedition, it was a joint British/French/American attack on the newly installed Bolshevik government in Russia. The U.S. sent an expeditionary force of 5,000 troops to join with British and French forces to intervene in the Russian Civil War on the side of the Czar. While other reasons were given for the intervention, such as saving some supplies and rescuing a stranded Czechoslovak Legion, the U.S. force stayed on to fight the Red Army from September 1918 to July 1919, eight months after the Armistice had ended WWI on November 11, 1918.[70]

The U.S. soldiers were primarily from Michigan and Wisconsin and trained at Fort Custer in Battle Creek, Michigan:

> When American troops reached their destination in early September, they joined an international force commanded by the British that had been sent to northern Russia for purposes never made clear. Whatever the reasons for the intervention, however, the force was fighting the Bolsheviks who had taken power in Petrograd and Moscow the previous winter.... A winter of fighting Bolsheviks and wondering why they were still in combat when the war with Germany had ended, led to severe morale problems among the American troops, including an alleged mutiny in March 1919 by members of one company in Archangel, and the presentation of an antiwar petition by members of another company in the same month.[71] Bentley Historical Library, University of Michigan

After the next great clash of empires, World War II, it was only the threat of nuclear retaliation that kept the West from attacking the Union of Soviet Socialist Republics (USSR) led by Russia, who had been our ally in WWII. This allowed the flawed autocratic socialist USSR government to peacefully coexist with the capitalist democracies during the Cold War. No one is here to defend the brutal murderous excesses of Vladimir Lenin and Joseph Stalin. But the U.S. sought to overthrow the Russian Revolution not because it was undemocratic, autocratic, and totalitarian—which it certainly became—but because it was socialist.

And when the USSR did collapse, America's policy that required Russia's embrace of free market capitalism, caused the Russian people's poverty rate to go from a minuscule 1.3% to a staggering 49% in just a few years.[72]

Saudi Arabia

Another example of a country with a similarly dismal record on human rights is Saudi Arabia. When he was President, Donald Trump visited, donned their dress, and danced with their leaders.[73] After Trump lost the 2020 election to Joe Biden, his son in law Jared Kushner was rewarded with a $2 billion investment in his startup private equity investment company (hedge fund) Affinity Partners from Saudi funds controlled by none other than the Saudi Crown Prince Mohammed bin Salman himself.[74] This despite Mr. Kushner's complete lack of experience in running a hedge fund.

Whether or not Saudi Arabia is democratic is of little concern to US policy makers. The important thing is that Saudi Arabia is not a socialist country, and if it was a socialist country there would have been a CIA-sponsored coup there decades ago. Even after the Saudi Crown Prince sent government assassins to its embassy in Turkey to kill Saudi-born journalist Jamal Khashoggi, who lived in the U.S and was a critic of the Saudi regime, our government only slapped a few sanctions on the Crown Prince's associates, but otherwise refused to criticize him personally.[75]

Iran

In 1951, Dr. Mohammad Mossadegh was democratically elected as prime minister of Iran by the Iranian parliament.[76] British oil company Anglo Iranian Oil Company, which became British Petroleum Company in 1954 and eventually BP in 2000, had the oil rights in Iran. Because of the Cold War between the U.S. and the Union of Soviet Socialist Republics (USSR, Soviet Union), there was pressure on the U.S. to treat the Third World countries better, so that they would not switch their support to the Soviet Union. As such the major U.S. oil companies operating in Venezuela in 1948 and in Saudia Arabia, Kuwait and Iraq in 1950, agreed to pay the host countries a 50% tax on their income from exported crude oil.[77] Britain, who was more dependent on income from Iranian oil, refused to change their arrangement in Iran.[78]

In 1950, Prime Minister Mossadegh, with the support of the Iranian people and the entire parliament, nationalized the Iranian oil fields, to be effective in 1951. The United Kingdom would have none of the nationalization of their oil income stream and conspired with U.S. intelligence to overthrow Mossadegh. A coup attempt was unsuccessful on August 15, 1953. Dozens of arrests were made and the Shah, who was to have replaced Mossadegh fled the country.

U.S. Central Intelligence Agency (CIA) headquarters sent the following cable (declassified in 2017) to the station chief in Iran:

> Operation has been tried and failed and we should not participate in any operation against Mossadegh which could be traced back to US... Operations against Mossadegh should be discontinued.[79]

Kermit Roosevelt, grandson of President Teddy Roosevelt, was the top CIA officer in Iran. Whether he ignored the cable and continued on with the coup (Operation Ajax) on his own, or he read into it that it was okay with headquarters to go on with the operation as long as it could not be traced back to the U.S. is not now clear from the released CIA materials.

The next day, August 19, 1953, with "rented" crowds arranged by the CIA under Kermit Roosevelt, the coup succeeded. The nationalist hero, Prime Minister Mossadegh was jailed and the monarchy was restored under Shah Mohammad Reza Pahlavi. Mossadegh had hoped to establish a democracy in Iran, instead Iran was subjected to 26 years of brutal excesses under the Shah until he was finally replaced by the 1979 Islamic Revolution.

Expert Witnesses: Names Withheld

On Dec. 6, 1979, the nation's oldest continuously published daily college student newspaper, the Harvard Crimson published this account from Iranian students afraid to be identified, even though the Shah had been deposed by revolution and had managed to safely make it to the U.S. as a "private citizen," for treatment of his cancer:

> The Shah systematically dismantled the judicial system of Iran and the country's guarantees of personal and social liberties. His regime consistently violated the codes of law and justice, destroying the dignity of our people by treating them like backward savages to be pulled with an iron hand out of the middle ages into the light of the modern era. Nearly every source of creative, artistic and intellectual endeavor in our culture was suppressed.
>
> The media said little about the 80 percent of peasant families remaining landless, about the growing shanty towns holding the displaced peasants, the misery and alienation of these people ripped from their traditional way of life and subject to new economic and cultural pressures.
>
> SAVAK [Shah's secret police] conducted most of the torture, under the friendly guidance of the CIA. which set up SAVAK in 1957 and taught them how to interrogate suspects. Amnesty

> International reports methods of torture that included "whipping and beating, electric shocks, extraction of teeth and nails, boiling water pumped into the rectum, heavy weights hung on the testicles, tying the prisoner to a metal table heated to a white heat, inserting a broken bottle into the anus, and rape..."[80]

Because of the joint British/CIA coup against a socialist leader who seemed to be on track to making his country a better place to live for his people, Iran got the brutal Shah. And after the Shah, Iran got the 1979 Islamic Revolution against the despised leader who was put in place with the help of our government. After all this in Iran, it hardly matters who is right or what is right, our past actions now leave us confronted with an Iran that is in no mood to trust us.

On a broader scale, the Capitalist/Socialist Divide leaves us unable to solve the climate crisis and other crises confronting *Spaceship Earth*. Reining in capitalism with a little socialism like public schools, police and fire departments, public water, sewers, parks, highways, ports, canals, airports, and broadband computer access does not damage our social fabric. It will only make us stronger. Reining in capitalism with environmental legislation, which is literally needed to save life as we know it, will not hurt our country. It will only make us stronger. Reducing the number of billions our billionaires possess by a few; while making life more livable for the many will not turn us into a reincarnation of the Soviet State. It will only make us stronger. Switching to a publicly created money system enables us to pay for the things we desperately need, conversely the bank-created debt-money system never seems to have the money to properly fund that which we desperately need. Publicly created money only makes us stronger.

---

1. Peralta, Eyder, "Socialism, Capitalism: Merriam-Webster's Odd-Couple Words of the Year," NPR, WBEZ Chicago, Dec 5, 2012, https://www.npr.org/sections/thetwo-way/2012/12/05/166579843/socialism-capitalism-merriam-websters-odd-couple-words-of-the-year
2. McMillan, Jonathan, *Capitalism and the Market Economy,* Zero/One Economics GambH, Zurich, 2024, p. 4.
3. *Ibid.,* pg. 4-5.

4. Casey, Lauren, "Monopoly: Financial Prosperity in the Depression," Pennsylvania Center for the Book, https://pabook.libraries.psu.edu/literary-cultural-heritage-map-pa/feature-articles/monopoly-financial-prosperity-depression#:~:text=According%20to%20Tim%20Walsh%2C%20board,the%20rest%20of%20his%20life.
5. Library of Congress, "The Game of Monopoly is Patented," Research Guides, This Month in Business History, https://guides.loc.gov/this-month-in-business-history/december/game-of-monopoly-patent
6. Pilon, Mary, "Monopoly's Lost Female Inventor," National Women's History Museum, Sept 1, 2018, https://www.womenshistory.org/articles/monopolys-lost-female-inventor
7. *Ibid.*
8. *Ibid.*
9. *Ibid.*
10. Bellis, Mary, "Charles Darrow and the Monopoly of Monopoly," May 30, 2019, https://www.thoughtco.com/monopoly-monopoly-charles-darrow-4079786#:~:text=Darrow%20accepted%20and%20permitted%20Parker,to%20earn%20that%20-much%20money
11. Pilon, Mary, "The secret history of Monopoly: the capitalist board game's leftwing origins," The Guardian, April 11, 2015, https://www.theguardian.com/lifeandstyle/2015/apr/11/secret-history-monopoly-capitalist-game-leftwing-origins
12. McMahon, Brian, "How board games helped Free POWs," Mental Floss, Dec 7, 2007, http://www.cnn.com/2007/LIVING/wayoflife/12/05/mf.waropoly/index.html
13. Burns, Nick, "In Defense of Sparta," The New Republic, Aug 7, 2019, https://newrepublic.com/article/154685/defense-sparta
14. Montero, Roman, "The Sources of Early Christian Communism," Church Life Journal, University of Notre Dame, July 20, 2019, https://churchlifejournal.nd.edu/articles/the-sources-of-early-christian-communism/
15. Schwaller, Tyler M., "The Use of Slaves in Early Christianity: Slaves as Subjects of Life and Thought," Harvard Library Office of Scholarly Communication, Abstract, https://dash.harvard.edu/handle/1/37925650
16. Encyclopedia of Business, "Socialism and Communism," Background, https://www.referenceforbusiness.com/encyclopedia/Sel-Str/Socialism-and-Communism.html
17. Marc'hadour, Germain P., "Thomas More," Encyclopedia Britannica, https://www.britannica.com/biography/Thomas-More-English-humanist-and-statesman/Years-as-chancellor-of-England
18. Ball, Terence & Dagger, Richard, "Socialism," Encyclopedia Britannica, March 1, 2021, https://www.britannica.com/topic/socialism
19. Encyclopedia Britannica, "Digger -- English Agrarian Movement," https://www.britannica.com/event/Digger
20. Encyclopedia Britannica, "Henri de Saint-Simon," Oct 13, 2021, https://www.britannica.com/biography/Henri-de-Saint-Simon
21. Encyclopedia Britannica, "New Harmony," https://www.britannica.com/place/New-Harmony
22. Ball, Terence & Dagger, Richard, "Socialism," Encyclopedia Britannica, March 1, 2021,
23. Stanford Encyclopedia of Philosophy, "Hegel's Dialectics," Revised Oct 2, 2020, https://plato.stanford.edu/entries/hegel-dialectics/#HegeDescHisDialMeth

24. Liulevicius, Vejas Gabriel, "The Communist Manifesto and the Revolutions of 1848," The Great Courses Daily, June 21, 2020, https://www.thegreatcoursesdaily.com/the-communist-manifesto-didnt-spark-the-revolutions-of-1848/
25. Encyclopedia Britannica, "The Revolutions of 1848," https://www.britannica.com/topic/history-of-Europe/Cultural-nationalism
26. *Ibid.*
27. Cam, Tanner & Kayaoglu, Mustafa, "Marx's distinction between socialism and communism," International Journal of Human Sciences, 2015, Abstract, https://j-humansciences.com/ojs/index.php/ijhs/article/view/3152
28. Pruitt, Sarah, "How Are Socialism and Communism Different," History.com, Nov 4, 2020, https://www.history.com/news/socialism-communism-differences
29. *The Oxford Handbook of Karl Marx*, "Marx's Concept of Socialism," Peter Hudis, online publication Sept. 2018, abstract, https://www.oxfordhandbooks.com/view/10.1093/oxfordhb/9780190695545.001.0001/oxfordhb-9780190695545-e-50
30. *The Oxford Handbook of Karl Marx*, "Marx's Concept of Socialism," Peter Hudis, online publication Sept. 2018, abstract
31. Danforth, John; Ginsberg, Ben; Griffith, Thomas B; Hoppe, David; Luttig, J. Michael; McConnell, Michael W; Olson, Theodore B; Smith, Gordon H, "LOST, NOT STOLEN: The Conservative Case that Trump lost and Biden won the 2020 Presidential Election," July 2022, https://drive.google.com/file/d/1aqorZ61AYFqZU-EDQBBzjqfvAoC5nKcB/
32. Egnatz, Nick, Money Creation 101, Amazon, 2023, p. 220.
33. National Security Archive, "1953 Iran Coup: New U.S. Documents Confirm British Approached U.S. in Late 1952 About Ousting Mosaddeq," George Washington University, Aug 8, 2017, https://nsarchive.gwu.edu/briefing-book/iran/2017-08-08/1953-iran-coup-new-us-documents-confirm-british-approached-us-late
34. Kornbluh, Peter, "Chile and the United States: Declassified Documents Relating to the Military Coup, September 11, 1973," National Security Archive Electronic Briefing Book No. 8, George Washington University, Sept 11, 1998, https://nsarchive2.gwu.edu/NSAEBB/NSAEBB8/nsaebb8i.htm
35. Wilson, Scott, "Venezuelan Military Says Chavez Is Ousted," Washington Post, April 12, 2002, https://www.washingtonpost.com/archive/politics/2002/04/12/venezuelan-military-says-chavez-is-ousted/c01b2fc5-e427-4ecb-a2d4-db827abcf10a/
36. Coles, T.J., "The CIA's View of Venezuela: What We Learn from Archives," tela-SUR, Feb 29, 2019, https://www.telesurenglish.net/opinion/The-CIAs-View-of-Venezuela-What-We-Learn-from-Archives-20190227-0019.html
37. Congressional Research Service, "Venezuela: Overview of U.S. Sanctions," Nov 30, 2022, https://crsreports.congress.gov/product/pdf/IF/IF10715#:~:text=Terrorism%2DRelated%20Sanctions&text=The%20most%20recent%20determination%20was,retransfers%20to%20Venezuela%20since%202006.
38. U.S. Department of State, "U.S. Recognition of Venezuela's 2015 National Assembly and Interim President Guaidó," Ned Price, Press Statement, Department Spokesperson, Jan 4, 2022, https://www.state.gov/u-s-recognition-of-venezuelas-2015-national-assembly-and-interim-president-guaido/
39. Lawler, Dave, "U.S. no longer recognizes Guaidó as Venezuela's president, Biden official confirms," Axios, Jan 4, 2023, https://www.axios.com/2023/01/04/us-stops-recognizing-juan-guaido-venezuela

40. Seelke, Clare Ribando, "Venezuela: Overview of U.S. Sanctions," Congressional Research Service, Nov 1, 2023, chrome-extension://efaidnbmnnnibpcajpcglclefindmkaj/https://crsreports.congress.gov/product/pdf/IF/IF10715
41. Main, Alexander, "Honduras: The Deep Roots of Resistance," Dissent Magazine, Spring 2014, https://www.dissentmagazine.org/article/honduras-the-deep-roots-of-resistance/
42. Johnston, Jake, "How Pentagon Official May Have Encouraged a 2009 Coup in Honduras," The Intercept, Aug 29, 2017, https://theintercept.com/2017/08/29/honduras-coup-us-defense-departmetnt-center-hemispheric-defense-studies-chds/
43. Physicians for Human Rights, "Honduras: Constitutional Crisis and Coup D'Etat (2009)," https://phr.org/honduras-constitutional-crisis-and-coup/
44. Pruitt, Sarah, "How Are Socialism and Communism Different," History.com, Nov 4, 2020
45. American Historical Association, "Can Russians Own Personal Property?" https://www.historians.org/about-aha-and-membership/aha-history-and-archives/gi-round table-series/pamphlets/em-46-our-russian-ally-(1945)/can-russians-own-personal property
46. PoliticalDictionary.com, "safety net," https://politicaldictionary.com/words/safety-net/
47. USA Gov, "Food Assistance," https://www.usa.gov/food-help
48. Reich, Robert, "The state of Joe Biden's union: The return to democratic capitalism," Feb 6, 2023, Substack.com, https://robertreich.substack.com/p/the-state-of-joe-bidens-union-the?utm_source=post-email-title&publication_id=365422& post_id=100925959&isFreemail=false&utm_medium=email
49. *Ibid.*
50. *Ibid.*
51. American Experience, "The Industrial Workers of the World," Emma Goldman Article, PBS, https://www.pbs.org/wgbh/americanexperience/features/goldman-industrial-workers-world/
52. Parfitt, Steven, "The Justice Department Campaign Against the IWW, 1917-1920," University of Washington -- Civil Rights and Labor History Consortium, 2016, https://depts.washington.edu/iww/justice_dept.shtml
53. Grossman, Jonathan, "Fair Labor Standards Act of 1938: Maximum Struggle for a Minimum Wage," U.S. Department of Labor, https://www.dol.gov/general/about dol/history/flsa1938
54. Cole, Peter, "The Law that Changed the American Workplace," Time, June 24, 2016, https://time.com/4376857/flsa-history/
55. Romig, Kathleen, "Social Security Lifts More People Above the Poverty Line Than Any Other Program," Center on Budget and Policy Priorities, Jan 31, 2004, chrome-extension://efaidnbmnnnibpcajpcglclefindmkaj/https://www.cbpp.org/sites/default/files/atoms/files/10-25-13ss.pdf
56. Vance, Lawrence M., "Eighty Years of Socialism," The Future of Freedom Foundation, August 12, 2015, https://www.fff.org/explore-freedom/article/eighty-years-socialism/
57. Green, Mathew, "Back in the Day, Medicare Had Its Haters Too," KQED Public Radio, https://www.kqed.org/lowdown/19169/50-years-ago-medicare-had-its-haters-too-and-we-never-did-awake-to-socialism
58. *Ibid.*

59. Skidmore, Max J., "Ronald Reagan and 'Operation Coffee Cup': A Hidden Episode in American Political History," Journal of American Culture, Wiley Online Library, Fall 1989, https://onlinelibrary.wiley.com/doi/abs/10.1111/j.1542-734X.1989.1203_89.x
60. Atomic Heritage Foundation, "Soviet Atomic Program -- 1946," Atomic Heritage Foundation & National Museum of Nuclear Science & History, June 5, 2014, https://www.atomicheritage.org/history/soviet-atomic-program-1946
61. Gever, John, "The AMA's Bogus Lenin Scare Tactic Quote", Medpage Today, June 13, 2019, https://www.medpagetoday.com/publichealthpolicy/healthpolicy/80448
62. *Ibid.*
63. Robinson, William I., *Promoting Polyarchy -- Globalization, US Intervention, and Hegemony,* Cambridge University Press, 1996, p. 21-24.
64. CNN, "2019 State of the Union: Read the full transcript," Feb. 6, 2019, https://www.cnn.com/2019/02/05/politics/donald-trump-state-of-the-union-2019-transcript
65. Crehan, Kate, *Gramsci, Culture and Anthropology,* University of California, 2002, p.100.
66. CNN, "2019 State of the Union: Read the full transcript."
67. Egnatz, Nick, "Capitalism's War on Socialism," OpEdNews.com, https://www.opednews.com/articles/Capitalism-s-War-on-Social-by-Nick-Egnatz-Capitalism_Capitalism-Failures_Capitalism-Over-Humanity_Capitalism-A-Love-Story-190402-993.html
68. Blum, William, *Killing Hope -- U.S. Military and CIA Interventions Since World War II,* Common Courage Press, Monroe, ME, 2004.
69. Rubin, Neal, "'Polar Bear' memorial in Troy marks a largely forgotten GI mission in WWI Russia," Detroit News, May 22, 2019, https://www.detroitnews.com/story/news/local/michigan/2019/05/27/polar-bear-memorial-world-war-i-russia-troy/3745930002/
70. Rubin, Neal, "'Polar Bear' memorial in Troy marks a largely forgotten GI mission in WWI Russia."
71. Polar Bear Expedition History, Bentley Historical Library, University of Michigan, https://bentley.umich.edu/research/catalogs-databases/polar-bear/polar-bear-expedition-history/
72. Klein, Naomi, *The Shock Doctrine -- The Rise of Disaster Capitalism,* Henry Holt & Co, New York, 2007, pp. 275-331
73. The Guardian, "Trump joins ceremonial sword dance in Saudi Arabia – video," Source: AP/Reuters, May 27, 2017, https://www.theguardian.com/us-news/video/2017/may/21/trump-joins-ceremonial-sword-dance-in-saudi-arabia-video
74. Getahun, Hannah, "Jared Kushner's private equity firm concealed the origins of Saudi-backed funds and used the SEC's own rules to help them do it, report says," Business Insider, Feb 12, 2023, https://www.businessinsider.com/kushners-2-billion-investment-saudi-backed-fund-concealed-sec-rules-2023-2
75. Kirchgaessner, Stephanie, "US finds Saudi crown prince approved Khashoggi murder but does not sanction him," The Guardian, Feb 26, 2021, https://www.theguardian.com/world/2021/feb/26/jamal-khashoggi-mohammed-bin-salman-us-report
76. Mossadegh Initiative, "Who Was Mohammad Mossadegh?" Northeastern Illinois University, https://www.neiu.edu/academics/college-of-business-and-technology/mossadegh-initiative/who-was-mohammad-mossadegh

77. Fakhimi, Ghobad, *Thirty Years Iran Oil: From Nationalization to Islamic Revolution*, Amazon, 2016, pp. 29-32.
78. Freidman, Jeremy & Liu, Jingyu, "Mossadeq's Gambit: The US, UK, and Iranian Oil Nationalization," Faculty & Research, Harvard Business School, June 2022, https://www.hbs.edu/faculty/Pages/item.aspx?num=62650
79. Allen, Bethany, ""64 Years Later, CIA Finally Releases Details of Iranian Coup," Foreign Policy, June 20, 2017, https://foreignpolicy.com/2017/06/20/64-years-later-cia-finally-releases-details-of-iranian-coup-iran-tehran-oil/
80. Names Withheld, "Life Under The Shah," The Harvard Crimson, Dec 6, 1979, https://www.thecrimson.com/article/1979/12/6/life-under-the-shah-pit-was/

EIGHT

Russia's Democracy Sacrificed on the Altar of the Free Market

Author's note: As *Spaceship Earth* journeys through the heavens, Russia's February 24, 2022, invasion of Ukraine has led me to give a more fulsome explanation here of how the Soviet Union ended. Originally this was to be covered in just a few paragraphs. If Russia had just instituted a publicly created money system in lieu of embracing the free-market capitalist system that we required of them in 1991, it is extremely unlikely that a democratic Russia would have invaded their peaceful neighbor Ukraine in 2022.

Vladimir Putin Invades Ukraine, February 24, 2022

Russian President Vladimir Putin has invaded Ukraine and made war on their civilian population. The Ukrainian people, many of them Russian speaking and with Russian heritage, have shown unbelievable courage and love of country in resisting Putin's war of aggression and acquisition. Fear of nuclear Armageddon has kept the U.S. and NATO (North Atlantic Treaty Organization) from using troops to support Ukraine, although arms have been provided. We have witnessed the destruction of Ukrainian cities and the people who live in them on our TV screens. The irony that Russian Lieutenant Colonel Stanislav

Petrov saved humanity from a nuclear disaster thirty-nine years ago and today Russian President Vladimir Putin's butchery may very well bring us to the brink again is frightening indeed.

Full Disclosure

In 2013 and 2014 I was personally much more open to Russia's claims in Crimea and the Donbas regions of Ukraine than I am today. I recognized that many of the residents of these areas spoke Russian and had been discriminated against by some Ukrainians. What I did not understand at this time was the tremendous propaganda narrative that Russia had instigated to push this view of Ukraine, along with assorted conspiracy theories, upon the unsuspecting members of the American public who were like me, open minded to a legitimate criticism of our own government when warranted. The proof of this is evidenced in the determination, courage, and will of the Ukrainian people, both Ukrainian speaking and Russian speaking, in their fight to preserve their democracy. This in turn has convinced me that they want nothing to do with Mr. Putin. Their actions in fighting Putin's war crimes and brutal assault against a peaceful, civilian populations have truly inspired the world.

In the U.S., I will continue to critique our government's policies when they are wrong, as they often have been. I will also continue to criticize our Constitution and laws when I think it is warranted. But I believe such critiques and corresponding reforms must be made from within our own legal system. I now recognize that Russia under dictator Vladimir Putin has successfully used social media to extensively undermine the American people's view of our own government with the explicit goal of destroying our own democracy.[1] [2] As such, a few misguided people in the anti-war movement have fallen prey to siding with Putin and his lackey, president Donald Trump, over America and our admittedly imperfect democracy.

When the Soviet Union ended, I was blissfully ignorant of what was going on behind the scenes, as were I assume most of my fellow Americans. It was only twenty or so years later, after reading Naomi

Klein's book *The Shock Doctrine*,[3] while immersed in anti-war activism against our own U.S. wars in Iraq and Afghanistan, that I began to understand what had transpired decades earlier. Russia had a budding democracy in the late 1980s. If the U.S.-led Western capitalist system had allowed Russia to continue to nurture their growing democracy, Russia would not today be under the control of dictator Vladimir Putin. Russia would have no reason to invade its peaceful neighbor Ukraine, and the entire world would be a better place, peacefully coexisting with democracies in both Russia and Ukraine.

Mikhail Gorbachev's Vision of Joint Mountain Climbing

In the late 1980s, Soviet Union Premier Mikhail Gorbachev attempted to bring the USSR in from the Cold War and into the Western capitalist community of nations. Gorbachev's plan was to do so as a Scandinavian-style democracy, guaranteeing the Soviet people a strong social safety net within a regulated market economy. It was really quite remarkable, as my generation had looked at the Russians/Soviets/communists as the ultimate enemy of freedom and democracy. Yet in the late 1980s with his twin policies of glasnost and perestroika (openness and restructuring), Gorby, (as he affectionately began to be referred to in the U.S. press) had proposed an end to all this nonsense of brinkmanship and possible nuclear annihilation. He was *Time* magazine's 1987 Man of the Year and won the 1990 Nobel Peace Prize as he brought about democratic reforms in the Soviet Union and attempted to transition slowly from a centrally planned, state-run economy to a mixture of capitalism and socialism.

Why was a hardline communist like Mikhail Gorbachev motivated to junk communism for capitalism? In a 1992 *Time* magazine account, "The Holy Alliance," American investigative journalist Carl Bernstein outlined the five-part U.S. plan under President Ronald Reagan that began in early 1982:

1. The increased U.S. defense buildup resulting in an arms race that the Soviets could not afford.

2. U.S. covert operations targeted to encourage reform movements in Warsaw Pact counties Hungary, Czechoslovakia and Poland. (The Warsaw Pact was a joint defense treaty signed by the Soviet Union and her satellite states in Central and Eastern Europe in 1955—Albania, Bulgaria, Czechoslovakia, East Germany, Hungary, Poland, and Romania. Albania had withdrawn in 1968.[4])
3. Giving financial aid to Warsaw Pact countries based on their willingness to undertake political and free market economic reforms.
4. Economically isolate the USSR and deny her U.S. and Japanese technology.
5. Increased use of Radio Liberty, Voice of America, and Radio Free Europe to transmit U.S. messages [propaganda] to the peoples of Eastern Europe.[5]

One can argue whether or not the U.S. had the moral high ground in its struggle with the Soviet Union. We will leave that for others to debate. The simple fact is that this Holy Alliance described by Mr. Bernstein, combined with the financial drain on the USSR from its Afghanistan War (1979-89) was successful in convincing Soviet Premier Gorbachev to transform the Soviet Union and end the Cold War.

Gorbachev understood that Soviet Union could not bring about the change by itself. The USSR needed the financial help of the Western nations, just as the capitalist Western states needed the cooperation of the USSR and her satellite states to begin to safely dismantle the Soviet nuclear arsenal. In a 1987 trip to Prague, Gorbachev described what he believed to be the level of cooperation necessary to succeed: "Like mountain climbers on one rope, the world's nations can either climb together to the summit or fall together into the abyss."[6]

Chicago School/Neoliberalism/Washington Consensus v. Stockholm on the Volga

Unfortunately, the capitalist West, under the leadership of U.S. Presidents Ronald Reagan and George H.W. Bush, was in no mood for any sort of mutual mountain climbing. The USSR was monetarily exhausted (broke) after their arms race with the United States and 10-year war in Afghanistan. Since no one in the Soviet Union had exhibited any knowledge of publicly created money, the Soviets were forced to borrow money from the Western bank-created debt-money system. They needed loans from the West to gradually convert from an economy organized by the Communist Central Committee to Gorby's vision of a Stockholm on the Volga, so to speak.

The U.S. and the West at the time were completely mesmerized by the policies of the Chicago School. [Do not confuse the Chicago School policies with the *Chicago Plan*, a system of publicly created money proposed during the Great Depression and then completely ignored by U.S. policy makers.] The Chicago School, made famous by economist Milton Friedman, laid the foundations for what is now known as 'neoliberalism' or the 'Washington Consensus.' The Chicago School stood for free trade, free markets, no governmental intervention, tax cuts for the rich, and the privatization of everything public. Ronald Reagan,[7] who departed the White House in January 1989, and his successors George H.W. Bush[8] in 1989 and Bill Clinton[9] in 1993 all generally subscribed to these policies, as did the majorities in both houses of Congress.

The term 'Washington Consensus' was originally used to indicate the level of agreement between the U.S. Department of Treasury, the International Monetary Fund, and the World Bank,[10] who jointly held the purse strings for loans to the Third World. The term was first used in 1989 by American economist John Williamson:

> The term "Washington Consensus" was coined in 1989. The first written usage was in my background paper for a conference that the Institute for International Economics convened in

> order to examine the extent to which the old ideas of development economics that had governed Latin American economic policy since the 1950s were being swept aside by the set of ideas that had long been accepted as appropriate within the OECD [Organization for Economic Cooperation and Development].[11]

Dr. Williamson does not specifically mention the Chicago School in this quote from his paper, "A Short History of the Washington Consensus." I do believe that Dr. Williamson does not want to be mistaken as the architect, so to speak, of the Chicago School policies, which have been for decades now also referred to as the Washington Consensus, for the simple reason that said policies were disastrous for the peoples that were subjected to them. Nor should Dr. Williamson be thought of as such. University of Chicago Economist Dr. Milton Friedman, inspired by Adam Smith's 1776 *The Wealth of Nations*, is widely considered the architect of the Chicago School's system of neoliberalism dubbed the Washington Consensus.[12] What the policies are now called is not nearly as important as the devastation they caused to peoples all across the globe. Here we limit our discussion to their influence on how the West responded to breakup of the Soviet Union and one of her former satellites, Poland.

Gorbachev's vision of harmony among nations working toward a common goal of peace and prosperity was rudely interrupted by the response from those that held the Western purse strings. If the Soviets wanted loans they would have to accede to the demands of the Western financial establishment, who were only too happy to cut the Soviet's mountain-climbing rope and watch them drop into the abyss if they did not. The G7 (group of the top 7 Western economic powers) turned down Gorbachev's loan request in July 1991. In keeping with Friedman's ideology, the West wouldn't offer any loans unless they were accompanied by an abrupt transition to the free trade, free markets, no government intervention, and privatization that they demanded.[13]

The Soviets under Gorbachev's leadership in the late 1980s and into 1991 had already, on its own initiative, achieved quite a level of democracy. Russia had a budding free press, elected Parliament, elected local councils, an elected president and vice president, and a constitutional court.[14] But to ask the Soviets to make an immediate shift to unrestrained free market capitalism from their state-run economic system was like asking the driver of speeding car to shift it into reverse without slowing down and stopping first. In addition to ruining your car's transmission, you just might cause a horrific accident, killing everyone in the crash.

What if the speeding car containing the Russian people did not want to reverse into unrestrained free market capitalism, but rather wanted to gradually brake and downshift into a mixture of a capitalist market with a strong socialist safety net like President Gorbachev wanted? What if the five-point plan that Carl Bernstein described above was used by the U.S. with the intention, not to assist the Russian people in achieving the type of economy and democracy they were aspiring to, but to instead make them subservient to the West?

U.S. Version of Democracy-Promotion—Also Known as Polyarchy

U.S. foreign policy in 1980, after decades of promoting all manner of dictators across the globe in the name of the Cold War, turned away from outright support of dictators and began a policy called democracy-promotion. American sociologist William I. Robinson uses the term "polyarchy" to describe the type of democracy that was the goal of the U.S. foreign policy of democracy-promotion. Our foreign policy was not to promote the Lincoln ideal many of us aspire our government to be, "of the people, by the people and for the people." The democracies being promoted included a system of unrestrained free market capitalism coupled with a democracy-lite system of elections controlled by wealthy elites.[15]

The U.S. did not create the movements for democratization that were already beginning all across the globe in 1980. The U.S. policy was to use an alphabet soup of NGOs (non-government organizations) such as USAID or AID (Agency for International Development) and

NED (National Endowment for Democracy) to infiltrate any sort of organic or people-based democracy and turn it into a support network for unrestrained free market capitalism. It was also U.S. policy to get the people to support elections, while ensuring that these elections ultimately ceded power to the international financial class. The NED spent an impressive $50.5 million ($131 million in 2023 dollars) from 1984–92 within the Soviet bloc to promote a system of polyarchy.[16]

The Union of Soviet Socialist Republics (USSR) was composed of 15 republics—Russia, Ukraine, Georgia, Belorussia, Uzbekistan, Armenia, Azerbaijan, Kazakhstan, Kyrgyzstan, Moldova, Turkmenistan, Tajikistan, Latvia, Lithuania, and Estonia. In 1985 Gorbachev became the General Secretary of the Communist Party and the unquestioned leader of the USSR. On March 15, 1990, the Congress of the People's Deputies of the Communist Party of the Soviet Union elected Gorbachev as the first president of the Soviet Union. Giving Gorbachev the title of president seems to have been part of the overall democratization process. He was the USSR's first and only president. Future elections were to have been by popular vote, instead of by the Communist Party officials. Boris Yeltsin was soon to be elected the president of Russia. Since Russia was only one state within the USSR, albeit the major one, Gorbachev outranked Yeltsin. But all of this was soon to change.

Communist Old Guard Attempts Coup Against Gorbachev's Reforms

Boris Yeltsin was elected president of Russia on June 12, 1991. Two months later, on August 19, 1991, a group of the Communist old guard drove tanks up to the Russian Parliament building in a coup attempt against Gorbachev, Yeltsin, and democracy. A large group of Russian citizens surrounded the tanks, ready to die for their fledgling democracy. Yeltsin climbed on one of the tanks and denounced the "cynical, right-wing coup attempt."[17] But instead of further supporting the brave people standing for democracy and defying the tanks outside the building, Yeltsin then went into the Parliament building and descended into a safe bunker underneath the building, joining two other unnamed officials for a night of feasting and drinking cognac, vodka, and whiskey. At daybreak, when it became clear that the Communist tanks had retreated, Russian President Yeltsin and his two friends, had to be helped out of their bunker hideaway under Parliament. They had imbibed so much they could not walk on their own. According to Pavel Voschanov, Press Secretary to Boris Yeltsin:

> Had there been an attack, those people outside the White House [parliament building] would have died, because they were there defending democracy, defending a new Russia. But those who were downstairs in the bunker drinking vodka, did not bother about the new Russia. They were thinking of themselves.[18]

The Baltic Way

In the mid-1980s the Baltic States of Latvia, Estonia, and Lithuania were struggling for independence from the Soviet Union. All three countries had made their native tongues their official state language and declared their intent to secede from the Soviet Union by 1989. On August 23, 1989, they showed the world their intentions. Their independence movement, called The Baltic Way, was a demonstration for independence in which two million people [22% of the entire population of the 3 nations] joined hands to form a united human chain spanning more than 600 kilometers linking together the 3 Baltic capitals—Vilnius, Riga, and Tallinn.[19]

In 1990, Lithuania and Latvia declared independence. On January 13, 1991, the Soviets promptly sent elite KGB troops into Vilnius, Lithuania, to take control of the TV and radio stations that were broadcasting news of Lithuanian independence. The Lithuanian people rushed to the aid of their media, putting their bodies between the Russian tanks and the TV tower. In what became known as the Vilnius Massacre the tanks rammed into the unarmed demonstrators while Russian troops fired into the crowd. Fourteen people supporting Lithuanian democracy died and hundreds were wounded, as the TV and radio stations went silent. The next day the Russian troops went to the Lithuanian Parliament where thousands of democracy supporters had again taken a stand. Gorbachev, alarmed at the bloodshed of the previous day, had the troops stand down.[20] It is unclear whether or not Gorbachev had advance knowledge of the Vilnius Massacre. However, the troops involved were under the command of Boris Pugo, who would become one of the plotters behind the coup attempt against Gorbachev seven months later.

After the Vilnius Massacre, an estimated one-third of tiny Latvia's two million people demonstrated their own independence from the Soviet Union by building barricades around the key public buildings in their capital of Riga. The feared Soviet OMON black beret forces proceeded to kill five people manning the barricades, as the Soviet Communist Party declared that "fascism was reborn in Latvia," echoing the claims Russian dictator Vladimir Putin would make decades later as a pretext for his invasion of Ukraine. Latvians honor the memory of those who died to purchase their freedom every January during the anniversary of The Barricades.[21]

Estonia followed suit by declaring independence on August 21, 1991. Two weeks later, on September 6, 1991, the independence of all three Baltic States was finally recognized by Gorbachev and the Soviet Union. *The Baltic Way* had eventually proved successful for Latvia, Estonia, and Lithuania.

The End of the Soviet Union and the Rebirth of Russia and Ukraine

Yeltsin's public defiance of the aborted old guard revolt did for a time make him very popular with the Russian people. This in turn gave him the stature to pull off one of the most virtuoso political feats in history. Early in December 1991, President Yeltsin secretly met with newly elected President Leonid Kravchuk of Ukraine and Stanislav Shushkevich, the leader of Belorussia (or Belarus as it is now called), in Viskuly, Belarus. Together the leaders of the three countries declared their independence from the USSR by forming the

Commonwealth of Independent States (CIS), effectively ending of the Soviet Union.[22] It was one thing for the three tiny Baltic States to be independent of the USSR and quite another for Russia, Ukraine, and Belarus to secede from the USSR. Effectively, the USSR without Russia was nothing. As Shushkevich explained:

> It is the opening statement of our agreement, the only one which was adopted without any arguments. "The USSR, as a geopolitical reality, and as a subject of international law - has ceased to exist." And I was the first to say that I would sign up for this.[23]

Just weeks later on December 25, 1991, Mikhail Gorbachev resigned as president of the USSR and the Soviet hammer and sickle flag was lowered from the Kremlin, replaced by the tri-color flag of Russia on the same day. Gorbachev was out and the tremendous responsibility of leading the Russian state was now in the hands of President Boris Yeltsin.[24]

Thus, Russia, Ukraine and Belarus recognized each other as independent countries in December 1991. The Russian Federation also agreed to recognize Ukraine as an independent country and respect its borders when it jointly signed the Budapest Memorandum with the United States and United Kingdom in 1994. The Budapest Memorandum guaranteed Ukraine's status as an independent country within its 1994 borders, in return for Ukraine releasing what at the time was the world's third largest nuclear arsenal to Russia, so as to be dismantled in a nuclear arms agreement between the signatory parties.[25]

In the Budapest Memorandum the Russian Federation under President Boris Yeltsin had agreed to:

> "To respect the independence and sovereignty and *the existing borders* of Ukraine"[26] (emphasis added).

It is beyond irony that Russia and Ukraine jointly declared their independence from the Soviet Union in 1991 and affirmed it three years later. Fast forward three decades and Russian President Vladimir Putin has made war on Ukraine on the basis that it is not an independent country and belongs to Russia.[27]

Two Options—Really?

Moscow mayor Gavriil Popov described the two options for breaking up the Russian centrally controlled economy:

> Property can be divided among all members of society, or the best pieces can be given to the leaders.... In a word, there's the democratic approach, and there's the nomenklatura, apparatchik approach.[28]

Yeltsin was soon directed by the U.S. economic team which of Moscow Mayor Popov's two options was available to Russia. If it was to have any hope of obtaining the desperately needed financing, Russia was to immediately begin the privatization of all the state's assets (industry, mines, natural resources, etc.) before any economic assistance would be available. Russia's tremendous natural and industrial assets were then sold to selected apparatchiks of the Communist Party for less than pennies on the dollar. Many of these bargain-basement acquisitions were financed using the money eventually provided by U.S. loans to make the purchases.[29] These men became Russia's multi-billionaire oligarchs, with their yachts, corruption, and jet-setter lifestyles that we hear about today on the news.

Naomi Klein, author of *The Shock Doctrine*, documents the plight of the Russian people—they did not want their economy organized by a Communist central committee, but they did believe in some wealth redistribution and an activist government to accomplish it. A 1992 poll showed that 79% of Russians polled thought maintaining full employment was a core function of government and 67% favored privatization to be done through worker cooperatives, in lieu of connected individuals. But they were in a state of shock; the USSR, the only government most of them had ever known, no longer existed. They wanted to keep their new democracy, and they felt that they had to trust the democratic Western nations to help them in their transition to what would be a mixture of capitalism and socialism.[30]

Western Neoliberalism Creates Russian Poverty

At the insistence of the West, Parliament gave Yeltsin dictatorial powers for one year to enact the draconian economic programs which were soon to make beggars of the Russian people. On October 28, 1991, Yeltsin lifted the price controls on the basic commodities that the Russian people used in their daily life.[31] Two months later, after the end of the Soviet Union, Yeltsin instituted free trade policies and the first phase of the rapid-fire privatization of the country's 225,000 state-owned companies.[32] In 1989, with Gorbachev as president of the USSR, Russia had a scant 1.3% poverty rate (existence on less than $4/day). In the first year alone of the drastic reforms from 1991 to 1992, one-third of the Russian people had fallen into poverty. Under Yeltsin's leadership, the capitalist financial reforms demanded by the U.S. caused the Russian poverty rate to soar to 49% by 1996.[33]

The Russian people and Parliament eventually refused to continue to go along with the free market reforms that had Russian citizens selling their belongings on street corners so that they could survive. (I remember the U.S. news media at the time presenting this selling of family heirlooms as some sort of a successful example of their transfer to capitalism.) In March of 1993, Parliament voted to end the dictatorial powers that they had given to President Yeltsin. Boris I, as Yeltsin had taken to calling himself, went on television and declared a state of emergency, which restored his imperial powers. Three days later, Russia's independent Constitutional Court ruled by a 9–3 vote that President Yeltsin had violated the constitution that he had sworn to uphold. This put Russia's budding democracy and Parliament on a collision course with its president, Boris Yeltsin. Meanwhile, in the West both the U.S. and the European Union continued to support

Yeltsin, whom U.S. President Bill Clinton referred to as "genuinely committed to freedom and democracy, genuinely committed to reform."[34]

Yeltsin put together a hasty referendum asking voters if they agreed that early elections should be held for the president and for Parliament. While more referendum voters did support early elections for both president and Parliament, it still amounted to less than half of the people voting in both categories. The Constitutional Court had previously ruled that a majority of voters was necessary to change the constitution.[35] Ms. Klein reports that the Russians looked upon the referendum as a failed propaganda exercise.[36]

American economist Lawrence Summers, then U.S. Treasury Undersecretary, testified to the Senate Foreign Relations Committee on September 7, 1993, "We urge Russia to reinvigorate and intensify its reform process so that it can fully secure the benefits on offer from the international financial community."[37] This was a clear indication that the U.S. required acquiescence to the Chicago School/neoliberal/Washington Consensus policies euphemistically referred to as reforms. An official at the International Monetary Fund (IMF) leaked out that the IMF was rescinding a $1.5 billion loan to Russia as the IMF was "unhappy with Russia's backtracking on reforms."[38] After informing Congress of the Chicago School/neoliberal/Washington Consensus demand to Russia, Dr. Summers would go on to be Secretary of the Treasury under President Bill Clinton, director of the National Economic Council under President Barack Obama, and president of Harvard University.[39]

Yeltsin Issues Pinochet Option

Yeltsin responded by issuing what became known as the "Pinochet option," referring to when Chilean dictator Augusto Pinochet instituted similar "economic reforms" at the urging of the U.S twenty years earlier. In Chile, the reforms came along with a great deal of brutality against the Chilean people.[40] Years later and Chile has officially recognized at least 40,018 victims of dictator Augusto Pinochet that were either killed, tortured, or imprisoned for political reasons.[41] Yeltsin's "Pinochet option" that he issued was known as decree 1400. In a stroke, he dissolved Russia's Parliament and abolished its constitution. Parliament responded by voting 636–2 to impeach Yeltsin. This was the same Parliament that had two years earlier supported Yeltsin and the "economic reforms" that he was initiating at the demand of the West. The Constitutional Court again ruled Yeltsin's actions illegal, yet U.S. President Clinton and Congress continued to support Yeltsin by voting to give him $2.5 billion in aid.[42]

In response to his impeachment, Yeltsin shut off the power, phone lines, and heat to the Russian parliament building (called the White House). With Parliament in session inside the building, President Yeltsin surrounded the parliament building with soldiers and tanks. The Director of the Institute of Globalization Studies in Moscow, Boris Kagarlitsky, reported that Russian citizens who supported democracy:

> …were coming in by the thousands trying to break the blockade. There were two weeks of peaceful demonstration confronting the troops and police forces, which led to partial unblocking of the parliament building, with people able to bring food and water inside. Peaceful resistance was growing more popular and gaining broader support every day.[43]

Ms. Klein related that the natural compromise to resolve the standoff would have been for both sides to agree to immediate elections for both president and Parliament. But then news came in from Poland that the Solidarity Party had just been decisively defeated at the polls.

Poland's Solidarity

The Solidarity Movement began in Poland in 1980, when laid-off electrician Lech Walesa climbed over a steel fence to join thousands of protesting workers in Gdańsk, Poland. They were protesting the Polish Communist Party's decision to raise the price of meat by barricading themselves inside the Lenin Shipyards. Within a year, Solidarity had become a huge revolutionary movement with ten million members. They wanted democracy and a mixture of capitalism and socialism, with the power of government vested in the people through workers councils. The following statement is from Solidarity's Program, adopted by their First National Congress:

> We demand a self-governing and democratic reform at every management level and a new socioeconomic system combining the plan, self-government and the market. The socialized enterprise, should be the basic organizational unit in the economy. It should be controlled by the workers council representing the collective and should be operatively run by the director, appointed through competition and recalled by the council.[44]

Moscow eventually ordered a crackdown on Solidarity, and Polish General Wojciech Jaruzelski declared martial law in Poland in December 1981. Tanks surrounded factories and Solidarity members were rounded up, arrested, and jailed, with the leaders like Walesa imprisoned for years (Walesa was awarded the Nobel Peace Prize in 1983 while in prison).

In 1982 a covert U.S./Vatican program was launched in support of Solidarity. In 1984 the U.S. government-funded National Endowment for Democracy (NED) took over the support of Solidarity and channeled money through the Free Trade Union Institute (FTUI) in coordination with the CIA.[45] There was certainly nothing wrong with the U.S. government supporting Solidarity. However, the U.S. government was only supporting Solidarity so as to get Poland to support the same type of radical free market capitalism that we were soon to foist upon the Russia, instead of the balanced mixture of capitalism and socialism that both Solidarity in Poland and the USSR/Russia under Gorbachev were striving to achieve.

In Poland, the repression against Solidarity eventually began to subside, and by 1988, workers again began launching massive strikes. The Polish economy was in freefall and with the moderate Gorbachev leading the USSR, the Communist Party was finally forced to recognize Solidarity. Elections were held and Solidarity won 260 out of 261 seats contested in Parliament. Since only a minority of seats in Parliament were up for election, the 260 seats themselves were not enough for a majority. But by forming coalitions with a few minor parties, they soon had their majority and Poland introduced the first non-communist government within the Soviet bloc.[46]

But what had Solidarity won? Lech Walesa famously and prophetically assessed the victory: "To our misfortune, we have won!"[47] Solidarity inherited a $40 billion debt, 600% inflation rate, severe food shortages, and a thriving black market.[48] Solidarity leaders had gone from prison to leading the government in the blink of an eye. Now they were given the task of governing a country which was broke and in debt up to its ears to international bankers, all without a system of publicly created money to get them to a solid financial footing. The U.S. and the West insisted that Solidarity adopt the same Neoliberal/Chicago School/Washington Consensus policies of free trade, free markets, no governmental intervention, tax cuts for the rich, and privatization of everything public that were also presented later as an ultimatum to Russia. That is if there were to be any loans extended to either Poland or Russia. Both countries would soon meet with disastrous consequences after acquiescing to the West's monetary blackmail.

American economists Jeffrey Sachs and David Lipton wrote out the fifteen-page plan for Poland to transition from a managed central economy to a hoped-for Chicago School free market paradise in a single night.[49] Those of us who have had our academic challenges can think of it as an all-nighter writing that term paper on the French Revolution or trying to cram a semester's worth of Economics 101 into your brain over the course of one evening for the final exam the next day. But economists Sachs and Lipton weren't writing a term paper or taking a test, they were writing the blueprint for Poland's future. The blueprint of the Chicago School's economic shock therapy that came out of their all-nighter was hardly what the Solidarity Union members had struggled and gone to prison for. The union wanted the socialized enterprise to be the basic organization of the economy, with workers councils making the decisions. Desperate for funding and with no knowledge of publicly created money, the Solidarity Party debated which course to take and eventually held their nose and swallowed the Chicago School's poison pill—unrestrained free market capitalism. The result of the Chicago School free market paradise: Poland's poverty rate skyrocketed from 15% in 1989 to a whopping 59% in 2003.[50]

The West had forced Solidarity to renounce its entire agenda of mixing capitalism and socialism under the direction of workers councils, all done to keep Poland under the thumb of the bank-created debt-money system. The same fate would soon await Russia. Poland and Russia needed exactly what the American colonies had needed centuries earlier (*History of Money 101:* Chapter 4) and what America and every other nation needs today—a system of publicly created money.

Russian Democracy Massacred

With the news of Solidarity's election defeat, Yeltsin and his Western economic advisors saw the writing on the wall and abandoned any further thought of negotiations or elections. Yeltsin has never been accused of being a deep thinker. After witnessing the once tremendously popular Solidarity Party get trounced in the polls in Poland, there was no way Boris Yeltsin was going to jeopardize his own once quite popular presidency in another free election. Ms. Klein believes that either the U.S. or the European countries could have forced Yeltsin back to the negotiating table with a clear signal, but instead he received only their directives to establish the Chicago School/neoliberal policies now known as the Washington Consensus.[51]

Meanwhile in Moscow, democracy supporters, upset that the state-run television stations were not accurately reporting the standoff at Parliament, marched to the Ostankino TV station only to be met with deadly force in a horrific massacre. Boris Kargarlitsky, who took part in the protests, reports that on October 3, 1993, crowds of

Parliament/democracy supporters "marched to the Ostankino TV center to demand that news be announced. Some people in the crowd were armed, but most were not. There were children in the crowd. The marchers were met by Yeltsin's troops and machine-gunned."[52]

Expert Witness: Naomi Klein—Author: *The Shock Doctrine: The Rise of Disaster Capitalism*

Ms. Klein's book is largely responsible for enlightening me on the events that led to the end of the Soviet Union. Those of us who lived through the Cold War were shocked to wake up one day and discover that our arch adversary the Soviet Union no longer existed. It took Ms. Klein's book written in 2007, sixteen years after the breakup of the Soviet Union, to bring this story to the world's people.[53] She reports an estimated 100 people were killed in the Ostankino TV Center Massacre. On the next day, October 4, 1993, President Boris Yeltsin ordered the Russian army to attack the seat of the budding Russian democracy, their parliament building the White House, with the entire Parliament and staff inside. Naomi Klein reports:

> Communism may have collapsed without the firing of a single shot, but Chicago-style capitalism, it turned out, required a great deal of gunfire to defend itself. Yeltsin called in five thousand soldiers, dozens of tanks and armored personnel carriers, helicopters and elite shock troops armed with automatic machine guns—all to defend Russia's new capitalist economy from the grave threat of democracy.[54]

The Russian people's parliament building with the Parliament members and staff inside was shelled and burned to the ground, with Klein estimating that 500 people inside were killed and another 1,000 wounded.[55] Ms. Klein uses several different sources to arrive at these horrific figures. Radio Free Europe reported that the same Russian government that carried out the massacres listed 187 dead and 437 wounded in both the TV station massacre and the hours-long shelling and burning of the parliament building.[56] The U.S. demand for Russia to be a laissez-faire capitalist country at all costs resulted in the present autocratic regime now led by Vladimir Putin supported by billionaire oligarchs ruling over a poverty-stricken people. This brief distillation of Russia's budding democracy being sacrificed to the Western insistence that Russia embrace capitalism first and foremost is largely based on Naomi Klein's account in *The Shock Doctrine*.[57]

The U.S.-led West's demands to end the Soviet social safety net and privatize what Vladimir Lenin had referred to in 1922 as the "commanding heights" of the economy—mineral resources, mines, energy production, manufacturing, and transportation[58]—directly resulted in the impoverishment of half the Russian people.[59]

Putin Uses Kompromat to Become President

Boris Yeltsin had two terms as president, yet he left office with a hasty resignation in December 1999 with a year left in his second term, after first appointing Vladimir Putin as his successor as president. Putin, who was the head of the FSB (Federal Security Service, Russian secret police), had surprisingly been appointed prime minister by Yeltsin only four months earlier.[60] This was done to reward Putin for getting rid of Prosecutor General Yury Skuratov, who had been investigating President Yeltsin for taking bribes from a Swiss firm trying to secure lucrative contracts for Kremlin renovations. Putin released kompromat (compromising material/blackmail) on Prosecutor General Skuratov that ran on the evening news. It showed a person who looked like Prosecutor General Skuratov in bed with two prostitutes. This promptly torpedoed the investigation on Yeltsin and ended Prosecutor General Shuratov's career.[61] Soon after this, Yeltsin resigned as president of Russia and appointed Putin as his successor. If Putin had kompromat on the prosecutor Skuratov, why should we not believe that he would also have kompromat on Yeltsin himself? [62]

Russian Democracy Would Have Been Compatible with Publicly Created Money

Yeltsin began the destruction of Russia's fledgling democracy at the behest of the West, so as to conform to the Chicago School/neoliberal/Washington Consensus policy of free market capitalism and privatized public assets. Putin then completed the job, using the system of oligarch apparatchiks who owed allegiance to him as they jointly bled Russia dry.

But Russia was bankrupt only because it used the same bank-created debt-money system that the Western nations use. Evidence for this will be provided in the following chapter. Only after Russia agreed to sell off its natural assets and industry at below bargain-basement prices, did the U.S. agree to loan Russia $4.5 billion.[63] In 2015 the European Parliament estimated the worth of Russian mineral wealth to be $75 trillion.[64] The $4.5 billion 1991 dollars the U.S. loaned Russia was the equivalent of $7.8 billion in 2015 dollars, yet the mineral assets of the Russian state were worth $75 trillion. Russia's assets were worth more than 9,600 times as much as the amount the West begrudgingly lent them at the point of a financial gun, demanding that they bankrupt their people to do so. In other words, the Western bank-created debt-money system reluctantly loaned Russia $1 for every $9,600 that Russia had in natural resource assets as collateral for the loans.

But to get the loans, Russia was required to basically give away all these and other assets to Communist Party apparatchiks (connected Communist Party officials) so as to qualify for the loan assistance from the West. Soviet and Russian law was convoluted and constantly changing on the issue of foreign and Russian ownership of property.[65] Privatization was required as an offering to the altar of free market capitalism. The fickle and unsettled nature of property ownership in Russia facilitated the fire sale of Russian assets to the apparatchiks who would soon become oligarchs. The Western-led bank-created debt-money system would obviously have preferred direct ownership of the Russian assets. But the international bankers were forced to content themselves with putting the ownership of Russia's vast resources into the hands of Yeltsin and his oligarchs-to-be. And in December 1999 this became Vladimir Putin and his oligarchs.

Russia and Poland could have just begun to create their own money, free and clear of the debt-money system. A Russian publicly created money system would have had $75 trillion in mineral assets to provide any backing that the Western debt-money system might require if there was a reluctance to recognize Russia's fundamental right to create its own circulating medium of currency. Poland, while not possessing the natural resources of Russia, did have the labor of 10 million Solidarity union workers to back what would have been their own publicly created Polish money.

Both countries would have been able to slowly transition to whatever mixture of capitalism and socialism was agreeable to the majority of their respective peoples. Half of the Russian people would not have been forced into poverty and Russia would have been able to grow its budding democracy. In Poland they could have avoided impoverishing 59% of their people. Solidarity could have continued to set an example for the rest of the world, as a beacon of democracy. If the Russian people had been allowed to keep their fledgling democracy, it seems highly unlikely that they would have allowed themselves to be put under the thumb of authoritarianism that Vladimir Putin and his apparatchik oligarchs would subsequently impose upon Russia and later attempt to put upon Ukraine.

---

1. Kelly, Meg & Samuels, Elyse, "How Russia weaponized social media, got caught and escaped consequences," Washington Post, Nov 18, 2019, https://www.washingtonpost.com/politics/2019/11/18/how-russia-weaponized-social-media-got-caught-escaped-consequences/
2. Nixon, Angela, "Clemson Media Forensics Hub digs into Russian 'narrative laundering,'" Clemson University, https://news.clemson.edu/clemson-media-forensics-hub-digs-into-russian-narrative-laundering/
3. Klein, Naomi, *The Shock Doctrine -- The Rise of Disaster Capitalism,* Henry Holt & Co, New York, 2007, pp. 275-331.
4. North Atlantic Treaty Organization, "What Was the Warsaw Pact?", https://www.nato.int/cps/us/natohq/declassified_138294.htm
5. Bernstein, Carl, "The Holy Alliance," Time, Feb 24, 1992, p. 30.

6. Church, George J., "The Education of Mikhail Sergeyevich Gorbachev," Time, Jan 4, 1988, http://content.time.com/time/subscriber/article/0,33009,966393-15,00.html
7. Steger, Manfred B. & Roy, Ravi K., "First-wave neoliberalism in the 1980s: Reganomics and Thatcherism," Oxford Academic, January 2010, Abstract, https://academic.oup.com/book/705/chapter-abstract/135378613?redirectedFrom=fulltext
8. Johnson, Rachel, "George H.W. Bush Was an Enemy of the Working Class," In These Times, Dec 5, 2018, https://inthesetimes.com/article/george-herbert-walker-bush-enemy-working-class-death-labor-unions
9. Stein, Judith & Lichtenstein, Nelson, "Bill Clinton Campaigned as a Progressive. Why Didn't He Govern Like One?" Mother Jones, Sept 8, 2023, https://www.motherjones.com/politics/2023/09/bill-clinton-a-fabulous-failure-nelson-lichtenstein-judith-stein/
10. Hurt, Stephen R., "Washington Consensus," Encyclopedia Britannica, https://www.britannica.com/topic/Washington-consensus
11. Williamson, John, "A Short History of the Washington Consensus," Peterson Institute for International Economics, Sept 24, 2004, https://www.piie.com/commentary/speeches-papers/short-history-washington-consensus
12. PBS, Excerpt from Daniel Yergin & Joseph Stanislaw, Commanding Heights, 1998, pp. 145-149, https://www.pbs.org/wgbh/commandingheights/shared/minitext/ess_chicagoschool.html
13. Klein, Naomi, *The Shock Doctrine -- The Rise of Disaster Capitalism,* pp. 276-277.
14. Klein, Naomi, *The Shock Doctrine -- The Rise of Disaster Capitalism,* p. 276.
15. Robinson, William I., "Democracy or Polyarchy?" North American Congress on Latin America, Sept 25, 2007, https://nacla.org/article/democracy-or-polyarchy
16. Robinson, William I., *Promoting Polyarchy–Globalization, US Intervention, and Hegemony*, Cambridge University Press, 1996, pp. 322-323
17. Frontline, "Return of the Czar," PBS, May 9, 2000, Sherry Jones, writer & producer, https://www.pbs.org/wgbh/pages/frontline/shows/yeltsin/etc/script.html
18. *Ibid.*
19. Baltic Defense College, "Restoration of Independence in the Baltics," https://www.baltdefcol.org/1243#:~:text=On%206th%20September%201991%2C%20the,Latvia%20on%2031%20August%201994
20. Emerging Europe, "Lithuania remembers January 13th, 1991," Jan 13, 2021, https://emerging-europe.com/news/lithuania-remembers-january-13-1991/
21. The Museum of the Barricades of 1991, Riga, "The Baltic Initiative and Network," Cold War Sites, https://coldwarsites.net/country/latvia/the-museum-of-the-barricades-of-1991-riga/
22. Office of the Historian, "The Collapse of the Soviet Union," Department of State, United States Government. https://history.state.gov/milestones/1989-1992/collapse-soviet-union
23. Newman, Dina, "How three men signed the USSR's death warrant," BBC News, Dec 24, 2016, https://www.bbc.com/news/magazine-38416657
24. Office of the Historian, "The Collapse of the Soviet Union," Department of State, United States Government.
25. Bunn, Matthew, "Budapest Memorandum at 25: Between Past and Future," Harvard Kennedy School, March 2020, https://www.hks.harvard.edu/publications/budapest-memorandum-25-between-past-and-future

26. Soldatenko, Mykhailo, "Constructive Ambiguity of the Budapest Memorandum at 28: Making Sense of the Controversial Agreement," Lawfare, Feb 7, 2023, https://www.lawfaremedia.org/article/constructive-ambiguity-of-the-budapest-memorandum-at-28-making-sense-of-the-controversial-agreement
27. Baker, Sinead, "Putin denies planning to revive the Russian empire after declaring that Ukraine is not a real country and sending troops there," Business Insider, Feb 22, 2022, https://www.businessinsider.com/putin-denies-reviving-russian-empire-says-ukraine-not-real-country-2022-2
28. Reddaway, Peter & Glinski, Dmitri, *The Tragedy of Russia's Reforms: Market Bolshevism against Democracy,* United States Institute for Peace Press, Washington, DC, 2001, p. 253
29. Klein, Naomi, *The Shock Doctrine -- The Rise of Disaster Capitalism,* p. 275-331
30. Klein, Naomi, *The Shock Doctrine -- The Rise of Disaster Capitalism,* p. 282.
31. Dahlburg, John-Thor, "Once More, Yeltsin Puts Himself in Line of Fire: Russia: His strategy is treacherously double-edged: If his reforms fail, so do his political fortunes." Los Angeles Times, Oct 29, 1991, https://www.latimes.com/archives/la-xpm-1991-10-29-mn-723-story.html
32. McClintick, David, "How Harvard Lost Russia," Institutional Investor, Jan 1, 2006, https://www.institutionalinvestor.com/article/b150npp3q49x7w/how-harvard-lost-russia
33. Klein, Naomi, *The Shock Doctrine -- The Rise of Disaster Capitalism,* pp. 199-200.
34. Ifil, Gwen, "Clinton Meets Russian on Assistance Proposal," New York Times, March 25, 1993.
35. Encyclopedia.com, "Referendum of April 1993," https://www.encyclopedia.com/history/encyclopedias-almanacs-transcripts-and-maps/referendum-april-1993
36. Klein, Naomi, *The Shock Doctrine -- The Rise of Disaster Capitalism,* p. 285.
37. C-Span, "U.S. Aid to Russia," Testimony Honorable Lawrence H. Summers, Under Secretary for International Affairs, U.S. Treasury Department, U.S. Senate Committee on Foreign Relations, Sept 7, 1993, 29 minute mark, https://www.c-span.org/video/?50083-1/us-aid-russia
38. Reddaway, Peter & Glinski, Dmitri, *The Tragedy of Russia's Reforms: Market Bolshevism against Democracy,* p. 294
39. Famouseconomists.net, "Lawrence Summers," https://www.famouseconomists.net/lawrence-summers
40. Mizrahi, Alina, "Support for Authoritarianism: The Case of Augusto Pinochet," University of Pennsylvania, Scholarly Commons, 2020, https://repository.upenn.edu/cgi/viewcontent.cgi?article=1290&context=curej
41. Associated Press, "Chile dictatorship victim list bumped to 40,018," Canadian Broadcasting Corporation, Aug 18, 2011, https://www.cbc.ca/news/world/chile-dictatorship-victim-toll-bumped-to-40-018-1.998542
42. Klein, Naomi, *The Shock Doctrine -- The Rise of Disaster Capitalism,* p. 286
43. Boris Kargarlitsky quoted in Klein, Naomi, *The Shock Doctrine -- The Rise of Disaster Capitalism,* p. 286
44. Raina, Peter, *Poland 1981: Towards Social Renewal,* Allen & Unwin, London, 1985, pp. 236-380.
45. Robinson, William I., *Promoting Polyarchy–Globalization, US Intervention, and Hegemony*, p. 322.

46. Newsweek Staff, "The Berlin Wall Was Not the First to Fall," Newsweek Nov 2, 2009, https://www.newsweek.com/berlin-wall-was-not-first-fall-76651
47. Glyn, Andrew, editor, *Social Democracy in Neoliberal Times*, Kowalik, Tadeusz, "Why the Social Democratic Option Failed: Poland's Experience of Systemic Change," Oxford University Press, 2001, p. 223
48. Weschler, Lawrence, "A Grand Experiment," The New Yorker, Nov 13, 1989, https://www.newyorker.com/magazine/1989/11/13/a-grand-experiment
49. Klein, Naomi, *The Shock Doctrine -- The Rise of Disaster Capitalism,* pp. 241-242.
50. Klein, Naomi, *The Shock Doctrine -- The Rise of Disaster Capitalism,* pp. 241-242.
51. Klein, Naomi, *The Shock Doctrine -- The Rise of Disaster Capitalism,* pp. 286-287
52. Boris Kargarlitsky quoted in Klein, Naomi, *The Shock Doctrine -- The Rise of Disaster Capitalism,*
p. 287
53. Klein, Naomi, *The Shock Doctrine -- The Rise of Disaster Capitalism,* pp. 275-331.
54. Klein, Naomi, *The Shock Doctrine -- The Rise of Disaster Capitalism,* p. 288
55. Kargarlitsky, Boris, *Square Wheels,* translated by Leslie A. Auerbach, Monthly Review Press, New York, 1994, p. 218.
56. Foltynova, Kristyna, "The Day The Russian White House Was Shelled," Radio Free Europe/Radio Liberty, Oct. 24, 2019, https://www.rferl.org/a/white-house-shelled/29525525.html
57. Klein, Naomi, *The Shock Doctrine -- The Rise of Disaster Capitalism,* pp. 275-331.
58. Kling, Arnold & Schultz, Nick, "The New Commanding Heights," National Affairs, Summer, 2011, https://www.nationalaffairs.com/publications/detail/the-new-commanding-heights
59. Klein, Naomi, *The Shock Doctrine -- The Rise of Disaster Capitalism,* pp. 199-200
60. Rosenberg, Steve, "The man who helped make ex-KGB officer Vladimir Putin a president," BBC News, Dec 17, 2019, https://www.bbc.com/news/world-europe-50807747
61. Ioffe, Julia, "How State-Sponsored Blackmail Works in Russia," *The Atlantic*, Jan 11, 2017, https://www.theatlantic.com/international/archive/2017/01/kompromat-trump-dossier/512891/
62. Ioffe, Julia, "How State-Sponsored Blackmail Works in Russia," *The Atlantic*, Jan 11, 2017.
63. Congressional Research Service Report for Congress, "U.S. Assistance to the Former Soviet Union 1991-2001: A History of Administrative and Congressional Action," Jan 15, 2002, https://www.hsdl.org/?view&did=446614
64. European Parliamentary Research Service Blog, "Russian Natural Resources," March 12, 2015, https://epthinktank.eu/2015/03/16/the-russian-economy-will-russia-ever-catch-up/eprs-ida-551320-russian-natural-resources/
65. Schneider, Richard C. Jr., "Privatization in One Country: Foreign Investment and the Russian Privatization Dynamic," Hastings International and Comparative Law Review, Vol 17, Number 4, Summer 1994, https://repository.uchastings.edu/cgi/viewcontent.cgi?article=1386&context=hastings_international_comparative_law_review

NINE

Darkness Reigns Amidst the Capitalist/Socialist Divide

Recapping the Bleak, Bank-Created Debt-Money System

As *Spaceship Earth* continues her journey, there is a simple reason why almost none of us understand how our present money system works. Those that hold the Money Power (power to create our money) do not want us to know that they hold this power. Their best chance of retaining this power lies in keeping the American people in the dark, completely ignorant about how they create our money out of thin air when they loan it to us at interest, making us debt slaves in the process.

In a functioning democracy, the people are sovereign, possessing supreme political power. But a sovereign people who do not understand how the money system operates are like a rudderless ship adrift in the sea, with captain and crew unable to determine and navigate a course to safety. Knowledge of the dysfunctional, bank-created debt-money system gives us the chance to implement a system of publicly created money. This in turn, allows us to expand the level of liberty, equality and democracy in our society, moving us toward the more perfect union we have been seeking since our nation's founding.

Within the dysfunctional bank-created debt-money system, a repayment of even a relatively small amount of the overall debt load of people and government would reduce the money supply, sending us into financial collapse. As presented in *History of Money 101*, the Panic of 1907 was caused by the U.S. sending only 1% of our gold to the United Kingdom, which reduced our money supply by just 2.5%. As a result, the big banks refused to let people withdraw their own money from the banks.[1] Today our money is no longer backed by gold. So, a similar reduction in the money supply would be triggered by our people and/or our government repaying a certain percentage of loans, without anyone else taking out new loans —thus reducing our supply of money. If enough existing loans were repaid without a corresponding amount of new loans being taken out, it could very well cause a depression. The only tool our government has to avert such a collapse would be for our government to borrow more money, going into greater debt to increase the money supply, so that our economy can function, we can have jobs and pay our bills.

The structural problem with the debt-money system is that we (you, I, and our government) must be in debt for there to be money in existence and society can function. Japanese economist Dr. Kaoru Yamaguchi said it best. As quoted in *Money Creation 101*: Chapter 9, "If all debts are repaid, money ceases to exist. This is the essence of a debt money system."[2]

On the other hand, a system of publicly created money would allow the people to build up wealth and financial security, without the requirement of society increasing its debt. A humming, functioning economy, which is up to the challenge of real climate action and gives all our people the pathway to individual financial security, is only possible within a system of publicly created money. While conversely, true liberty is an impossibility within a system of bank-created debt-money that requires us to be in debt for society to simply be able to function.

Private creation of money as debt is the antithesis of equality. Public creation of money will not magically change our society, into one in which we all have an equal amount of money. But it will inject money into our economy so that we can create millions of good-paying jobs rebuilding our infrastructure, fighting climate change with clean renewable energy and doing so without creating debt. It will allow our federal government to fund programs for those of us who have lost their jobs or small businesses to pandemics, Artificial Intelligence, or whatever surprises the future holds for us. Publicly created money then stays in the economy, providing jobs and security for our people, in contrast to the bank-created debt-money that is destroyed by the banks when the loans are repaid and the interest has been sucked out of us. While publicly created money will not make our society exactly equal, it will make it dramatically more equal.

A nation of debt slaves is incapable of democracy. When we are forced to owe someone else to simply exist as a modern society, we do not have the freedom necessary to have a democratic government. All our decisions are framed by the existential fact that whenever we need money (individual needs or the collective needs of our local, state, and federal governments), we must borrow it, at interest from private banks. Of course, in our present system we can work for our money, as most of us do. But that money that we work to earn is only in the system because somebody, somewhere, went into debt for it to exist.

The insidiousness of this depraved money system is compounded by the fact that its operation has carefully been kept secret from us. Those who have been entrusted by society to understand, study, and ultimately teach us about that which is the most necessary component of our lives have been either unable or unwilling to tell us how our money is created. The economics profession has evolved over the last century into a sort of religious cult in which blind obedience to free markets and the debt-money system is the prerequisite to membership. Up-and-coming economists are fully aware that questioning the bank-created debt-money system is almost certainly a sure path to career suicide. Those who refrain from such questions may advance. And for the few who might want to ask such questions, there is no forum available for them to bring their concerns to the public.

The Money Power's Seven Tactics to Stay in Power, presented in *Money Creation 101*, demonstrated how those who currently hold the power to create our money have rigged the system to keep us from understanding how it functions.

Money Power's 7 Tactics to Stay in Power:

1. The first line of defense used to ensure the continuation of a toxic money system is to keep the people confused and in the dark about the present system of bank-created debt-money and the democratic alternative—publicly created money.
2. The second line of defense is to tell us we are too stupid to understand it.
3. The third line of defense is to create textbooks that lie to us about how our money is created.
4. The fourth line of defense is to stop teaching monetary history, even in the most prestigious economics programs.
5. The fifth line of defense is to simply ignore papers critical of the debt-money system or supportive of publicly created money.
6. The sixth line of defense is to control economics journals so that they will not publish papers critical of the debt-money system or supportive of publicly created money.
7. The seventh line of defense is to make it clear to up-and-coming young economists that for them to buck the debt-money system is career suicide.

Evidence for the above tactics is provided throughout *Money Creation 101*. Two university professors from schools with top rated economics programs were interviewed anonymously at their request. Neither one was able to clearly explain how our money is created. A Federal Reserve macroeconomist, who I am quite sure knows that our money is privately created by banks when they make loans, refused to answer the question himself, instead referring the question to the Federal Reserve Public Relations Department, which has failed to respond to me.

Mayday for Money!

Mayday! Mayday! Mayday!, the International Distress Signal, is given out when a pilot is experiencing distress and declares an emergency, requiring other aircraft to switch their own communications with Air Traffic Control to a different frequency, so that the aircraft in distress is given the entire attention of Air Traffic Control and airport personnel.[3] As a former Air Force Air Traffic Controller, which included one year controlling aircraft in the Vietnam war zone, I am well aware of such signals. Now, more than half a century after that service, I am also well aware that the emergency of half of our people having no net worth, combined with the emergencies of global warming, dying oceans, disappearing species, and collapsing ecosystems demands the entire attention of our society.

On May 17, 2024, the Alliance for Just Money, joined by the American Monetary Institute, 14 other organizations, and 47 individuals delivered the following letter to the Chicago Federal Reserve:

> Dear Dr. Goolsbee and the Federal Reserve Bank of Chicago Board of Directors:
>
> Mayday! Mayday! Mayday for Money! The Alliance for Just Money (AFJM), allied organizations, and citizens are gathering together in Chicago this weekend to issue the international distress call about the US Federal Reserve System and related monetary systems worldwide.
>
> May 18th, 2024 marks the 110th anniversary of the formal signing of the Federal Reserve Bank of Chicago's organization certificate.[a] In passing the Federal Reserve Act in December 1913, Congress surrendered its Constitutional authority—under Article I Section 8—to create all U.S. money and regulate the value thereof. Congress instead ceded that power to the commercial banks nationwide. Over a century later, We the

---

[a] Chicago Fed History: 1907-1914, www.chicagofed.org/utilities/about-us/history/chicago-fed-history-1907-1914.

People declare "Mayday for Money," calling for a sovereign public money system.

We and a growing number of citizens recognize that, no matter how officially established and protected it has been, the private, debt-based modern money system is inherently unjust, unsustainable, and undemocratic.[b] Our current money system is structurally incapable of serving our people and planet. Earth is warming and its species, oceans, and ecosystems are dying. Our government and people are drowning in debt; wealth inequity is growing exponentially; wars are multiplying; and the money supply is bigger than ever. Yet we are told there is simply not enough money to care for our people and planet! We must change this narrative and demand a sovereign public money system.

We are at a historical juncture regarding monetary policy and financial systems worldwide. With the rise of digital currencies, we invite you to dialogue with us to enact Just Money rather than allow our financial institutions to continue our private, debt-based money system. **We call upon you to work with us and our elected officials to pass the American Monetary Reform Act of 2024, that will establish and transition us to a sovereign public money system.**[c] [4] (Emphasis in letter)

---

[b] Omarova, S. T. (2020, March 20). Technology v technocracy: Fintech as a regulatory challenge. *Journal of Financial Regulation, 6(*1), 75–124 (https://academic.oup.com/jfr/article/6/1/75/5858319). See also International Movement for Monetary Reform, internationalmoneyreform.org/members/; legal scholars of money at JustMoney.org; and regenerative and distributive economics efforts of DoughnutEconomics.org

[c] The American Monetary Reform Act (AMRA) of 2024 is based on the H.R. 2990 National Emergency Employment Defense (NEED) Act of 2011 which was updated and improved upon by AFJM. It and a two-page factsheet on it are on AFJM's Archive page (www.monetaryalliance.org/archive-afjm/) and directly at www.monetaryalliance.org/wp-content/uploads/American-Monetary-Reform-Act.pdf, and www.monetaryalliance.org/wp-content/uploads/AMRA-Fact-Sheet.pdf.

We had contacted the Chicago Federal Reserve well in advance of the Mayday date and requested that a small group of us be allowed to present this letter and other supporting materials to the Federal Reserve Board of Directors. We were told no. We then asked that two or three of us be allowed to present the letter to Federal Reserve staff and again were told no. We went to the Chicago Federal Reserve Bank and were turned away, forced to then find the nearest U.S. Post Office and mail the Mayday letter and supporting materials to the Chicago Federal Reserve. This is a perfect example of the Federal Reserve System representing the Money Power by shunning the idea of monetary reform, all the while *Spaceship Earth* travels the heavens in a Mayday emergency status.

Expert Witness: Dr. Kaoru Yamaguchi

Japanese economist Dr. Kaoru Yamaguchi, who received his doctorate in economics from the University of California, Berkeley, was later terminated from his position teaching economics with a System Dynamics Method of analysis at the prestigious Doshisha University, Kyoto, Japan. Dr. Yamaguchi's crime? He used System Dynamics modeling to show that publicly created money was vastly superior to our bank-created debt-money system. It took five years before Dr. Yamaguchi was again given a full professorship, this time at Ankara University, Turkey.

Dr. Yamaguchi explaining the bank creation of money:

> Commercial banks then create credits under a fractional reserve banking system by making loans to producers and consumers. These credits constitute a great portion of the money supply. In this way, money and credits are only created when commercial banks and government as well as producers and consumers come to borrow at interest. Under such circumstances, if all debts are repaid, money ceases to exist. This is the essence of a debt money system. The process of creating money is known as money out of nothing.[5]

I have been fortunate enough to meet Dr. Yamaguchi on two occasions before he was fired for speaking the truth about our crisis-prone money system. A great man; his employment termination remains as an indictment against the bank-created debt-money system.

Expert Witness: Jonathan McMillan—Author: 2014, *The End of Banking - Money, Credit, and the Digital Revolution;* 2024, *Capitalism and the Market Economy - Bringing Back Together What Banking Pulls Apart*

McMillan defines banking:

> We adopt a macroeconomic perspective and define *banking* as the creation of money out of credit.[6]

What does Jonathan McMillan have in common with Expert Witnesses Michael Chambers from Chapter 1 and Professor Plastics from Chapter 4? Although none of the three mentioned are AI beings out to take our jobs, none of them are real people. Mr. Chambers was a character on the TV show *The Twilight Zone* and Professor Plastics was a wonderful cartoon caricature by the American Chemistry Council who now no longer exists. Jonathan McMillan is a pseudonym for a pair of former schoolmates who went on to become a macroeconomist and an investment banker. Why did they write their books anonymously? Dr. Yamaguchi was fired for speaking out, did they likewise fear for their careers? Or were they just bashful? Actually, after years the macroeconomist has outed himself, but the investment banker still remains hidden behind the McMillan moniker. All this fuss for just telling us that our money system is not what we have thought it to be.

Forget the Capitalist/Socialist Divide

Putting our society and *Spaceship Earth* on the proper course is the challenge we face. The stakes are far too great to allow ourselves to become embroiled in a divisive debate between capitalism and socialism. Both systems are theoretical and neither has ever successfully existed in its pure form for any length of time. Attempts at unrestrained free-market capitalism resulted in the Great Depression (1929–1941) and more recently the Great Recession/Global Financial Crisis, lasting from 2007–2009 for banks and continuing for the poor and working class. Capitalism is a theory that an invisible, all-powerful, all-knowing, and beneficent guiding hand ensures that the free market dispenses justice to the people. The reality is that no such free market exists in nature and the so-called free market that currently dominates our society is a creation of government laws. The weaker the laws are and the more this alleged free market is unrestrained and unregulated, the greater the concentration of wealth and power in the hands of an elite few, as monopolies benefit the wealthy at the expense of the many.

People collectively fight back, hopefully getting their democratically elected representatives to legislate reforms that restrain the power of monopolies. But this yin and yang between democratic self-governance vs. powerful interests ultimately depends upon being able to regulate and constrain huge corporations and special interests when necessary. True free-market capitalism does not allow for this type of restraint. And when our government does apply some form of regulation to the huge corporations, they squeal like stuck pigs. The invisible hand of the free market jerks around the lives of poor and working-class people like puppets on a string, while the wealthiest amongst us profit, from both the inflating of and the bursting of bubbles. The stock market crash in 1929 that led to the Great Depression, the real estate bubble that burst in 2008, and the dot-com bubble that burst in March 2000 are good indicators that the market is neither all-knowing nor a dispenser of justice.

Dot-Com Bubble

Excessive speculative investment in internet-based technology stocks pumped up the dot-com bubble from 1995 to 2000. The NASDAQ Composite Index rose 400% from 1995 to 2000. When the bubble burst in March 2000, it fell 78% from its peak by October of the same year.[7] This classic stock market bubble created big winners and losers. As for the free market's alleged omniscience (possessing universal or complete knowledge), one could say the winners were all-knowing, while the losers were just casualties of the system. But that is the essence of the free market: there can be no winners in the free market without there also being losers to finance their winnings.

The Great Depression and the Great Recession/Global Financial Crisis

The real estate bubble was triggered by the repeal of the 1933 Glass-Steagall Act, which separated retail commercial banking from investment banking. The Great Depression had been attributed to the reckless actions of investment bankers. President Franklin Delano Roosevelt and Congress were able to pass the 1933 and 1935 Banking Acts which contained the Glass-Steagall separation of the retail and investment banks[8] and the birth of the Federal Deposit Insurance Corporation.[9] While these two reforms were certainly much needed, Roosevelt's New Dealers were so proud of this feat that they failed to see the big picture. Sure, banking needed to be regulated and separated from reckless speculation, but more important was liberating the power to create money from the banking system and giving it back to the people through their Congress. This they failed to do or even consider.

The Chicago Plan[10] could have been enacted during the Great Depression. It would have given us the system of just, publicly created money that we still so desperately need as a society. *History of Money 101* chronicles our country's history from the early colonial days as a search and struggle for a just system of money. Instead of realizing that centuries long quest for a just system of money, we got the lipstick on the pig reforms of the Glass-Steagall Act to the bank-created debt-money system.

Without a public money system in place, we were then hit hard by the Great Recession/Global Financial Crisis in 2008. Ten million families lost their homes to foreclosure during the aftermath of the Great

Recession.[11] In 2008, the average U.S. family was 3.15 people. The 10 million families thus represented 31.5 million people, or 10% of the American people. The National Association of Realtors believed that less than one-third of these American families would ever become homeowners again.[12] These and other forgotten families just might take issue with those experts who commonly list the duration of the Great Recession/Global Financial Crisis from 2007 to 2009. That was simply the period that the big banks were in distress. Perhaps we should ask those who lost everything as a result of the chicanery of the big banks, if their misery continues today? Absent their voice, the K-shaped recovery says it all: a fantastic increase for those who were already blessed by wealth and a dramatic drop for the rest of the pack.

After that chronology of failures in our own economic and monetary system, let's take a look at what went wrong in the Soviet Union.

Socialism's Failure in the Soviet Union

Socialism failed miserably in the USSR, in part because the capitalist West did everything in its power to reverse the 1917 socialist/communist Russian Revolution for fear that it would spill over to their own countries. Those in charge of the Russian Revolution, as a policy of self-preservation, understood that moving in the direction of democracy would endanger their own hold on power. They correctly determined that the capitalist West would try to foment a counter-revolution to overthrow their communist/socialist government. In Chapter 7 we presented the Polar Bear Expedition a joint U.S./British/French military expedition into Russia that was an attempt to do just that — overthrow the Russian Revolution.

One would think that theoretically socialism would embrace democracy. Yet Russia and later, the Soviet Union, felt the need to entrench into a totalitarian system of one-party rule they called communism. This set the standard for future authoritarian governments —all efforts must be channeled into staying in power. After the Bolsheviks took over in Russia, they continued to fight the White forces in a civil war to return Czar Nicholas II to power. The

Bolsheviks clearly understood that if the Czar was returned to power, they would all be killed. As the White forces approached the Yekaterinburg house near the Ural Mountains where the Romanov Czar Nicholas II and his family were being kept by the Bolsheviks, the decision was made by Russian leader Vladimir Lenin to execute them all.

On the night of July 16, 1918, Nicholas, his wife, Alexandra, their five children, and four servants were ordered to dress and go down to the cellar. They were photographed alive in a group photo and told the reason that the photo was being taken was to quash rumors that they had escaped. Suddenly armed gunmen came into the room and shot them all. Those still alive were stabbed with bayonets. They were then buried. The czar's death was announced in the press, but the fate of the family members was unclear for several years. A disinformation campaign muddied the waters as to whether the family had been killed or were still alive. Only after Lenin's death in 1924 was the fate of the entire Romanov family finally admitted to in 1926, with the caveat that Lenin's cabinet members had not participated in issuing the order. It was not until USSR President Mikhail Gorbachev brought the Soviet Union in from the cold in the late 1980s that the Soviet Union officially announced the existence of the remains of the Romanov royal family. Finally in 1991, after the fall of the Soviet Union, the Russian state sent a team to dig up the remains and run DNA analysis confirming that these were the remains of the Romanov family.[13]

Whether or not the Soviet Union would have become more democratic without the constant fear of attack from the Western capitalist countries, we will never know. All we know for sure is that existentially threatened by the West, the USSR reflexively retreated from any democratic leanings that they might have developed over time.

The Communists Used the Same Bank-Created Debt-Money System We Use

Years ago as I began to research and learn about our debt-money system, I was flabbergasted upon learning that the Soviet Union used the same bank-created debt-money system that we use in the West. And just like the majority of people in the Western countries, the people in the Soviet Union and its satellites in Eastern Europe were just as uninformed as we are. George Garvey explains in his book *Money, Banking and Credit in Eastern Europe,* published in 1966 by the Federal Reserve Bank of New York:

> In the communist countries, money is created in the same way as in capitalist countries—through the extension of bank credit. This fact is not generally recognized or accepted in the various countries of Eastern Europe. The result is that a good deal of confusion emerges from their economic literature with regard to the nature of money and the role of monetary process and the function of the banking system.... Since Marx identified money with gold, the official theory holds that paper money to be merely a substitute for gold and ignores deposit money [bank-created debt-money].[14]

The communists used the same fraudulent dysfunctional bank-created debt-money system that we use. The communists were kept equally in the dark about the money system as we are. No wonder that they failed their people, just as our capitalist leadership is now failing our own people. When I stood bullhorn in hand, on a street corner with my friends for peace and social justice every Saturday from 2005–2020, I would say, "End the wars overseas and end the war on the poor and working class at home." I said this for years before gaining the knowledge that the war on the poor and working class at home begins with the bank-created debt-money system. It was only years later that I discovered that the poor and working class in communist/socialist countries behind the Iron Curtain were also subjected to the same treacherous bank-created debt-money that we are in America.

The Battle for Democracy in America

Thinking that the U.S. cannot become a rigid, one-party, totalitarian, fascist state is putting on rose-colored glasses. For the last two decades I have been an outspoken critic of U.S. democracy, not because I was against it but rather because I felt it was not democratic enough. But in the 2020, 2022 and 2024 elections I did everything in my power to save the low level of democracy we have. Junking our admittedly flawed democracy for a man who refuses to follow the law and accept election results that have been fully adjudicated within our legal system would be the end of U.S. democracy.[15]

Plotting *Spaceship Earth's* future course, the best way to keep the low level of democracy that we presently enjoy is to avoid the capitalist/socialist divide. Our system has always been a mixture of both capitalism and socialism, and our job as citizens is to constantly test and adjust the mixture, while publicly objecting to those who insist on perpetrating the divide. Our military, police, fire departments, schools, libraries, sewers, roads, and parks are socialist operations. Although there have been attempts, some successful, to privatize them, most people understand that this is lunacy. When public figures scornfully disparage socialism, they are attacking the social fabric of our country and many of the very institutions which build and protect our communities.

Getting the Right Mixture: Capitalism/Socialism

Arguing capitalism over socialism or vice versa is just so much wasted hot air. With *Spaceship Earth* overheating we certainly don't need counterproductive arguments. With Artificial Intelligence threatening to take 36 million U.S. jobs and very possibly take control of humanity itself (as forecasted by Dr. Stephen Hawking),[16] we cannot helplessly ignore our present perilous position. The COVID depression required the creation of trillions of dollars of debt-money just to allow poor and working-class people to get by and carry on until we could return to some form of normalcy. With other unknown viruses and environmental crises sure to follow, we certainly don't need to be fighting amongst ourselves.

We need to fix the system we have. That system has never been a pure capitalist or a pure socialist system. It has always been a mixture. Our job is to become informed private citizens and fight for change, so as to get the mixture right. Bank-created debt-money can only give us debt. Publicly created money is the only way to improve the lives of our people, by putting us to work at saving our planet, without putting us deeper and deeper into debt.

Donald Trump Wins 2024 Presidential Election

That man who refused to accept the results of the 2020 Presidential Election, Donald Trump, has now been elected president for the second time in 2024. Whether or not he will end American democracy and become an authoritarian strongman is up to him. He has said he will terminate the Constitution[17] which is the embodiment of the Rule of Law. Despite his history of playing fast and loose with the truth, there is no reason to doubt him at his word here.[18] [19]

---

1. Friedman, Milton & Schwartz, *A Monetary History of the United States 1867-1960,* Princeton University Press, 1971, p. 161
2. Yamaguchi, Kaoru, *Workings of A Public Money System of Open Macroeconomies – Modeling the American Monetary Act Completed – (A Revised Version),* 2011, Doshisha University, http://www.muratopia.org/Yamaguchi/doc/DesignOpenMacro.pdf
3. Federal Aviation Agency, "Emergency Procedures: Section 3. Distress and Urgency Procedures," https://www.faa.gov/air_traffic/publications/atpubs/aim_html/chap6_section_3.html
4. Alliance For Just Money, "Mayday for Money! Open letter to the Federal Reserve Bank of Chicago Board of Directors," May 17, 2024, https://docs.google.com/forms/d/e/1FAIpQLSd8bwyS6osb01a83mAxlbctVUq39zvcJsw93I9uBoHCZNMISA/viewform
5. Yamaguchi, Kaoru, *Workings of A Public Money System of Open Macroeconomies – Modeling the American Monetary Act Completed – (A Revised Version)*, p. 17, chrome-extension://efaidnbmnnnibpcajpcglclefindmkaj/http://www.muratopia.org/Yamaguchi/doc/DesignOpenMacro.pdf
6. McMillan, Jonathan, *The End of Banking*, Zero/One Economics GmbH, Zurich, 2014.

7. Folger, Jean, "5 Successful Companies that Survived the Dotcom Bubble," Investopedia, June 25, 2019, https://www.investopedia.com/financial-edge/0711/5-success ful-companies-that-survived-the-dotcom-bubble.aspx
8. Maues, Julia, "Banking Act of 1933 (Glass-Steagall)," Federal Reserve History, https://www.federalreservehistory.org/essays/glass-steagall-act
9. Federal Deposit Insurance Corporation, "History of FDIC," https://www.fdic.gov/about/history/#:~:text=On%20June%2016%2C%201933%2C%20Presi dent,of%20which%20established%20the%20FDIC
10. Paul H. Douglas, University of Chicago; Irving Fisher, Yale University; Frank D. Graham, Princeton University; Earl J. Hamilton, Duke University; Willford I. King, New York University; Charles R. Whittlesey, Princeton University, "A Program for Monetary Reform," July, 1939, https://faculty.chicagobooth.edu/amir.sufi/research/monetaryreform_1939.pdf
11. Andres, Tommy, "Divided Decade: How the financial crisis changed housing," Marketplace.org, Dec. 17, 2018, https://www.marketplace.org/2018/12/17/what-we-learned-housing/
12. Kusisto, Laura, "Many who lost homes to foreclosure won't return -- NAR," Wall Street Journal, April 20, 2015, https://www.wsj.com/articles/many-who-lost-homes-to-foreclosure-in-last-decade-wont-return-nar-1429548640
13. Blakemore, Erin, "Why the Romanov Family's Fate Was a Secret Until the Fall of the Soviet Union," History.com, March 29, 2019, https://www.history.com/news/romanov-family-bodies-discovery-coverup
14. Garvey, George, *Money, Banking and Credit in Eastern Europe*, Federal Reserve Bank of New York, 1966, pp. 42-43
15. Danforth, John; Ginsberg, Ben; Griffith, Thomas B; Hoppe, David; Luttig, J. Michael; McConnell, Michael W; Olson, Theodore B; Smith, Gordon H, "LOST, NOT STOLEN: The Conservative Case that Trump lost and Biden won the 2020 Presidential Election," July 2022, https://drive.google.com/file/d/1aqor Z61AYFqZU-EDQBBzjqfvAoC5nKcB/
16. Cellan-Jones, Rory, "Stephen Hawking warns artificial intelligence could end mankind," BBC News, Dec 2, 2014, https://www.bbc.com/news/technology-30290540
17. Holmes, Kristen, "Trump calls for the termination of the Constitution in Truth Social post," CNN, Dec 4, 2022, https://www.cnn.com/2022/12/03/politics/trump-constitution-truth-social/index.html
18. Danforth, John; Ginsberg, Ben; Griffith, Thomas B; Hoppe, David; Luttig, J. Michael; McConnell, Michael W; Olson, Theodore B; Smith, Gordon H, "LOST, NOT STOLEN: The Conservative Case that Trump lost and Biden won the 2020 Presidential Election," July 2022, https://drive.google.com/file/d/1aqor Z61AYFqZU-EDQBBzjqfvAoC5nKcB/
19. "False or misleading statements by Donald Trump," Wikipedia, https://en.wiki pedia.org/wiki/False_or_misleading_statements_by_Donald_Trump

TEN

A More Perfect Union

During her journey, *Spaceship Earth* has witnessed the founding of our country on the values of liberty, equality and democracy more than two centuries ago. But as Americans we are left to reconcile these lofty ideals with the grim reality that U.S. Constitution has in the past enabled: the continuation of African American slavery, the theft of native American lands, the killing of Native Americans with near absolute impunity, and the denial of basic rights to women and LGBTQ+ people. In other words, our Constitution originally was far from perfect, and it is our job as citizens to continue the struggle to make our Constitution and Union more perfect.

The word 'genocide' was first coined by Polish-Jewish jurist Raphael Lemkin in his 1944 book *Axis Rule in Occupied Europe*. Mr. Lemkin personally survived the deaths of 49 family members, including both parents, in killing centers, concentration camps, the Warsaw ghetto and death marches during the Holocaust.[1] This term 'genocide' was not available when the crimes listed in the previous paragraph were committed. Today, it would be difficult to argue that the word genocide does not reflect the reality of our nation's historic treatment of the First Americans.

Expert Witness: Howard Zinn

Boston University Professor of Political Science, Howard Zinn's *A People's History of the United States* is as relevant today, as the day it was published in 1980. Millions of copies have been sold, it has been assigned reading in high schools and colleges across the country, and it was runner-up for the National Book Award in 1980. In contrast to histories that are written from the perspective of the conquerors, Dr. Zinn sought the point of view and "words of America's women, factory workers, African Americans, Native Americans, working poor and immigrant laborers."[2]

Dr. Zinn concludes his opening chapter, "Columbus, the Indians, and Human Progress":

> Columbus and his successors were not coming into an empty wilderness, but into a world which in some places was as densely populated as Europe itself, where the culture was complex, where human relations were more egalitarian than in Europe, and where the relations among men, women, children and nature were more beautifully worked out than perhaps any place in the world.
>
> They were people, without a written language, but with their own laws, their poetry, their history kept in memory and passed on, in an oral vocabulary more complex than Europe's, and accompanied by song, dance, and ceremonial drama. They paid careful attention to the development of personality, intensity of will, independence and flexibility, passion and potency, to their partnership with one another and nature.
>
> John Collier, an American scholar who lived among Indians in the 1920s and 1930s in the American Southwest, said of their spirit: "Could we make it our own, there would be an eternally inexhaustible earth and a forever lasting peace."
>
> Perhaps there is some romantic mythology in that. But the evidence from the European travelers in the sixteenth, seventeenth, and eighteenth centuries, put together recently by an

American specialist on Indian life, William Brandon, is overwhelmingly supportive of much of that 'myth." Even allowing for that imperfection of myths, it is enough to make us question, for that time and ours, the excuse of progress in the annihilation of races, and the telling of history from the standpoint of the conquerors and leaders of Western civilization.[3]

Admitting and denouncing the sins of the past witnessed by *Spaceship Earth*, gives us the freedom to move forward and develop that more perfect Union that our next expert witness addresses.

Expert Witness: Barack Obama

Human bondage or slavery does not come dressed-up in the form of a newly created word. We leave it to then candidate for president Barack Obama to provide insight into the issue of slavery within the American experiment. An excerpt from his 2008 More Perfect Union Speech given at the Constitution Center in Philadelphia:

> "We the people, in order to form a more perfect union ..." — 221 years ago, in a hall that still stands across the street, a group of men gathered and, with these simple words, launched America's improbable experiment in democracy…
>
> The document they produced was eventually signed but ultimately unfinished. It was stained by this nation's original sin of slavery, a question that divided the colonies and brought the convention to a stalemate until the founders chose to allow the slave trade to continue for at least 20 more years, and to leave any final resolution to future generations.
>
> Of course, the answer to the slavery question was already embedded within our Constitution — a Constitution that had at its very core the ideal of equal citizenship under the law; a Constitution that promised its people liberty and justice and a union that could be and should be perfected over time.
>
> And yet words on a parchment would not be enough to

> deliver slaves from bondage, or provide men and women of every color and creed their full rights and obligations as citizens of the United States. What would be needed were Americans in successive generations who were willing to do their part — through protests and struggles, on the streets and in the courts, through a civil war and civil disobedience, and always at great risk — to narrow that gap between the promise of our ideals and the reality of their time.[4]

Expert Witness: Ruth Bader Ginsberg

Supreme Court Justice Ruth Bader Ginsberg was a champion for equality. This from her 2020 article "The Equal Rights Amendment: What You Need to Know."

Justice Ginsberg first tells us that the "sex discrimination" in the Equal Rights Amendment text is intended to be synonymous with other terms such as sex-based discrimination, gender discrimination, or gender-based discrimination, gender identity, gender expression and or sexual orientation. In other words, all these very important issues are included in the Equal Rights Amendment:

> Neither "women" nor "sex" are words that appear in the Constitution, revealing the limits of the Founding Fathers' narrow understanding of women as equal citizens. The Constitution was written by and for white men with means, which reserved its principle of equal justice under law for the sole benefit of the authors and their privileged peers. This meant that women and people of color, among others, were openly regarded as less than full citizens and thus excluded from many legal protections because of their sex, race, and/or ethnicity.
>
> Even without an explicit mention of sex in the Constitution, many of the legal protections that seek to promote women's equality—and equality across the gender spectrum—are rooted in the Constitution's equality principles and a modern under-

> standing of equality that has surpassed outdated prejudices and stereotypes…
>
> Ratifying the ERA [Equal Rights Amendment] would affirm that sex discrimination is inconsistent with the nation's core value of equal protection under the law, and it would send a clear message about a national commitment to the inherent equality of all people.[5]

Just admitting the original sins of our nation — genocide, slavery, denial of women's and LGBTQ+ rights, and sexual discrimination of all kind is a good start at democratizing our constitutional republic and achieving that more perfect union. Sunlight is a great disinfectant and the more we examine and admit our past mistakes, the better our chances are for the future.

Citizens United v. Federal Election Commission: Unlimited Dark Money in Elections v. Democracy

In 2010, the U.S. Supreme Court ruled in favor of unlimited dark money in elections in a narrow 5–4 decision: *Citizens United v. Federal Election Commission*. The Supreme Court ruled that corporations and other outside groups could spend unlimited funds on elections. Writing in the court's opinion, Justice Anthony Kennedy said that limiting "independent political spending" from corporations and other groups violates the First Amendment right to free speech. In other words, the Supreme Court proclaimed that corporations and other groups had the same First Amendment rights as people, at least with respect to free speech within our all-important electoral system.

A rational citizen who believes in our democratic experiment can only assume that the justices, from their lofty ivory tower who voted with the majority, assumed that independent spending would not be corrupt and that this independent spending would be transparent. Unfortunately, both assumptions have proven to be incorrect. The *Citizens United* ruling overturned more than a century of Supreme

Court precedent that had supported restrictions on spending so as to prevent corruption.[6]

Expert Witness: Sheila Krumholz—Executive Director OpenSecrets

> In our 35 years of following the money, we've never seen a court decision transform the campaign finance system as drastically as *Citizens United.* We have a decade of evidence, demonstrated by nearly one billion dark[a] money dollars, that the Supreme Court got it wrong when they said political spending from independent groups would be coupled with necessary disclosure.[7]

Expert Witness: Move to Amend—Move to Amend ~ Sign the Petition

Move to Amend is a citizens' initiative to overturn the Supreme Court's *Citizens United* ruling that corporations have the rights of people. In February 2024 the Move to Amend petition had more than 500,000 signatures:[8]

> We, the People of the United States of America, reject the U.S. Supreme Court's Citizens United ruling and other related cases, and move to amend our Constitution to firmly establish that money is not speech, and that human beings, not corporations, are persons entitled to constitutional rights.[9]

The Move to Amend petition, has more than 90 Democratic Congress Members sponsoring it, in addition to the 500,000 citizens that have signed the petition online.

---

[a] Dark money in politics is money that the public does not know from whence it came.

The Scheme to Capture the U.S. Supreme Court and Judiciary—Expert Witness: U.S. Senator Sheldon Whitehouse—Senior Member of the Judiciary Committee, Chairman of Subcommittee on Federal Courts, Oversight, Agency Action, and Federal Rights

In 2010, Senator Whitehouse was just trying to understand why the Senate with a Democratic majority was unable to take action on climate change legislation that had already passed the House of Representatives. It was especially perplexing, since Republican Senator John McCain had a strong climate platform in his unsuccessful 2008 presidential campaign. This Republican inaction on climate change led Senator Whitehouse to investigate why the bipartisanship had stopped and ultimately to write his 2023 book *The Scheme — How the Right Wing Used Dark Money to Capture the Supreme Court.*[10] Senator Whitehouse relates:

> Then in January 2010 all that bipartisanship stopped, as if a switch had been turned off. Climate progress died. The Sudden shift came immediately after a bare majority of Republican-appointed justices set loose unlimited political spending in the Supreme Court's disastrous Citizens United decision…
>
> This is the Scheme: a decades-long, behind-the-scenes manipulation of our political and justice systems to capture our courts – especially the Supreme Court – as a way to control the future of our democracy.[11]

Senator Whitehouse soon discovered that the scheme to capture our court system was financed by dark money. Testimony before the Senate Judiciary Subcommittee originally uncovered $400 million in dark money behind the scheme. In 2021, Lisa Graves, president of the Center for Media and Democracy provided sworn testimony that the known dark money behind the court grab scheme was $580 million.[12] Of course dark money is just that, dark and extremely hard to find. The multi-millionaires and billionaires that shovel it into our elections, judicial system and ultimately our democracy, don't want you to know anything about it.

Leonard Leo's Role in the Right-Wing Federalist Society's Capture of Our Judicial System

Oh, but it gets much worse than the $580 million of known, conservative, dark money influencing our judicial system uncovered by the Center for Media and Democracy. In 2022, the New York Times and ProPublica reported that conservative, secretive, Chicago businessman Barre Seid had given $1.6 billion in what was intended to be dark money to Leonard Leo's Marble Freedom Trust. Mr. Leo is the judicial kingmaker behind the activist, conservative Federalist Society. Leo's Marble Freedom Trust and Federalist Society[b] now have $1.6 billion in additional funds to capture and control our judicial system. [13] [14] All to be done with the end goal of putting corporations above poor and working-class people as was done in 2010 *Citizen's United*, and to further erode women's reproductive rights as was done in 2022 *Dobbs v. Jackson Women's Health Organization* when the Supreme Court ended the 49 years of precedent that women had a right to an abortion, in striking down *Roe v. Wade*.[15]

So, while a rational citizen might hope that the Justices that voted for *Citizens United* just made incorrect assumptions that independent spending would not be corrupt and would be transparent, Senator Whitehouse disagrees. He says it was intentional, with the end game of capturing the court system. From Senator Whitehouse's September 13, 2022 speech before the U.S. Senate:

---

[b] The Federalist Society is a conservative and libertarian society of lawyers who advocate limiting federal power, safeguarding individual liberty and an original interpretation of the Constitution. This also means that they believe in fewer environmental and health care regulations, allowing businesses to refuse service to customers, and denying protections to LGBTQ+ people. President Trump's three picks for the Supreme Court: Neil Gorsuch, Brett Kavanaugh and Amy Coney Barrett all came from a Federalist Society list submitted to Trump.

This is the 18th time that I have come to the floor to expose the dark money scheme that has captured and controlled our Supreme Court. Over the last 2 years, I have, over and over, exposed how dark money operatives, working from the shadows, have installed Supreme Court Justices handpicked—handpicked—by the minions of far-right donors. I have exposed the key front groups through which this Court-packing operation is driven and the tactics that the schemers have used to hide the dark money donors who pull its strings. And when you take a close look at the scheme, the little spider that you find at the center of the dark money web behind it is a character named Leonard Leo.

From his perch at the dark money-funded Federalist Society, Leo crafted a reputation as the Court-capture scheme's puppet master. The key to his craft is an armada of phony front groups that shuffle dark money back and forth, around and amongst each other, to deploy as spin, as propaganda, as political ads, or as hidden campaign funding…

Last month, ProPublica and the New York Times broke the news that a reclusive, far-right billionaire supercharged Leo's dark money operation with a $1.6 billion donation to a Leo front group. You heard that right, $1.6 billion into this dark money operation.

The man behind this new slush fund is a billionaire named Barre Seid, and even the way the donation was made was creepy and clandestine. Seid and Leo devised a plan to transfer all the shares in an electronics company to Leo's front group, on the way to selling that company. So, when that company sold for $1.6 billion, it all went straight to Leo's group and, by the way, helped Seid avoid what would have been roughly $400 million in taxes.

Seid has a long history of funding far-right front groups. Here is how ProPublica characterized what Seid calls his 'attack philanthropy:'

"Seid has funded climate denialism as well as a national

network of state-level think tanks that promote business deregulation and fight Medicaid expansion. He's also supported efforts to remake the higher education system in a conservative mold, including to turn one of the nation's most politically influential law schools into a training ground for future generations of rightwing judges and justices."[16]

Expert Witness: Nancy Northup—President & CEO Center for Reproductive Rights

> The Court's opinion delivers a wrecking ball to the constitutional right to abortion, destroying the protections of Roe v. Wade, and utterly disregarding the one in four women in America who make the decision to end a pregnancy.[17]

Tips & Gratuities Go to Servers & Bartenders, Not to Mayors & Justices

Since 2004, Supreme Court Justice Clarence Thomas has received in excess of $4.7 million in gifts involving private yacht trips, private jet travel, lavish vacations, his mother's home mortgage paid off, his nephew's private tuition paid, his luxury motorhome loan paid off etc. Justice Thomas received 193 such gifts since 2004 but has reported only 27 of these gifts on his financial disclosures and many of these were only reported after public outcry in the press. Deceased Justice Antonin Scalia from 2004–2016 received the second highest figure of $210,000 in gifts, followed by Justice Samuel Alito receiving $170,000 in gifts.[18] [19] Many of these gifts were given to the Supreme Court Justices by wealthy right-wing donors who directly benefit from Supreme Court decisions.

Snyder v. United States

June 27, 2024 the Supreme Court ruled that while bribes for public officials continue to be illegal, gratuities are not. Portage, Indiana is a city nearby to your author. In 2014 Portage Mayor James Snyder was financially strapped and personally needed money. He went to the Great Lakes Peterbilt truck company that only the year before had been awarded contracts by the city of Portage for the purchase of over $1 million in trucks and asked for some money. Peterbilt gave Snyder a check made out to him personally for $13,000. Republican Snyder was convicted of bribery and of soliciting a bribe in 2021 and sentenced to 21 months in prison, well below the recommended sentencing guideline of 46 to 57 months.[20] In 2024, the U.S. Supreme Court overturned Snyder's conviction, ruling his erstwhile bribe a gratuity.[21] How nice of the supreme justices to be so generous to the mayor.

Since we are talking about the Supreme Court, please allow me to use legal language: I object! My last job was tending bar at the Radisson Hotel in Merrillville, Indiana near Portage. The Radisson complex contained the Star Plaza Theatre and a separate Convention Center. It was, before the owner stupidly demolished it, the hub of Northwest Indiana events, meetings and business. I surely must have waited on the Peterbilt Truck Dealer owner at one time or another and I was never given a $13,000 gratuity and I probably gave him better service than the mayor did. Leave it to the current Supreme Court to get it wrong. Tips and gratuities go to those of us in the food, beverage and service industries that are waiting on you hand and foot—they don't go to mayors and Supreme Court Justices.

A Supreme Court that can't tell a mayor or a justice from a server or bartender needs help. The Court needs to be able to differentiate between a bartender and a mayor, who needs an extra 13 grand to pay his bills, or a server and a fellow justice, with his hand out looking for a jet setter vacation on a rich guy's yacht.

But with our current Supreme Court it doesn't stop with tips, gratuities, yachts, private jets and paying off a mother's mortgage. Justices Clarence Thomas and Samuel Alito have also both refused to recuse themselves from the Supreme Court cases involving the January 6 insurrection to stop the peaceful transfer of power and Donald Trump's role in it.

Ginni Thomas Wants to Release the Kraken

Ginni Thomas, wife of Supreme Court Justice Clarence Thomas, serves on the board of the right-wing Council for National Policy Action (C.N.P. Action) advocacy group that circulated an "action steps" document after the 2020 Presidential Election that called for challenging the results of the election in Georgia, Pennsylvania and Arizona that President Biden had won. C.N.P. Action told its members to "pressure" the Republican lawmakers in these states to appoint "fake" alternate slates of electors.[22]

The 2020 election was on Nov. 3. On Nov. 7 CNN, followed shortly by all other networks called Pennsylvania for Biden. This put Biden over the 270 electoral votes making him President-elect.[23] Even the right-wing Fox News joined in calling the election for Biden on Nov. 7.[24] Obviously these are not official results, yet the handwriting was on the wall as different recounts and court appeals went forward, with Trump losing more than 60 of them and winning only a minor case that had no bearing on the final result of a Biden victory.[25] In spite of this, Ginni Thomas, wife of a Supreme Court Justice, sent these texts to Trump's Chief of Staff Mark Meadows:

> (Nov. 10, 2020) "Help This Great President stand firm, Mark!!! ... You are the leader, with him, who is standing for America's constitutional governance at the precipice. The majority knows Biden and the Left is attempting the greatest Heist of our History,"

> (Nov. 19, 2020) "Sounds like Sidney and her team are getting inundated with evidence of fraud. Make a plan. Release the Kraken and save us from the left taking America down." [Sidney would seem to refer to attorney Sidney Powell, who

had referred to herself as the Kraken, an ancient mythological sea creature.]

(Nov 24, 2020) “I can’t see Americans swallowing the obvious fraud. Just going with one more thing with no frickin consequences... the whole coup and now this... we just cave to people wanting Biden to be anointed? Many of us can't continue the GOP charade.”[26] [The coup she refers to here is obviously not the January 6, 2021 coup attempt to overturn the Biden victory which is 6 weeks in the future. She is calling the normal election process in which Biden won and the peaceful transfer of power a coup.]

Flag Waving at the Alito Home & Beach House

Supreme Court Justice Samuel Alito and his wife Martha-Ann became embroiled in a flag flying scandal in 2024. Mrs. Alito said that flying the American flag upside-down at their Fairfax County, Virginia home in January 2021 after the January 6 insurrection was “an international signal of distress.”[27] Actually, Mayday! Mayday! Mayday! Is the international distress signal. But Mrs. Alito is close to being right, “The flag should never be displayed with the union down, except as a signal of dire distress in instances of extreme danger to life or property.”[28] (4 U.S. Code § 8 - Respect for flag)

I know this because comrades and friends in the anti-war movement would at times have upside-down flags at marches and vigils in which we protested the Afghanistan and Iraq Wars. Protesting what we felt were illegal and immoral wars that certainly endangered life and property of innocent people was all the justification needed to fly the flag upside-down.

Mrs. Alito’s justification was either that Trump had lost the election to Biden and that made her angry or that she didn’t want to look from her house, across the pond at another homeowner flying a Pride flag during pride month.[29] One would think that both of the Alitos would be aware that the January 6 insurrection featured many in the mob that stormed the Capitol carrying upside-down flags. They did so because the disillusioned followers of the former president have listened to the Big Lie[30] out of Mr. Trump's mouth so often that they actually believe that the 2020 Election was stolen from him. And that flying the flag upside-down would be interpreted as solidarity with Mr. Trump's claim that he won and should be the rightful President. It would be helpful if Mr. and Mrs. Alito would explain to us whether or not they believe in Mr. Trump's Big Lie, since their actions clearly indicate that they do believe it.

In addition to the upside-down flag at their primary residence, we also find out that the Alitos also flew an "Appeal to Heaven" flag at their New Jersey beach home in 2023. This flag has been adopted by Christian nationalists.[31] Many Christian nationalists were involved in the January 6th insurrection and carried the Appeal to Heaven flag as they stormed the Capitol.[32]

Failure to Recuse

These are hardly the neutral positions the people should expect from two Supreme Court Justices who sit in judgement on cases concerning Mr. Trump and the January 6th insurrection. 28 U.S. Code § 455 - Disqualification of justice, judge, or magistrate judge states: "Any justice, judge, or magistrate judge of the United States shall disqualify himself in any proceeding in which his impartiality might reasonably be questioned."[33]

It really doesn't matter if both Justices are capable of divorcing themselves from these entanglements when they make their decisions. If their impartiality can be reasonably questioned, they have a duty to recuse themselves from these cases in which they have much more than just the appearance of impropriety. But the two Justices refuse to recuse.

The Constitution states, "The Judges, both of the supreme and inferior Courts, shall hold their Offices during good Behavior…" (Article III, Section 1.) Justice Thomas has raked in $4.7 million in gifts and gratuities and Justice Alito $170,000. Much of this has been unreported on their financial disclosure forms or reported only after it has come out later in the press and the justices then go back and change their already submitted disclosure forms.

In 2008, conservative billionaire Paul Singer flew Justice Alito to Alaska for a luxury fishing trip hosted by another rightwing businessman, Leonard Leo, was also on the trip. Alito described the fishing lodge as, "comfortable but rustic" that served "homestyle fare." A fishing guide used a grander description of "chefs [that] served multi-course meals of Alaskan king crab legs or Kobe filet [imported Japanese steak]. On the last evening, a member of Alito's group bragged that the wine they were drinking cost $1,000 a bottle."[34] If Justice Alito would have chartered a private jet flight back and forth from Alaska, ProPublica estimates the cost for just the plane trip would have exceeded $100,000. In the years following this "rustic" vacation, billionaire buddy Paul Singer's hedge fund appeared before the Supreme Court at least ten times. In 2014 the Supreme Court resolved a key issue in a long-standing battle between Singer's hedge fund and Argentina that resulted in Singer's hedge fund being paid $2.4 billion. Alito did not recuse himself or disclose that he had received the luxury fishing vacation trip from Singer, six years before he voted to give Singer's hedge fund the $2.4 billion.[35]

Supreme Court Grants Trump Broad Immunity for Official Acts, Placing Presidents Above the Law

On July 1, 2024 the Supreme Court ruled 6-3 along ideological party lines granting Trump, more than 3½ years after the alleged crimes had been committed, two newly created categories of immunity that are not recognized in the Constitution: *absolute immunity* for core official acts and *presumptive immunity* for unofficial acts. While failing to tell us exactly which of his actions are core official acts and which are unofficial acts, they did classify that the act of instructing officials at the Justice Department to obstruct the results of the election was a core official act with the benefit of absolute immunity.[36]

"Under our constitutional structure of separated powers, the nature of Presidential power entitles a former President to absolute immunity from criminal prosecution for actions within his conclusive and preclusive constitutional authority. And he is entitled to at least presumptive immunity from prosecution for all his official acts." (Trump v. United States)

These acts for which the Supreme Court has deemed Trump immune from prosecution, also cannot be used as evidence in providing motive for other crimes in which he is being investigated.

Expert Witness: Justice Sonia Sotomayor

Donald J. Trump v United States
From Justice Sotomayor's Dissent:

Today's decision to grant former Presidents' criminal immunity reshapes the institution of the Presidency. It makes a mockery of the principle, foundational to our Constitution and system of Government, that no man is above the law. Relying on little more than its own misguided wisdom about the need for "bold and unhesitating action" by the President, the Court gives former President Trump all the immunity he asked for and more. Because our Constitution does not shield a former President from answering for criminal and treasonous acts, I dissent…

The President of the United States is the most powerful person in the country, and possibly the world. When he uses his official powers in any way, under the majority's reasoning, he now will be insulated from criminal prosecution. Orders the Navy's Seal Team 6 to assassinate a political rival? Immune. Organizes a military dissenting coup to hold onto power? Immune. Takes a bribe in exchange for a pardon? Immune. Immune, immune, immune….

In every use of official power, the President is now a king above the law… With fear for our democracy, I dissent.[37]

Expert Witness: President Joe Biden

"There are no kings in America. Each of us is equal before the law. No one, no one is above the law, not even the president of the United States," Biden said in a speech from the White House.

"(With) today's Supreme Court decision on presidential immunity, that fundamentally changed. For all practical purposes, there are virtually no limits on what the president can do. It's a fundamentally new principle and it's a dangerous precedent because the power of the office will no longer be constrained by the law even including the supreme court of the United States."[38]

PACs and Super PACs

PACs (Political Action Committees) had been limited to $5,000 contribution per candidate, but that went out the window after the 2010 *Citizens United* decision. Just two months later, a federal appeals court used the logic from *Citizens United* in *Speechnow.org v. FEC* to rule that outside groups could accept unlimited contributions from both individual donors and corporations, as long as they didn't give directly to candidates.[39]

The direct result of these two rulings has been the creation of super PACs which allow multi-millionaires and billionaires to use shadowy nonprofit organizations that can hide their names, as they inject huge sums into our election process. They can't give the money directly to the candidate, but they can give it to PACs and Super PACs, so as to fund the endless negative TV commercials, online advertising and mailings attacking their pet candidate's opponent. It is actually more effective for the super PACs to do the dirty negative campaigning apart from the campaign of their favorite candidate. It allows both the candidate supported and the wealthy donors to keep their hands somewhat clean from the mud they are slinging.

For years Senator Sheldon Whitehouse (D-R.I.) has put legislation into the U.S. Senate called the DISCLOSE Act that would require dark money groups to disclose the names of all donors who contribute more than $10,000.[40] President Joe Biden is on record saying that he supports and would sign the DISCLOSE Act.[41] The political reality is that the ridiculous Senate filibuster rule, requiring 60 votes to move legislation forward, enables Republicans to keep this legislation from even getting a hearing. In addition, the Republican majority in the 2024 House of Representatives torpedoes any Democratic legislation, especially legislation that might shine a little sunlight on dark money or the Supreme Court.

The single largest example of known dark money giving was the above mentioned 2022 gift of $1.6 billion from electronics manufacturing mogul Barre Seid to conservative activist Leonard Leo's Marble Freedom Trust. Mr. Leo is the same gentleman who is behind the conservative Federalist Society that has supported ultra-conservative appointments to our federal court system. All three of former President Trump's Supreme Court Appointments were first vetted by the Federalist Society. The only reason we know of this massive dark money political donation from Mr. Seid is because an insider tipped off a New York Times reporter.[42]

While it is easy to use this issue to beat up on the Republicans, the nonprofit Open Secrets organization reported that of the known $1 billion in dark money spending in the 2020 presidential election, more went to the Democratic Party than to the Republican Party.[43] This even though it has only been the Democratic Party that has made attempts at campaign finance and ethics reform.

In 2019, the Democratic majority in the House of Representatives made campaign finance reform the first bill they introduced into the new Congress. The House then passed the For the People Act,[44] "which proposed a ban on contributions from companies with significant foreign investments, a disclosure requirement for dark money groups and a six-to-one matching system for small dollar donations to federal elections."[45] It then went to the Senate, where the Republican majority was able to keep it from seeing the light of day. It needed 60 votes to advance under the Senate filibuster rule but received only the 50 Democratic Senators votes, with all 50 Republicans voting to shelve it.[46]

And these are but tepid reforms in relation to what we propose here —an end to all private spending on our elections and judiciary. Is democracy possible if millionaires and billionaires are allowed to spend unlimited amounts of money to influence our elections, officials, and justices who then turn presidents into kings?

Increasing Equality with the Ultra-Millionaire Tax Act of 2024

Switching to a system of publicly created money is certainly why the three books of the *People, Planet & Power of Money Project* exist and doing so will make our society more equal. But with the massive level of inequality that currently exists, the ultra-wealthy will continue to have too much wealth for their own good.

Senator Elizabeth Warren (D-MA), U.S. Representatives Pramila Jayapal (D-WA) and Brendan Boyle (D-PA) have reintroduced the Ultra-Millionaire Tax Act that would bring in an estimated $3 trillion revenue over a 10-year period by requiring the American super-rich to annually chip in 2 cents for every dollar of wealth that they have over $50 million.[47] For those of you reading who might be feeling a twinge of angst over our wealthy having to pay two cents on the dollar, they can never go broke with this program. They pay no extra tax on their first $50 million in wealth, so the closest they can get to broke with the Ultra-Millionaire Tax Act would be $50 million in wealth tax-free. We can all rest assured that these ultra-millionaires won't have to make any trips to a food pantry or a homeless shelter.

I am sure that Amazon founder Jeff Bezos with a net worth of $203 billion might have to pay what seems like a lot of money to us, 2% of $203 billion equals $4.06 billion, but he will still have almost $199 billion left to get by on. But actually, it seems like Mr. Bezos won't have to pay anything near $4 billion with the tax, since the wealth tax is only estimated to take in $300 million a year for ten years. Although the newly introduced version of the bill includes stronger rules on trusts through which the rich avoid taxes, Bezos and his rich buddies will probably still be able to keep from paying their fair share with the proposed law, but just maybe we can get them to pay something.

President Biden made this an important plank in his proposed tax policy:

> "A firefighter and a teacher shouldn't pay a higher tax rate than a billionaire pays. That's not right. My budget contains a Billionaire Minimum Income Tax to make sure billionaires pay their fair share."[48]

Taking Money Out of Politics: Locally and Nationally

The exponential growth of the amount of money to run a political campaign is truly breathtaking. My wife and I live in Indiana's 1st Congressional District. In the 2022 campaign for Indian's 1st, incumbent Democrat Frank Mrvan was up for reelection after his first term in Congress. His opponent was Republican Jennifer-Ruth Green. Mrvan won the 2022 Election 52.8% to Ms. Green 47.2%, in a seat that has been Democratic for 92 years.[49]

OpenSecrets listed the official campaign spending: Mrvan $2.5 million and Green $3.4 million.[50] In addition to both campaigns together officially spending almost $6 million for one Congressional seat, another $14.6 million in dark money was spent by outside groups and SuperPACs.[51] Of the dark money that OpenSecrets listed, $9.2 million was spent to support Ms. Green's bid to unseat a popular Democratic incumbent and 'only' $5.4 million was spent to return Congressman Mrvan to office.[52] Mrvan won despite being outspent by Green, $12.6 million to $7.9 million.

Of the $9.2 million in dark money that was lavished on Ms. Green's campaign, $7.4 million came from the Congressional Leadership Fund.[53] The Congressional Leadership Fund calls itself,

"The super PAC dedicated to electing Republicans to the House of Representatives."[54] For the 2022 Election the Congressional Leadership Fund listed spending more than $226 million on the 2022 Election: 90% against Democrats, 9% for Republicans, 1% against Republicans [one would assume this 1% spending against Republicans would have been in primary elections], and 0% for Democrats.[55] In Indiana's 1st District race, the Congressional Leadership Fund spent $6.3 million in negative advertising against Mrvan and $1 million in ads supporting Green.[56] I can personally attest to the negative advertising, as our home received at least one graphic oversized postcard almost every day for months, offering all sorts of gross perversions of the truth about Congressman Mrvan.

Full disclosure: I have met Congressman Mrvan, have contributed to his campaign and support him as my Representative in Congress. We had his yard sign in our front yard, and I marched with him and other supporters in the Highland, Indiana Fourth of July Parade. There were also negative ads against Ms. Green in this campaign that I researched on my own at the time. I believe these negative ads against Ms. Green were much more grounded in reality than the negative ads against Mrvan. That said, I believe that almost all citizens would be much happier with an end to the mudslinging and negative advertising on all sides. Taking all non-public money out of political campaigns would certainly help in doing that.

Let us contrast this with the 2018 Election in the same Indiana 1st Congressional District. Incumbent Democrat Pete Visclosky defeated Republican Mark Leyva. Congressman Visclosky served 36 years in Congress, and this was his last campaign. Visclosky spent just a tad over $1 million in official campaign spending. OpenSecrets had no data on how much challenger Leyva spent.[57] Visclosky won with 65% of the vote. Oh, and the dark money spent on the campaign. The Super PAC National Education Association Advocacy supported Visclosky with $67 and the Sierra Club with $10.[58] Not a misprint, a total of $77 in PAC money that was hardly dark. There are no figures for Mr. Leyva from dark money sources, as there were none for his official campaign spending. All figures provided by OpenSecrets.

So, in just 4 years, my Congressional District Election went from spending just over $1 million in official money and $77 in dark money that wasn't even dark in 2018, to spending almost $6 million in official money and $14.6 million in dark money. From $1 million to $20 million in four years! In all probability, the vast majority of the $14.6 billion in dark money and very well much, if not most of the official money in these campaigns has also come from outside our Congressional District. There has to be a better way for citizens to finance the campaigns in which we choose the individuals in charge of making some of the most momentous decisions that influence our lives and the very future of our planet.

Money is absolutely necessary for modern society to function. Yet if we are to have a democracy, we need to keep money out of our elections and political decisions. The only way to do that is pass legislation to have 100% public funding of election campaigns at the federal, state and local level. Endless TV commercials, postcards, online advertising, and illegitimate disinformation campaigns are very effective at confusing us and making us think that all politics and politicians are bad. Don't for a minute think I am advocating that our government take over the outlandish spending taking place today on politics and influence. Seemingly unlimited TV commercials telling us how terrible one candidate or the other is, that usually twist and elevate some minor statement or act by one's opponent into the image of that person being evil incarnate, are counterproductive to citizens making informed voting decisions. As were the daily postcards we received for months slandering Congressman Mrvan.

Should Billionaires Be Able to Buy Our Democracy?

Using a presidential campaign as an example: in 2024 we are presently in the billion-dollar plus range for what each official presidential campaign will be spending. Remember, that figure is just for the official campaign spending, exclusive of all the dark money that will also be spent by super PACs and others. OpenSecrets predicts a record $15.9 billion will be spent in the 2024 federal elections.[59] This figure includes both campaign and dark unofficial money and it includes the House and Senate races, in addition to the presidency. None of it should be allowed.

Tech billionaire Elon Musk, currently the world's wealthiest individual, gave almost $75 million to a pro-Trump super PAC. Miriam Adelson, heir to a casino fortune, put even more, $95 million into another super PAC backing Trump.[60] Shipping supplies magnate Dick Uihlein, added another $49 million to a pro-Trump super PAC.[61] Three people have invested $219 million in our election and that is only the money that we know about 3 weeks before the election. As business people, what do they expect as a return on investment? Is this any way to run a rodeo or a democracy?

Democratizing Our Democracy

What we desperately need in a democracy is for all citizens to be informed about the choices we have before us. Taking money out of the equation on how we are informed gives us the best chance to make the right decisions about our future.

Instead of letting billionaires buy our democracy, every news media outlet should be required to post side by side comparisons of the candidates as written by each respective campaign. For example, the TV news stations should be required to run periodic side by side short video clips of each candidate explaining his position on different issues. The print media would be required to do a similar side by side comparison of each candidate explaining her take on the different issues facing our country. The same for online news sites. The federal government would pay each news site a fee for providing this service. Political commercials would not be allowed, instead we would be able to access periodic side-by-side comparisons of each candidate's positions on key issues. Of course, the news media would certainly be able to and encouraged to, fact check all claims made by the candidates. Each candidate would also be provided the same amount of federal money to cover a small campaign staff and in person campaign events, etc. No other money could be used in the campaign. No matter how rich someone is, they could not use any of their money in a political campaign. All campaigns for the U.S. Congress and Senate would be funded in this manner. State and local election campaigns would also similarly be exclusively publicly funded at the state and local level.

Put the League of Women Voters Back in Charge of Presidential Debates

The League of Women Voters should be invited to run the presidential campaign debates, like they used to do prior to 1988 when the debates were taken over by the Democratic and Republican Parties using the Commission on Presidential Debates. The League was asked to continue to participate but declined when the Republican and Democratic national parties together agreed to move sponsorship of the debates to the two parties. The League of Women Voters stated:

> Between 1985 and 1987 the League challenged this move and sparked widespread public debate on the matter. The LWVEF argued that a change in sponsorship that put control of the debate format in the hands of the two dominant parties would deprive voters of one of the only chances they have to see the candidates outside of their controlled campaign environment.[62]

League of Women Voters United States President Nancy Neuman said it all in the League's statement to the press: The League of Women Voters had "no intention of becoming an accessory to the hoodwinking of the American public."[63]

That would be it. We would be informed of where each candidate stood on issues, with minimal influence from corporations and the wealthy. And it would then be up to an informed citizenry to vote.

Gerrymandering in Indiana and Wisconsin

Gerrymandering is the practice of drawing electoral districts in a way that unfairly favors one political party, usually by diluting the voting power of minority ethnic or linguistic groups. The name is derived from Massachusetts Governor Elbridge Gerry of Massachusetts, whose administration in 1812 redrew state senatorial districts to benefit his Democratic-Republican Party at the expense of the Federalist Party. The outline of one of these districts resembled a salamander. Someone combined Gerry's name to salamander and we are left with the undemocratic political process of gerrymandering.

My state Indiana has 9 Congressional Districts. In 2020 Trump got 57% of the vote and Biden 41%. In the Congressional election, the vote went 38.6% to the Democrats and 59.7% to the Republicans.[64] An even distribution of these votes would give us 3.5 Democrats and 5.4 Republicans in Congress. Well, we can't cut them into pieces, so we should have ended up with either 3 or 4 Democrats and 5 or 6 Republicans. Instead, we have 2 Democrats and 7 Republicans representing Indiana in the U.S. Congress.

But it gets worse in the state government. In 2024 the Indiana House of Representatives has 30 Democrats and 70 Republicans. This after Indiana voted Republican in 2020 in the Presidential election 57% to 41% and voted Republican 59.4% to 39.9% in the 2022 statehouse races.[65] This should have resulted in roughly 60 Republicans and 40 Democrats. Instead, we got a veto-proof supermajority of 70 Republicans and 30 Democrats.

Wisconsin is another example of extreme gerrymandering. Although generally close, the Democrats have won 8 of the last 9 presidential elections. Despite this historic electoral preference for Democratic presidential candidates, the Wisconsin Republican Party has figured out a way to maintain control of the state government. In the 2022 election for the State Assembly the Republicans received 53.6% of the statewide votes to the Democrats 44.6%, yet that 53.6% of the statewide vote resulted in 64 Republican State Assembly seats to the Democrats paltry 35 seats.[66] Giving the Republicans 64.6% of the State Assembly seats with only 53.6% of the vote.

Well, one might think that is severe gerrymandering, giving the Republicans an 11% bump in assembly seats over their percentage of the votes. Let's now take a look at the results of the state assembly elections just four years earlier in 2018, when the Democrats got the most votes. This time Democrats with 53% of the vote only got 36.6%/36 seats in the Assembly and the Republicans with only 44.8% of the vote were rewarded with 63.6%/63 seats in the Assembly.[67] Republicans got 18.8% more State Assembly seats than Republican votes. The Democrats won the election by 8%, yet got only 36 seats to the Republicans 63 seats. These are signs of severe gerrymandering!

Unfortunately, gerrymandering is not limited to Indiana and Wisconsin. It has been done across the country to benefit both sides, although the Republicans have proven themselves much more adapt at implementing it.

If only *Spaceship Earth* could save us from ourselves. But it doesn't work that way. She is merely a witness to our human frailty. We have to fix our democracy problem ourselves.

---

1. Holocaust Encyclopedia, "Coining a Word and Championing a Cause: The Story of Raphael Lemkin," United States Holocaust Memorial Museum, https://encyclopedia.ushmm.org/content/en/article/coining-a-word-and-championing-a-cause-the-story-of-raphael-lemkin
2. Zinn, Howard, *A People's History of the United States*, HarperCollins, New York, 2005, back cover.
3. Zinn, Howard, *A People's History of the United States*, pp. 21-22.
4. Obama, Barack, "Transcript: Barack Obama's Speech on Race," National Public Radio, WBEZ Chicago, March 18, 2008, https://www.npr.org/templates/story/story.php?storyId=88478467
5. Ginsberg, Ruth Bader, "The Equal Rights Amendment: What You Need to Know," Center for American Progress, Jan 29, 2020, https://www.americanprogress.org/article/equal-rights-amendment-need-know/
6. Lau, Tim, "Citizens United Explained," Brennan Center for Justice, Dec 12, 2019, https://www.brennancenter.org/our-work/research-reports/citizens-united-explained?ref=foreverwars.ghost.io
7. Evers-Hillstrom, Karl, "More money, less transparency: A decade under Citizens United," Open Secrets, Jan 14, 2020, https://www.opensecrets.org/news/reports/a-decade-under-citizens-united?category=Foreign+Influence
8. Move to Amend: End Corporate Rule. Legalize Democracy. 516,646 signatures, https://www.movetoamend.org/motion
9. Move to Amend: End Corporate Rule. Legalize Democracy. https://www.movetoamend.org/
10. Whitehouse, Sheldon with Mueller, Jennifer, *The Scheme – How the Right Wing Used Dark Money to Capture the Supreme Court*," The New Press, New York, 2022, Preface 2023.

11. Whitehouse, Sheldon with Mueller, Jennifer, *The Scheme – How the Right Wing Used Dark Money to Capture the Supreme Court*," The New Press, New York, 2022, Preface 2023, p.3.
12. "What's Wrong with the Supreme Court: The Big-Money Assault on Our Judiciary," Hearing Before the United States Senate Committee on the Judiciary Subcommittee on Federal Courts, Oversight, Agency Action and Federal Rights, 117th Congress 6 (2021) (testimony of Lisa Graves, president of the Center for Media and Democracy).
13. Vogel, Kenneth P. & Goldmacher, Shane, "An Unusual $1.6 Billion Donation Bolsters Conservatives," New York Times, Aug 22, 2022, https://www.nytimes.com/2022/08/22/us/politics/republican-dark-money.html
14. Perez, Andrew (The Lever) and Kroll, Andy & Elliott, Justin (ProPublica), ProPublica, Aug 22, 2022, https://www.propublica.org/article/dark-money-leonard-leo-barre-seid
15. Center for Reproductive Rights, "*Dobbs v. Jackson Women's Health Organization*," https://reproductiverights.org/case/scotus-mississippi-abortion-ban/
16. Whitehouse, Sheldon, "Scheme 18: Leonard Leo's $1.6 Billion Payday," Speeches, Sept 13, 2022, https://www.whitehouse.senate.gov/news/speeches/scheme-18_leonard-leos-16-billion-payday/
17. Center for Reproductive Rights, *"Dobbs v. Jackson Women's Health Organization,"* https://reproductiverights.org/case/scotus-mississippi-abortion-ban/
18. Irwin, Lauren, "Thomas has accepted $4M in gifts during career: Watchdog," The Hill, June 6, 2024, https://thehill.com/regulation/court-battles/4708390-thomas-has-accepted-4m-in-gifts-during-career-watchdog/
19. Fix the Court, "A Staggering Tally: Supreme Court Justices Accepted Hundreds of Gifts Worth Millions of Dollars," June 6, 2024, https://fixthecourt.com/2024/06/a-staggering-tally-supreme-court-justices-accepted-hundreds-of-gifts-worth-millions-of-dollars/
20. Kasadra, Bob, "U.S. Supreme Court agrees to hear former Portage Mayor Synder's bribery appeal," The Times, Dec 13, 2023, https://www.nwitimes.com/news/local/crime-courts/u-s-supreme-court-agrees-to-hear-former-portage-mayor-snyders-bribery-appeal/article_3780c2f4-99de-11ee-988e-07eaa8db9280.html
21. Lavalley, Amy & Kukulka, Alexandra, "What's next after the Supreme Court overturned James Snyder's bribery conviction," Post-Tribune, June 27, 2024, https://www.chicagotribune.com/2024/06/27/whats-next-after-the-supreme-court-over turned-james-snyders-bribery-conviction/
22. Durkee, Alison, "Justice Clarence Thomas's Wife Ginni Behind Group That Reportedly Pushed January 6 'Fake Electors' Scheme," Forbes, March 14, 2022, https://www.forbes.com/sites/alisondurkee/2022/02/22/justice-clarence-thomas-wife-ginni-behind-group-that-reportedly-pushed-january-6-fake-electors-scheme/
23. Collinson, Stephen & Reston, Maeve, "Biden defeats Trump in an election he made about character of the nation and the President," CNN, Nov 7, 2020, https://www.cnn.com/2020/11/07/politics/joe-biden-wins-us-presidential-election/index.html
24. Steinhauser, Paul & Singman, Brooke, "Biden wins presidency, Trump denied second term in White House, Fox News projects," Nov 7, 2020, https://www.foxnews.com/politics/biden-wins-presidency-trump-fox-news-projects
25. Danforth, John; Ginsberg, Ben; Griffith, Thomas B; Hoppe, David; Luttig, J. Michael; McConnell, Michael W; Olson, Theodore B; Smith, Gordon H, "LOST,

NOT STOLEN: The Conservative Case that Trump lost and Biden won the 2020 Presidential Election," July 2022, https://drive.google.com/file/d/1aqorZ61AYFqZU-EDQBBzjqfvAoC5nKcB/

26. Nobles, Ryan; Grayer, Annie; Cohen, Zachary: Gangel, Jamie, "Read the texts sent by Ginni Thomas to WH official urging overturn of 2020 election," CNN, KCRA 3, Sacramento, CA, March 24, 2022, https://www.kcra.com/article/texts-between-ginni-thomas-and-mark-meadows/39531243
27. Shelton, Shania, "Washington Post: Justice Samuel Alito's wife said upside-down American flag was an 'international signal of distress' in 2021," CNN, May 25, 2024, https://www.cnn.com/2024/05/25/politics/samuel-alito-wife-upside-down-flag/index.html#:~:text=Alito%20said%20the%20upside%2Ddown,attacking%20his%20wife%2C%20Alito%20said.
28. Cornell Law School, "4 U.S. Code § 8 - Respect for flag," https://www.law.cornell.edu/uscode/text/4/8#:~:text=The%20flag%20should%20never%20be%20carried%20flat%20or%20horizontally%2C%20but,always%20allowed%20to%20fall%20free.
29. Suebsaeng, Asawin & Perez, Andrew, "Martha-Ann Alito Condemns Pride Flags, the Left, and the Media," Rolling Stone, June 10, 2024, https://www.rollingstone.com/politics/politics-features/supreme-court-martha-ann-alito-pride-flags-left-media-1235037338/
30. Danforth, John; Ginsberg, Ben; Griffith, Thomas B; Hoppe, David; Luttig, J. Michael; McConnell, Michael W; Olson, Theodore B; Smith, Gordon H, "LOST, NOT STOLEN: The Conservative Case that Trump lost and Biden won the 2020 Presidential Election," July 2022, https://drive.google.com/file/d/1aqorZ61AYFqZU-EDQBBzjqfvAoC5nKcB/
31. Barron-Lopez, Laura & Popat, Shrai, "Flag associated with Christian nationalism flown at Alito's beach house, report says," PBS News Hour, May 23, 2024, https://www.pbs.org/newshour/show/flag-associated-with-christian-nationalism-flown-at-alitos-beach-house-report-says
32. Fields, Gary; Mascaro, Lisa; & Amiri, Farnoush, "The 'Appeal to Heaven' flag evolves from Revolutionary War symbol to banner of the far right," AP, May 23, 2024, https://apnews.com/article/alito-supreme-court-flags-history-symbol-protest-a5415aeba90e21a86a50f8489fc54b7a#:~:text=The%20%E2%80%9CAppeal%20to%20Heaven%E2%80%9D%20flag%20was%20among%20several%20banners%20carried,Bradley%20Onishi%2C%20author%20of%20%E2%80%9CPreparing
33. Cornell Law School, "28 U.S. Code § 455 - Disqualification of justice, judge, or magistrate judge," Legal Information Institute, https://www.law.cornell.edu/uscode/text/28/455
34. Pengelly, Martin, "Samuel Alito did not declare gifts from billionaire with case before US supreme court," Guardian, June 21, 2023, https://www.theguardian.com/law/2023/jun/21/samuel-alito-undisclosed-gifts-billionaire-paul-singer-supreme-court
35. Elliott, Justin; Kaplan, Joshua; & Mierjeski, Alex, "Justice Samuel Alito Took Luxury Fishing Vacation With GOP Billionaire Who Later Had Cases Before the Court," ProPublica, June 23, 2023, https://www.propublica.org/article/samuel-alito-luxury-fishing-trip-paul-singer-scotus-supreme-court

36. Sotomayor, J., dissenting, "Donald J. Trump, Petitioner v. United States," Supreme Court of the United States, July 1, 2024, p. 3 Sotomayor's dissent, chrome-extension://efaidnbmnnnibpcajpcglclefindmkaj/https://www.supremecourt.gov/opinions/23pdf/23-939_e2pg.pdf
37. *Ibid.*
38. Klein, Betsy; Williams, Michael; Forrest, Jack; & Lee, MJ, "Biden issues a warning about the power of the presidency – and Trump – after Supreme Court's immunity ruling," CNN, July 1, 2024, https://www.cnn.com/2024/07/01/politics/joe-biden-immunity-supreme-court/index.html
39. Federal Election Commission, "Speechnow.org v. FEC," March 26, 2010, https://www.fec.gov/legal-resources/court-cases/speechnoworg-v-fec/#:~:text=Documents-,Summary,them%2C%20violate%20the%20First%20Amendment.
40. Newell, Keith, "With Deadlocked Vote on Dark Money, DISCLOSE Act fails to clear in the Senate," Open Secrets, Sept 22, 2022, https://www.opensecrets.org/news/2022/09/with-deadlocked-vote-on-dark-money-disclose-act-fails-to-clear-senate/
41. Chatelain, Ryan, "Biden makes push to rid elections of 'dark money,'" Spectrum News NY1, Sept 20, 2022, https://ny1.com/nyc/all-boroughs/politics/2022/09/20/biden-makes-push-to-rid-elections-of--dark-money-
42. Chatelain, Ryan, "Biden makes push to rid elections of 'dark money,'" Spectrum News NY1, Sept 20, 2022,
43. Massoglia, Anna & Evers-Hillstrom, Karl, "Dark money topped $1 billion in 2020, largely boosting Democrats," Open Secrets, Mar 17, 2021, https://www.opensecrets.org/news/2021/03/one-billion-dark-money-2020-electioncycle
44. "H.R.1-For the People Act of 2019," 116th Congress (2019-2020), https://www.congress.gov/bill/116th-congress/house-bill/1/text
45. Champlin, Reid, "Where the 2020 Democrats stand on campaign finance reform," June 27, 2019, https://www.opensecrets.org/news/2019/06/2020-democrats-stands-on-campaign-finance/
46. Sprunt, Barbara, "Senate Republicans Block Democrats' Sweeping Voting Rights Legislation," NPR, WBEZ Chicago, June 22, 2021, https://www.npr.org/2021/06/22/1008737806/democrats-sweeping-voting-rights-legislation-is-headed-for-failure-in-the-senate
47. Warren, Elizabeth, "Warren, Jayapal, Boyle Reintroduce Ultra-Millionaire Tax on Fortunes Over $50 million," March 19, 2024, https://www.warren.senate.gov/newsroom/press-releases/warren-jayapal-boyle-reintroduce-ultra-millionaire-tax-on-fortunes-over-50-million
48. Center for American Progress Action, "You Probably Pay a Higher Tax Rate Than Jeff Bezos," April 6, 2022, https://www.americanprogressaction.org/article/you-probably-pay-a-higher-tax-rate-than-jeff-bezos/
49. Kang, Hanna & Cucci, Dorothy, "Results: Democratic Rep. Frank Mrvan defeats Republican Jennifer-Ruth Green in Indiana's 1st Congressional District election," Business Insider, Nov 9, 2022, tps://www.businessinsider.com/results-frank-mrvan-jennifer-ruth-green-indiana-1st-district-election-2022-11
50. OpenSecrets, "Indiana District 01 2022 Race," Total Raised and Spent, Open Secrets, "Indiana District 01 2018 Race," Pete Visclosky (D) Winner, https://www.opensecrets.org/races/candidates?cycle=2018&id=IN01&spec=N

51. OpenSecrets, "Indiana District 01 2022 Race," Outside Spending, https://www.opensecrets.org/races/outside-spending?cycle=2022&id=IN01&spec=N
52. *Ibid.*
53. *Ibid.*
54. Congressional Leadership Fund, https://congressionalleadershipfund.org/
55. *Ibid.*
56. *Ibid.*
57. OpenSecrets, "Indiana District 01 2018 Race," Pete Visclosky (D) Winner, https://www.opensecrets.org/races/candidates?cycle=2018&id=IN01&spec=N
58. *Ibid.*
59. Bryner, Sarah & Glavin, Brendan, "Total 2024 election spending projected to exceed previous record," OpenSecrets, Oct 8, 2024, https://www.opensecrets.org/news/2024/10/total-2024-election-spending-projected-to-exceed-previous-record/
60. Wright, David; Schouten, Fredreka; Holt, Matt & Matthews, Alex Leeds, "Elon Musk and other billionaires invest staggering sums into electing Trump, plus other takeaways from third-quarter filings," CNN Politics, Oct 16, 2024, https://www.cnn.com/2024/10/16/politics/fundraising-takeaways-elon-musk-billionaires-trump/index.html
61. Ray, Siladitya, "Billionaire Dick Uihlein Poured Nearly $49 Million into Pro-Trump PAC, Filings Show, Forbes, Oct 16, 2024, https://www.forbes.com/sites/siladityaray/2024/10/16/billionaire-dick-uihlein-poured-nearly-49-million-into-pro-trump-pac-filings-show/
62. "The League of Women Voters and Candidate Debates: A Changing Relationship," League of Women Voters, https://www.lwv.org/league-women-voters-and-candidate-debates-changing-relationship
63. *Ibid.*
64. "2020 Indiana House of Representatives election," https://en.wikipedia.org/wiki/2020_Indiana_House_of_Representatives_election
65. "2022 United States House of Representatives elections," Wikipedia, https://en.wikipedia.org/wiki/2022_United_States_House_of_Representatives_elections_in_Indiana
66. "2022 Wisconsin State Assembly election," Wikipedia, https://en.wikipedia.org/wiki/2022_Wisconsin_State_Assembly_election
67. "2018 Wisconsin State Assembly election," Wikipedia, https://en.wikipedia.org/wiki/2018_Wisconsin_State_Assembly_election

ELEVEN

Democratizing Our Constitutional Republic

As *Spaceship Earth* continues its journey, we continue our discussion on improving U.S. democracy, currently under attack from within and abroad. In addition, we examine power, specifically the Money Power (the power to create our nation's money), all done with the goal of creating a More Perfect Union.

Expert Witness: Merriam-Webster Online Dictionary:

Is the United States a *democracy* or a *republic*?

One of the most commonly encountered questions about the word democracy has nothing to do with its spelling or pronunciation and isn't even directly related to the meaning of the word itself. That question is "is the United States a democracy or a republic?" The answer to this, as with so many other questions about meaning, may be phrased as some form of "it depends."

Some people assert that a country calling itself a *democracy* must be engaged in direct (or pure) democracy, in which the people of a state or region vote directly for policies, rather

> than elect representatives who make choices on their behalf. People who follow this line of reasoning hold that the United States is more properly described as a *republic*, using the following definition of that word: "a government in which supreme power resides in a body of citizens entitled to vote and is exercised by elected officers and representatives responsible to them and governing according to law."
>
> However, both *democracy* and *republic* have more than a single meaning, and one of the definitions we provide for *democracy* closely resembles the definition of *republic* given above: "a government in which the supreme power is vested in the people and exercised by them directly or indirectly through a system of representation usually involving periodically held free elections."
>
> So, if someone asks you if the United States is a democracy or a republic, you may safely answer the question with either "both" or "it depends."[1]

In other words, all democracies have representation at some level. Ancient Athens is considered the birthplace of democracy. Yet, even in this early Athenian democracy there was representation for their ruling council called the boulē. It was made up of 500 citizens chosen by lot to serve one-year terms, with no citizen to serve more than two one-year terms.[2]

Questions to ponder as we consider the state of U.S. democracy: Is the United States a participatory democracy in which the people are actively involved in governance? Are our elected representatives responsive to the will of the majority of the people? Or are they responsive to the huge amounts of dark money shoveled into the electoral process, that has become necessary to get them elected into office in the first place?

Monopoly Is Not a Game to Be Played in Politics

One of the major critiques of U.S. democracy is the absolute electoral monopoly that the Democratic and Republican parties enjoy. It was certainly not given to them in the U.S. Constitution, as political parties were specifically omitted from it because our Founders were concerned that parties or factions would rip our new country apart as they did in England in the 17th Century.[3] Despite this original fear of political parties and their omission in the Constitution, we soon enough ended up with a two-party system of government, that by its very nature gives the two parties monopoly status.

After more than two centuries of basically two-party rule, state laws make getting on the ballot very difficult for candidates not belonging to the two monopoly parties. In my state of Indiana, to get a spot on the presidential primary ballot for either of our two monopoly political parties you need 4,500 signatures on a petition. To get a spot on the ballot as an independent, you need signatures representing 2% of the total votes cast in the last Secretary of State election in Indiana.[4] In 2020 this amounted to approximately 45,000 petition signatures needed to get on the ballot—ten times the number needed by the Democratic and Republican candidates

Ranked Choice Voting Can Save Us from the Lesser of Two Evils Dilemma

But the monopoly status of the two parties extends far beyond just getting on the ballot. The enforcement arms of the Democratic/Republican monopoly are state constitutions and Federal election law governing presidential elections. They enable a candidate to win an election with a plurality (more than anyone else, but less than a majority) of votes cast in the election. This forces the people voting into choosing between the lesser of two evils within the two monopoly-political parties, or wasting their votes on a minor party candidate who may represent their views exactly, but has no chance of winning.

Under this deplorable system, if too many of the voters choose to waste their vote on a third-party candidate, it can then enable the worse of the two monopoly party candidates to win. Because this is the cruel reality: it keeps the voters from supporting third-party candidates, even though third-party candidate are often the candidates who would best represent their views. Voters, who despite this fact, vote for the third-party candidate who has no chance of winning then will have four years until the next presidential election to kick themselves in the seat of the pants for doing so, wasting their vote, as they allowed the candidate, they dislike the most to win.

Don't Let My Stupid Mistake in 2016 Be Yours in 2024

In 2016 I had issues with Hillary Clinton's use of private email for government work as Secretary of State, so I wrote in Green Party Candidate Jill Stein for president. The result: we got the much greater of two evils—Donald Trump. I live in Indiana, and you could say my vote didn't matter, because Trump was going to win Indiana anyway. You would be right, but that doesn't make me feel any better. Because Trump won that first election over Hillary in 2016, he is today in June of 2024 an even money threat to winning the 2024 election and then proclaiming himself dictator.[5]

Ranked Choice Voting

Ranked choice voting (instant runoff elections) is the most practical way to allow other views to percolate to the top, democratizing our democracy. Ranked-choice voting gives voters the option to rank their votes for each office in order of preference. For example, if you are concerned about the environment, you would have the option in a three-person race to vote your environmental concern by ranking your first preference the Green Party candidate, and then rank second the Democratic Party candidate (who is always more environmentally focused than the Republican) and then to put the Republican Party candidate last in order of preference.

Under ranked-choice voting, after all the votes are cast and counted, a candidate who gets more than 50% of the votes wins outright. But if no one has a majority, the last place candidate is eliminated, and their votes go to whomever each of her individual voters ranked as their second-place preference. If there are only three candidates the election will then be decided in favor of the candidate with the most votes, who now has a majority of the votes cast. If there are more than three candidates in the race, the exact same procedure will keep eliminating the last place candidate until we eventually have a winner with a majority of the electorate supporting them. We will all have been able to vote for our top preference first and done so without wasting our vote. We will all have done our part to keep the candidate that we consider the worst in the field from winning. Yet, we will also have been able to show our preference for the candidate who best represents us. We will have become more democratic.

The 2020 Presidential Election: Biden Prevails

Because we do not have ranked choice voting, in the 2020 Presidential Election, I could not vote for the candidate I most preferred. Several years ago, I met Howie Hawkins at the annual American Monetary Institute Conference on Monetary Reform. Howie supports monetary reform and publicly created money. There is no doubt that he would support *The NEED Act Revisited* if and when we are able to get an updated version of the NEED Act into Congress again. Not only do I agree with Howie on most of his policy positions, but I was also drawn to him as a person. Howie Hawkins was the Green Party presidential candidate in 2020[6] and I did not vote for him. Not only did I not vote for Howie, but I did not donate to his campaign.

The Green Party has had a plank in their platform for several years supporting publicly created money called Greening the Dollar.[7] Several of the founders of Greens for Monetary Reform[8] are friends of mine in the struggle for publicly created money. Despite this, I ignored Howie's campaign. Instead, I used my vote to prevent the reelection of a man to the presidency who had numerous times failed to state that he would accept the result of the election,[9] [10] [11] who numerous times referred to the press as the enemy of the people,[12] [13] [14] [15] and whom I saw as the greatest threat to democracy in our country's history. I was forced by duty to our country to vote for a candidate who would have been my second choice in a ranked choice voting system.

With ranked choice voting, millions of Americans could have voted for the candidate who stood strongest on combating climate change and who supported publicly creating money, Howie Hawkins, while ranking Joe Biden their number two choice. Their votes would not have been wasted; they would have gone up the ladder to Biden if he initially received more votes than Hawkins, as he was almost sure to do. However, it would have sent Biden a message about how many people desperately wanted both real action on climate change and publicly created money.

Bush v. Gore: The 2000 Presidential Election Without Ranked Choice Voting

A classic example of how ranked choice voting could have changed an election and would have changed history was the 2000 U.S. presidential election. The final official results gave the election to George W. Bush with 271 electoral votes to Al Gore's 266. Before we as a nation got to this final result, we endured a month-long recount over Florida's 25 electoral votes. Two decades ago, Florida presidential elections were extremely close, with all sorts of accusations from both major political parties. Election day was November 7, 2000. Television and networks initially called Florida for Gore and then in the early morning hours retracted their call. Gore had called Bush and conceded, but then in the early morning, as Bush's lead had shrunk under 600 votes out of almost 6 million votes cast, Gore retracted his concession.

The closeness of the race triggered an automatic state machine recount that reduced Bush's lead, to 327 votes. Gore, as he was allowed to do under Florida state law, then asked for a manual recount in four counties. As the nation watched the recount with election workers looking at *hanging chads*—paper ballots with punch marks in them which had to be determined by election workers whether or not they were completely punched far enough through to show intent—Bush's lead was further reduced to 154 votes as the four-county recount was proceeding. On November 26, before the manual recount in the four counties was completed, Florida Republican Secretary of State Katherine Harris certified the election in Bush's favor by a 537-vote margin, although the not yet finished recount had cut his lead to 154 votes. Gore sued Harris because the recount had not been completed and on December 8, the Florida Supreme Court ruled 4–3 to order a statewide manual recount of the approximately 45,000 under-votes (ballots that machines recorded as not clearly expressing a presidential vote) and accepted some previously uncertified results in both Miami-Dade and Palm Beach counties, that had reduced Bush's lead, to a mere 154 votes.

Immediately Bush appealed to the U.S. Supreme Court, which ordered the recount halted on December 9, until it could hear arguments in the case.[16] [17] The Supreme Court heard oral arguments two days later on December 11th and the very next day handed down their decision. Contrast this with the current Supreme Court delaying the federal court cases against Trump for months and months. The end result being that Trump was able to avoid trial before the 2024 election, while also being given absolute and presumptive immunity for his conduct as President. The Supreme Court Justices that have allowed this to happen should be ashamed of themselves. The American people had a compelling interest in knowing before the election, whether or not Trump broke the law in both federal cases.

The Bush/Gore recount was eventually stopped by the 5–4 party line, U.S. Supreme Court Decision *Bush v. Gore* that ended the recount and allowed the election certification by Florida Secretary of State Katherine Harris to stand, thereby giving the election to Bush. The Supreme Court also said that their ruling in this case was not to be used as precedent for other cases.[18] This was absolutely baffling, since the job of the Supreme Court is to give us a system of justice and to use previous rulings or precedent to get there—not to make a ruling and say don't pay attention to it in the future. Later, different media recounts further complicated matters with differing reports of who actually won.

To his credit, Al Gore accepted the result of the Supreme Court decision, even though I doubt he personally agreed with it. Those of us who voted for Gore accepted the result, even though many of us believed that it had been stolen by the U.S. Supreme Court stopping the recount in Florida. This was a close election with Gore losing the presidency by 537 votes in Florida, despite receiving more than one half million more votes nationwide (537,179) than did Bush—Gore 48.4%, Bush 47.9%, Ralph Nader 2.7%.[19]

The final official Florida results had Bush with a scant 537 more votes than Gore out of almost 6 million votes cast. However, there were many votes cast for other candidates. Under a ranked choice voting system, those casting these votes would have been able to rank their preference of candidates if their first choice was eliminated. Green Party candidate Ralph Nader received 97,488 votes. One would assume that almost all of those voting for Nader would have preferred Al Gore to George W. Bush. After the election, Al Gore devoted his life to bringing the world's attention to global warming and climate change through his documentary *An Inconvenient Truth.*[20] Since environmental issues are at the core of the Green Party's platform and beliefs, there is little doubt that most of those voting for Nader would have preferred Gore as their second choice and not Bush.

There were also 17,484 votes for Reform Party candidate Pat Buchanan, and 16,415 for Libertarian Harry Browne, most of which we can assume would have gone to Bush as a second choice. There were an additional 6,640 votes cast for the Natural Law, Workers World, Constitution, Socialist and Socialist Workers Party's candidates. Add 36 write-in votes for a grand total of 138,063 Florida voters who were basically disenfranchised from both giving their second preference in the election and giving the people of Florida and America a true majority winner in Florida that decided the presidential election of 2000.

While we may make assumptions as to who these voters would have preferred as their second choice, we will never know. Only by adopting ranked choice voting will voters be able to tell us who their second and third choices are and thus give us an election winner who ultimately and democratically gets a majority of votes. This structural flaw in our system forces us as voters to settle for and vote for the Republican/Democratic candidate, instead of being allowed to vote for who we really believe in. Those who are not satisfied with the results our two-party system gives us might want to consider working to make ranked choice voting a reality.

Bulldozing Was Not Roadbuilding in the Jim Crow South

If no individual gets more than half the votes, Georgia and Louisiana laws call for runoff elections between the top two vote getters. This feature pertains to statewide offices in addition to U.S. Congress and the Senate. Presidential elections do not fall under the recount provision though. They are governed by federal law; the winner does not have to have 50% plus one of the total votes, just more votes than anyone else. But the Georgia and Louisiana laws are hardly examples of these states attempting to put more democracy into the electoral process. Instead, they are quite the opposite, vestiges of the post-Civil War, Jim Crow era of black voter suppression laws.[21] Think of them as one more hoop for a black candidate to jump through if she received the most votes, but not a majority of all votes cast. With a runoff election between the top two vote getters, there would be one last chance for white voters to coalesce around the white candidate, denying the black candidate the office.

An interesting and shameful tidbit of election history is the derivation of the term *bulldoze*. As a proud grandfather who watched his son many years ago and now his grandsons play for hours with toy bulldozers as I also did as a child, I was more than a little surprised to learn this history from the U.S. Vote Foundation:

> Physical violence was also commonly perpetuated against voters of color who dared to try to vote. Indeed, violent voter suppression was so common that the term *bulldoze* first came

into use in Louisiana in the 1870s, when the state was beginning its long embrace of Jim Crow laws and practices. [State or local laws that legalized racial segregation from the post–Civil War era until around 1968.[22]] While relatively innocuous today, the word *bulldoze* back then referred to the practice of giving prospective Black voters a "dose" of the bull whip in order to discourage them from voting. As the bull whip is generally considered too dangerous to use extensively on a 1,000-pound bull, much less a human, it's pretty obvious what the threat of being *bulldozed* meant to someone trying to exercise their right to vote.[23]

In ranked choice (instant runoff elections), as they can in the present system, whites could still stick exclusively with white candidates if that is their misguided solution to our nation's problems. The purpose of ranked choice/instant runoff elections is to allow divergent views, candidates, and parties a chance to get people to vote for them and show their support, thus sending the major party candidates a strong message that issues like climate, the environment, and publicly created money are gaining support. And under a system of ranked choice voting, if the major party candidates continue to ignore these types of issues, they may very well find that their major parties have become minor parties.

Ranked choice voting (also referred to as instant runoff elections) are vastly superior to the runoff elections now required in Georgia and Louisiana, because they only require one election. The Georgia and Louisiana system requires an entirely new election if no candidate gets more than half the votes. It is expensive, and both time and attention consuming on the people. Ranked choice voting gets the same basic results without the spending and effort on a new election, while encouraging alternate parties and candidates to join the process. This is all done without the voters having to worry about wasting their votes when they rank the alternative party candidate first on their ballots.

An End Run Around the Undemocratic Electoral College

A constitutional amendment to do away with the electoral college would also be helpful. The last two elected Republican Presidents Donald Trump and George W. Bush were both elected with a minority of the votes. This is no way to run a democracy. In 2000 George W. Bush was elected with only 47.9% of the popular vote. Al Gore had in excess of one-half million, 537,179 more votes than Bush, yet George W. Bush won in the Electoral College. (In 2004 George W. Bush was reelected with 3 million more than Democrat John Kerry. Yet if just 59,393 more votes had gone to John Kerry in Ohio, Kerry would have become president, despite losing the popular vote by almost 3 million votes.[24]) In 2016 Trump was elected with only 46.1% of the popular vote, 2.9 million less votes than Hillary Clinton. Is it even possible for us to imagine the response from Donald Trump in the 2016 election, if he was in Hillary's position winning the popular vote by 2.9 million votes nationwide and losing the election in the electoral college. Then in 2020 came Donald Trump's Big Lie, falsely claiming that he won the election,[25] despite receiving 7 million fewer votes than Joe Biden and losing the Electoral College 306-232.[26]

Democracy calls for the candidate who ultimately gets the majority of votes to be the next president. Unfortunately, under the undemocratic Electoral College system, enshrined in the Constitution, the candidate with the most votes often doesn't win. Let's take a look at how much your vote is worth in different states.

In 2024, California with a population of 38,889,770 people, has 54 electoral votes, amounting to 1 electoral vote for each 720,180 people. Wyoming with a population of 586,485 is given 3 electoral votes, amounting to 1 electoral vote for each 195,495 people in Wyoming.[27] [28] Thus, a Wyoming citizen's vote is 3.8 times more effective than a Californian's in determining who our next president is. A Vermont citizen's vote is 3.3 times and an Alaska citizen's vote is worth 2.9 times what a Californian's vote is worth in determining our next president.

National Popular Vote Interstate Compact

Doing away with the Electoral College and using the more democratic popular vote in presidential elections would also have the effect of making them national contests, instead of contests that seem to matter only in a handful of so-called battleground states. Yet, amending the Constitution to replace the Electoral College with the popular vote is a virtual impossibility in today's political climate. This for the simple reason that the current Republican Party is able win the Electoral College today with a minority of votes, while losing the national popular vote. Yet, it is entirely possible that this equation could flip with the Democratic Party benefitting at the expense of the Republican Party. We just showed that in 2004 Democrat John Kerry would have won the Electoral College and the election with 60,000 more votes in Ohio, despite Republican George W. Bush getting 3 million more popular votes nationwide.

The end run around the undemocratic Electoral College is the National Popular Vote Interstate Compact that began in 2006. It is an agreement among a group of states and the District of Columbia to award all their electoral votes to whichever presidential ticket wins the overall popular vote in the 50 states and the District of Columbia.[29]

The National Popular Vote law only takes effect when states with a total of 270 electoral votes agree to award all their individual state's electoral votes to the winner of the national popular vote. This regardless of the election outcome in each individual state in the compact. It would have the effect of awarding a block of the 270 electoral votes needed to the popular vote winner. The 270-vote threshold represents a majority of the 338 votes in the Electoral College. It is the number that is needed to win the presidential election.

In March 2024, the National Popular Vote law has been enacted by 16 states and the District of Columbia: California (54 electoral votes), Colorado (10), Connecticut (7), Delaware (3), Hawaii (4), Illinois (19), Maryland (10), Massachusetts (11), Minnesota (10), New Jersey (14), New Mexico (5), New York (28), Oregon (8), Rhode Island (4), Vermont (3), Washington (12), plus the District of Columbia (3). Four of these states would be considered small, nine are medium-sized and three are large, a representative sampling of our country. They currently represent 205 electoral votes, with 65 more electoral votes needed for the law to take effect.[30]

The National Popular Vote law has also passed at least one legislative chamber in 8 more states, representing 78 electoral votes: Arkansas (6 electoral votes), Arizona (11), Maine (4), Michigan (15), North Carolina (16), Nevada (6), Oklahoma (7), and Virginia (13). In Nevada and Maine, it has passed both houses but has not yet been enacted because of disagreements on the time elapsed between the different legislative bodies passing it.[31]

This leads one to believe that it indeed is possible that maybe there is an end-run around the dreadful, undemocratic Electoral College. However, before anyone becomes too excited about the National Popular Vote law, we have to assume that its constitutionality will be challenged in court.

Talking Power: Language, The Law, and the Money Power

Our legal system is the backbone of our country. Without it we have anarchy. For democracy to exist, we as citizens must agree that we accept the decisions of our legal system. Individually, we may not always agree with the decisions, but refusal to accept them, after all appeals have had their day in court, is anathema to democracy. Those under investigation, indictment and those who have been convicted naturally may not agree with abiding by our legal system's decisions. Yet, if we as citizens do not support our legal system, anarchy reigns.

The former president of the United States Donald Trump took the position before the elections in 2016, 2020 and continued to before the election in 2024, that he would not agree to accept the results if he lost the election. When he lost in 2020, he attempted a violent coup to stay in power. There is no reason to believe that he will not try another coup if he loses in 2024.

Throughout the three books of the *People, Planet & Power of Money Project* we have referred to the power to create money as the absolute power. I had a recent discussion with an attorney and a supporter of monetary reform. After reading *Money Creation 101*, he corrected my depiction of the Money Power as the absolute power. Without language we would not have society. Language enabled people to communicate and interact with each other and create a society. As they began to create this society, they needed to agree on rules to live by: The Rule of Law. After ancient societies developed language and organized society with rules or laws, their next step was to develop money. These first systems of publicly created money as accounting systems in the Fertile Crescent societies of Mesopotamia are covered in Chapter 3.

Philosopher's Stone

History of Money 101 tells the story of how gold and silver money systems were never successful, ultimately because there was never enough gold and silver to go around for everyone. Goldsmiths as early medieval bankers discovered that they could create money out of thin air when they made loans. They did this by writing paper receipts for up to 10 times more than the gold they held in their vaults and then loaning these receipts for gold that they did not possess to the unsuspecting population. (Federal Reserve, *Modern Money Mechanics*).[32] This gave the bankers the Money Power (power to create money), while medieval alchemists continued to fruitlessly search for the magic substance that would enable them to turn lead into gold—the Philosopher's Stone.[33] Although bankers couldn't create more gold or silver, they began to create what we now use for money by loaning it to people in the form of paper notes that were said to be redeemable in gold or silver. This is the basis for our present system of bank-created debt-money. Van Morrison's haunting melody "Philosopher's Stone" chronicles his own efforts hitting the road to find bookings for his band, as similar to the medieval alchemist pursuit of the philosopher's stone, the magic ingredient that would enable them to turn lead into gold.[34]

History of Money 101 also documents the story of ancient Greece and Rome using metallic systems of money of iron and bronze that were plentiful and had relatively no commodity value in themselves. The value of this publicly created money was that assigned to it by the state. These early systems of publicly created money were created by the state and not the private bankers. These Greek and Roman money systems were extensions and creatures of the Rule of Law. Seigniorage is the difference in the value assigned to the money and the cost of production. Within publicly created money systems such as the Greek and Roman, the seigniorage or the profit from the first use of the money belonged to the state.

Within the bank-created debt-money system, the profit from the first use of the money goes to the private banks that create it. True, in the U.S. the banks do pay the Federal Reserve System interest, but rest assured it is considerably less than the interest they charge you. The Federal Reserve System, after first paying all expenses and also paying dividends to the private banks that own the Federal Reserve Banks, turns over all excess funds to the U.S. Treasury and these funds are usually quite significant. But, the private banks within this system are allowed to keep all the interest they collect, less their expenses.

Another very important feature of the bank-created debt-money system, it is the banks that loan the money who determine what our money is used for. Within a publicly created money system, it is the people through our representative government who would determine what our money is used for.

Seigniorage and the Money Power

Our Constitution puts the power to create our nation's money squarely with Congress, "The Congress shall have Power … To coin Money, regulate the Value thereof," (Article I, Section 8).

This is discussed in detail in *History of Money 101*, Chapter 6: "The U.S. Constitution and Money Creation."

Whomever creates our nation's money benefits through its seigniorage (the profit difference between the total cost of creating money and the value assigned to the money). Who should create our money and benefit from its creation? Private banks or our government representing the people?

I completely agree with what my lawyer friend had said earlier. While I have referred to money creation or the Money Power as the ultimate power, it was always in context to the ultimate money power. *Money is an abstract legal power of the state that acts as a medium of exchange and a final means of payment, facilitating commerce, enabling all our people to have meaningful lives, and being there for society to confront the momentous crises of today and those which will inevitably arise in the future.* This is what money should be. Money exists within a society that itself exists, because people are able to communicate with each other through language and agree on a framework of laws to live by [The Rule of Law]. Money derives its power from the people, through our ability to speak and communicate with each other, so as to form a society. As the people form a society, they also create laws to live by, The Rule of Law. Our Constitution then assigns the Money Power to our government. (Book One: *Money Creation 101*, pages 14-15, *Book Two: History of Money*, Chapter 6).

Money is power. If you or I have enough money we have the ability to live relatively stress-free lives, certainly as far as our basic needs are concerned. That is a degree of power. If we are broke, jobless and homeless, we are powerless. Or if we are employed, but are not paid a living wage, we are powerless. Or if we are employed, but experience an illness in our family that breaks our family budget, we are powerless. Today, that is reality for far too many. If we are billionaires, we have the ability to exert all manner of control on different aspects of society and other people's lives. Power to a much greater degree than whatever you or I may have. Ultimately this power to create our money stems from our language and law and belongs to the people. *Spaceship Earth's* mission of safely transporting Earth's lifeforms across the heavens, would be much better served with publicly created money, than the present private bank-created debt-money we are currently saddled with.

1. Merriam-Webster Online Dictionary, "republic," https://www.merriam-webster.com/dictionary/republic
2. Cartwright, Mark, "Athenian Democracy," World History Encyclopedia, April 3, 2018, https://www.worldhistory.org/Athenian_Democracy/
3. Pruitt, Sarah, "The Founding Fathers Feared Political Factions Would Tear the Nation Apart," History Classics, Sept 29, 2023, https://www.history.com/news/founding-fathers-political-parties-opinion
4. BallotPedia, "Ballot access requirements for presidential candidates in Indiana," https://ballotpedia.org/Ballot_access_requirements_for_presidential_candidates_in_Indiana
5. Graham, David A., "Trump Says He'll Be A Dictator on 'Day One,'" The Atlantic, Dec 6, 2023, https://www.theatlantic.com/ideas/archive/2023/12/trump-says-hell-be-a-dictator-on-day-one/676247/
6. Weiss, Abby, "Howie Hawkins unsurprised by election results, hopeful for Green Party," The Daily Orange, Nov 11, 2020, http://dailyorange.com/2020/11/howie-hawkins-unsurprised-election-results-hopeful-green-party/
7. Green Party Platform, N: "Monetary Reform (Greening the Dollar)," IV. Economic Justice & Sustainability, https://www.gp.org/economic_justice_and_sustainability#monetary-reform
8. Greens for Monetary Reform, https://greensformonetaryreform.org/
9. Liptak, Kevin, "A list of times Trump has said he won't accept the election results or leave office if he loses," Sept 24, 2020, https://www.cnn.com/2020/09/24/politics/trump-election-warnings-leaving-office/index.html
10. Feuer, Will, "President Trump won't agree to accept 2020 election results as Biden leads in polls — 'I have to see,'" CNBC, Jul 19, 2020, https://www.cnbc.com/2020/07/19/president-trump-wont-agree-to-accept-2020-election-results-as-biden-leads-in-polls.html
11. BBC, "US election: Trump won't commit to peaceful transfer of power," Sept 24, 2020, https://www.bbc.com/news/election-us-2020-54274115
12. New York Times, "Trump Calls the News Media the 'Enemy of the American People,'" Feb 17, 2017, https://www.nytimes.com/2017/02/17/business/trump-calls-the-news-media-the-enemy-of-the-people.html
13. Stewart, Emily, "Trump calls media the 'true Enemy of the People' the same day a bomb is sent to CNN," Vox.com, Oct 29, 2018, https://www.vox.com/policy-and-politics/2018/10/29/18037894/donald-trump-twitter-media-enemy-pittsburgh
14. Smith, David, "'Enemy of the people': Trump's war on the media is a page from Nixon's playbook," The Guardian, Sept 7, 2019, https://www.theguardian.com/us-news/2019/sep/07/donald-trump-war-on-the-media-oppo-research
15. Stelter, Brian, "Why Trump's 'enemy of the people' smear will have long-lasting effects," Dec 28, 2020, CNN, https://www.cnn.com/2020/12/28/media/donald-trump-media-reliable-sources/index.html
16. National Constitution Center, "On this day, Bush v. Gore settles 2000 presidential race," Dec 12, 2022, https://constitutioncenter.org/blog/on-this-day-bush-v-gore-anniversary
17. Britannica, "United States presidential election of 2000," https://www.britannica.com/event/United-States-presidential-election-of-2000
18. NPR, , "Legal Precedent and the Bush-Gore Ruling," WBEZ, Chicago, https://www.npr.org/2006/08/20/5678490/legal-precedent-and-the-bush-gore-ruling

19. The American Presidency Project, University of California Santa Barbara, https://www.presidency.ucsb.edu/statistics/elections/2000
20. Internet Movie Database, *An Inconvenient Truth*, https://www.imdb.com/title/tt0497116/
21. U.S. Vote Foundation, "Georgia's Runoff Election: A Sordid History Underlies the Peach State's Election Process," https://www.usvotefoundation.org/georgiarunoff
22. Georgia College & State University, "Jim Crow Laws," https://www.gcsu.edu/sites/files/page-assets/node-2213/attachments/jim_crow_educational_resource_.pdf
23. U.S. Vote Foundation, "Georgia's Runoff Election: A Sordid History Underlies the Peach State's Election Process"
24. National Popular Vote, "Agreement Among the States to Elect the President by National Popular Vote," https://www.nationalpopularvote.com/written-explanation
25. Danforth, John; Ginsberg, Ben; Griffith, Thomas B; Hoppe, David; Luttig, J. Michael; McConnell, Michael W; Olson, Theodore B; Smith, Gordon H, "LOST, NOT STOLEN: The Conservative Case that Trump lost and Biden won the 2020 Presidential Election," July 2022, https://drive.google.com/file/d/1aqorZ61AYFqZU-EDQBBzjqfvAoC5nKcB/
26. David Leip's, "Atlas of U.S. Presidential Elections," https://uselectionatlas.org/
27. World Population Review, "US States – Ranked by Population 2024," https://worldpopulationreview.com/states
28. National Archives, "Distribution of Electoral Votes," Electoral College, https://www.archives.gov/electoral-college/allocation
29. National Conference of State Legislatures, "National Popular Vote," Updated March 11, 2015, http://www.ncsl.org/research/elections-and-campaigns/national-popular-vote.aspx
30. National Popular Vote, "Agreement Among the States to Elect the President by National Popular Vote," https://www.nationalpopularvote.com/written-explanation
31. *Ibid.*
32. Federal Reserve Bank of Chicago, "Modern Money Mechanics," Introduction: Who Creates Money, https://en.wikisource.org/wiki/Modern_Money_Mechanics
33. Merriam-Webster, "philosopher's stone," https://www.merriam-webster.com/dictionary/philosopher%27s%20stone
34. Morrison, Van, "Philosophers Stone," https://www.youtube.com/watch?v=T7YL5n_GA_c

TWELVE

The Lever to Change Our World—Publicly Created Money

As *Spaceship Earth* travels the heavens, think of the three books in the *People, Planet & the Power of Money Project* sending the international distress signal—Mayday! Mayday! Mayday! Warning the people of our fraudulent and structurally flawed bank-created debt-money system. Only by first becoming aware of the nature of our present system, will we be able to democratically consider an alternative system of publicly created money. Those who currently hold the Money Power are well aware that the best way for them to retain the power to create our nation's money is to keep you from understanding the present system: that almost the entirety of what we use for money is created out of thin air by banks when they loan it to us, charging us interest for the privilege. Our knowledge of this sorry fact is the key to a better world.

Getting the Right Mixture of Capitalism and Socialism

Money does not exist in a vacuum. It exists within the context of society's political and economic systems. Our job as citizens is to work jointly together, so as to get the best economic, political, and monetary systems. A reasonable mixture of capitalism and socialism: Senator

Bernie Sanders calls it democratic socialism and former Secretary of Labor Robert Reich calls basically the same thing democratic capitalism. I believe that a compromise mixture of capitalism and socialism could allow for the private ownership of individual lots, homes, small businesses, and farms, while excluding individuals or corporations from exclusive ownership of huge swaths of *Spaceship Earth's* natural resources. These natural resources should benefit us all. And they should be extracted and used in a safe, sustainable manner that is non-disruptive to Earth's surviving ecosystems.

Allowing a small number of people to amass huge wealth by owning and controlling Earth's natural resources creates tremendous inequality and takes the decisions about how these resources are used away from the nation's people. If we as a people choose to continue to allow private corporations to extract and use the natural resources of the Earth, then at the very minimum, laws must be enacted that give the planet and its ecosystems priority over corporate and individual interests—while also ensuring a healthy social safety net for both people and planet.

The Archimedes Lever to Change Our World

Greek mathematician Archimedes (287–211 BC) is generally considered one of the greatest mathematicians of all time.[1] My own memory of him from my early education was the story of his running into the street naked from his bathtub, shouting *Eureka!* immediately after discovering that he could measure the volume of an object by measuring how much water it displaced. Our son Nick reminded us of his other famous observation today. He texted my wife that he used a floor jack we had given him as a present to change the brakes on his car this morning. I said that given a large enough jack he could do anything; Nick reminded us that it was Archimedes who said, "give me a place to stand and a long enough lever and I can move the world." Changing our money system to publicly created money is the lever that will allow us to do the heavy lifting needed to change our world for the better.

Karl Marx, Environmentalist

I never used to think of myself as an environmentalist, although our son Nick likes to call me a tree-hugger. As a lifetime witness to the destruction of our Earth, its plants, animals, and ecosystems, I have become progressively more concerned. I guess the only reason I didn't consider myself an environmentalist in the past is that being concerned about these things should be a given for everyone. Those that do consider themselves environmentalists might be surprised to know that Karl Marx, writing in the mid-1800s, was also extremely concerned about the environment. His work on environmental issues was completely unknown to me until I read *The Ecological Rift—Capitalism's War on the Earth*[2] by John Bellamy Foster, Brett Clark, and Richard York. Marx's assessment in 1844 of the direct linkage from capitalism to the interruption of the natural order and destruction of ecosystems marks him as being one of the founders of the environmental movement. He was examining the relationship of humanity to ecosystems nearly a century before the word *ecosystem* was even coined by Oxford, England, biology student, Arthur Roy Clapham in 1935.[3]

Marx's lack of recognition as an early founder of the environmental movement is evidence of Antonio Gramsci's Theory of Cultural Hegemony that we introduced in Money Creation 101. Although the capitalist system is prepared to use all the force and violence necessary to stay entrenched in power, after years running the system, social institutions have become so entrenched into capitalist hegemony (DOMINATION[4]), that impositions of violence are now seldom necessary. Today, after decades of struggle, our society now considers environmentalism as a legitimate subject to be discussed. This itself has only happened because of the dire environmental emergency before us and the complete inability of the capitalist economic system and the bank-created debt-money monetary system to confront it.

But Karl Marx, as the number one historical critic of capitalism long before the modern environmental movement was even conceived, is not allowed to be recognized for his role in defense of the environment. I hardly consider myself a Marxist. I've already admitted that when I tried to read him years ago, I couldn't understand him. But when Marx has made his mark, so to speak on a subject, we need to consider it and then accept or reject it. We don't have to agree with everything Marx wrote to recognize him for his contributions to political economy and his pioneering concern for the environment.

Capitalism only exists because the dominant capitalist class unilaterally claimed the right to own the Earth and its resources. This is the bedrock of capitalism, without which capitalism could not exist. Another way to look at it is that capitalism puts the fox in charge of the henhouse, while under a socialist system the hens would be put in charge of their own henhouse.

In 1815 the term metabolism was used to describe "material exchanges within the body, related to respiration."[5] German chemist Justus von Liebig then gave the term a wider meaning, using it to refer to metabolic processes in the context of "tissue degradation" and as a key to understanding the processes at both the "cellular level and in the analysis of entire organisms."[6]

As capitalism began to expand in the 1800s, people flocked to the cities to work in the new industrial jobs. Chemists and agronomists in Germany, France, Britain, and the U.S. noticed that the agricultural fields of rural farms were becoming impoverished. The soil was losing its nutrients—nitrogen, potassium, and phosphorus. As capitalism took hold, factories sprouted up in the cities, and rural people migrated to work there. The rural farmers began to send their crops to the cities to be consumed by this new workforce. The waste containing nutrients that had originally come from the distant farm fields remained in or near the cities where the food was consumed. The rural fields became barren. Prior to the growth of capitalist cities, most agricultural products were consumed relatively near to where they were grown, with the waste also ending up relatively close. Liebig in 1859 termed the shipping of crops to distant cities a system of robbery, in lieu of rational agriculture. The land was being continuously depleted of its nutrients, losing its productivity.

Karl Marx Envisions Spaceship Earth

Karl Marx used the term *metabolic interaction* to refer to "the complex, dynamic interchange between human beings and nature." Marx contended that there is a necessary "metabolic interaction" between people and the Earth. "Man lives on nature" and is dependent on it, "nature is his body with which he must remain in continuous interchange if he is not to die." A sustainable social metabolism is "prescribed by the natural laws of life itself."[7] Marx was describing *Spaceship Earth* long before we had cars and planes, let alone spaceships.

Marx pioneered the concept of a metabolic rift—an ecological rupture in the metabolism of a system, as a direct result of man's actions, i.e., the interruption of the natural processes of an environmental system. Marx was talking about ecosystems, although the term was not coined until almost a century later when English botanist Arthur Tansley asked Arthur Roy Clapham, a young man in the Department of Botany at Oxford University, to think of a suitable word to denote the physical and biological components of an environment considered in relation to each other as a unit. Clapham then coined the term *ecosystem* and Tansley first used the Clapham-coined word in his own 1935 paper, "The use and abuse of vegetational concepts and terms," which appeared in the *British Journal of Ecology*.[8]

Marx contended that man naturally interacts with nature. We are part of nature. It is only when man disrupts the natural system that we have a metabolic rift in the natural system. Man became a major disrupter of the natural system with the advent of the industrial age and capitalism. People moved from the countryside to the cities to find employment. As a result, the landowners in the countryside began to ship their crops to the cities to feed an expanding industrial workforce. This interrupted the natural process of the nutrient-containing waste going back into the fields from which it had been taken. This metabolic rift could only be dealt with by bringing in nutrients from other locales and depositing them on the now barren fields. This in turn, created a chain reaction, disrupting the natural processes in the locations from which the nutrients were removed and the locations to which much of it ultimately goes—our oceans and fresh water.[9]

Another way to look at what Marx was saying is that the Earth and its ecosystems mirror the human body and its organs. Just as disease in individual organs will threaten the overall health and life of an individual, so too will harming, disrupting, and obliterating ecosystems affect the life of our Mother Earth. Indigenous people from all corners of the globe have intuitively understood this without the benefit of modern science to guide them. Marx understood that humans and the entire natural world together are the passengers on *Spaceship Earth.*

Juggling Tristan, Great Grandpa, Bombers & Seabirds with Karl Marx's Hand in Saving Capitalism

Our son Nick and his wife have three kids, Tristan, Kedzie, and Harrison, and our daughter Erin and her husband have two, Maddie and Leo. Tristan at thirteen is the oldest of our five grandchildren. When Tristan was seven, he was really into bombers. His great-grandpa, John Roth, my wife's dad, died a few years before Tristan was born. He was a great guy, a World War II vet, and a navigator on B-29 bombers. In 2019 we visited the Air Zoo Aerospace & Science Museum in Portage, Michigan with Tristan. They have a B-25 bomber on exhibit, almost the same as the B-29 that Great-Grandpa Roth flew in. Tristan would still be talking to the guide about it and his great-grandpa if we hadn't finally pulled him away.

Imagine standing on a rocky cliff overlooking the Pacific Ocean, looking to the west at nearby islands as sea birds plunge into the water. Scooping up anchovies for dinner and then dive bombing the islands with guano (bird dung), they are in effect using the islands as giant porta-potties. Well, maybe you can't quite imagine that scene, but it is the kind of thing I have thought about while researching and writing this book. Perhaps you might grant that I have been able to link all this in my dreams, but what on earth does it have to do with Karl Marx?

While Marx explained man's interdependence with nature, he wanted to keep the system intact the way it was. Others were content to react to the disruptions by finding and delivering a suitable replacement to the rural fields for the nutrients that had been lost to cities. The crisis in the fields imperiled capitalist agriculture, which in turn fed capitalist workers who lived in the cities and labored in the new industrial factories. The crisis of barren fields threatened capitalism to the core.

Bird Crap and Asian/Pacific Island Workers Rescue Capitalism

In the nineteenth century, there were rocky islands in the Pacific Ocean with copious deposits of guano from centuries of dive-bombing sea birds using the islands as their own porta-potties. The Chincha Islands off the coast of Peru were that place. Since it rarely rained there, the nitrates and other nutrients in the guano did not wash away. The sea birds had made their deposits over thousands of years and the nutrient-rich, rock-hard guano was piled hundreds of feet deep, just waiting for the ships from the British firm of Anthony Gibbs and Sons that were soon to come to take it to the impoverished fields of Britain.[10]

Guano is an extremely effective fertilizer because it contains an exceptionally high content of nitrogen, phosphate, and potassium, which are key nutrients essential to plant growth. Guano had been used for thousands of years in agriculture across the globe, but in a much less disruptive manner than what followed in the mid-nineteenth century. The Bible, 2 Kings 6:25, illustrates that dove's dung or guano was also in demand in biblical times. "There was a great famine in the city; the siege lasted so long that a donkey's head sold for eighty shekels of silver, and a quarter of a cab of seed pods (dove's dung) for five shekels."[11]

In 1841, the first ship with a full cargo of guano arrived in Britain. Marx was later to write in *Das Kapital* Vol. I that "the blind desire for profit" had "exhausted the soil" of England, thus driving "the manuring of English fields with guano" from Peru.[12] Guano was soon to be sought by U.S. farms and plantations that were also in desperate need of its nutrients. Congress passed the Guano Islands Act in 1856 that allowed U.S. citizens to take possession for the United States of unclaimed islands, rocks, and keys around the globe containing guano deposits. Under the Guano Islands Act, 94 islands were claimed and by 1903, 66 of them had become U.S. territories.[13]

Peru guano exports to Britain hit 95,000 tons per year in 1850 and increased to 200,000 in 1851. From 1866 to 1877 Peru annually exported worldwide 310,000 to 575,000 tons of guano. Peru had become dependent on the guano export trade. In the 1840s it represented only 5% of state revenue, but during the period of 1869–1875 the guano trade had become 80% of Peru's state revenue. Unfortunately, the indigenous people of Peru received little of the guano money. It all went to the wealthy oligarchy running the country.[14]

In the 1840s, Peru had developed a labor shortage in its silver mines and plantations. Maintaining the guano trade necessitated the importation of labor. Slavery had been abolished in Britain in 1834, but because of the Opium Wars and Taiping Rebellion in China, European merchants were able to get Chinese people to sign up as indentured labor. Using coercion, deceit, and outright kidnapping, tens of thousands of Chinese workers were sent from Portuguese Macao and Hong Kong to the guano fields. The voyage took five months, and the conditions were not much better than those on the slave ships from Africa to America. The mortality rate on just the voyage was 25 to 30 percent, with many of the men jumping overboard to end their suffering.[15]

Workers from China and India were also used to build railroads in the U.S., harvest sugar cane in Cuba, and work on plantations in various other British colonies. The pejorative term for these workers from China, India, and the Pacific Islands was "coolie." Ship captains and agents that dealt with the workers referred to the operation—signing them to a contract to pay for their passage and then ensuring that they never had enough money to pay off their contract and gain freedom—as the "pig trade." "Blackbirding" was the word coined to describe the coercion and outright kidnapping of Pacific Islanders to work as laborers/debt slaves in colonies throughout the Pacific. [16] The ship's owners, captains, and crews were called blackbirders, with a good number of the blackbirds landing on the Guano Islands to haul bird crap until expiring from sheer exhaustion.

From 1849–1874, more than 90,000 Chinese workers were shipped to Peru; the majority went to build railroads and work in sugar plantations. But those who were sent to work in the guano islands were given the most demoralizing work. They were required to use picks and shovels to pry the dried-out, rock-hard, thousand-year-old, dived-bombed bird crap loose, put it into bags, and then push it in a wheelbarrow to deposit in a chute to a ship's hold. Each worker was expected to repeat this process 80 to 100 times a day to the tune of five tons total. The heat was terrible, but the stench was said to have been even more unbearable.[17]

A.J. Duffield, writing in *Peru in the Guano Age*, describes what the guano laborers endured:

> No hell has ever been conceived by the Hebrews, the Irish, the Italians, or even the Scotch mind for appeasing the anger and satisfying the vengeance of their awful gods, that can be equaled in the fierceness of its heat, the horror of its stink, and the damnation of those compelled to labour there, to a deposit of Peruvian guano when being shoveled into ships.[18]

Slavery had been abolished in Britain in 1834, in Peru in 1854, and finally in the U.S. in 1865 with the ratification of the 13th Amendment to the Constitution after the defeat of the Confederate Rebellion. Cheap labor was needed to fill the hundreds of ships that were to come for the guano elixir that was to transform the barren fields of Britain, France, America and other capitalist countries into productive use again. Deceiving Asian and Pacific Islander people into signing contracts to repay the cost of their passage across the ocean to Peru and other destinations was the most popular and economical way to obtain that labor.

The robust guano trade saved large-scale, mechanized capitalist agriculture as it was just beginning to develop. This in turn saved the entire capitalist system from withering on the vine in imitation of the deteriorating agriculture fields that had been struggling to feed the new industrial workers. Foster, Clark, and York also provide an analysis of the guano trade as it pertains to which nations rule and which nations serve those that rule: "The international fertilizer [guano] trade ushered in decades of civil unrest, war, debt, and global asymmetries in the international hierarchy of nations."[19]

In 1865, Spain went to war with its former colonies Peru, Chile, Ecuador, and Bolivia by seizing the guano-rich Chincha Islands off the Peruvian Coast. This was the Chincha Islands War, also known as the Spanish-South American War. After two years of fighting, Spain was forced to withdraw, and its fleet had to circumnavigate the globe in order to return safely to Spain. Chile fought Peru and Bolivia from 1879 to 1884 in the War of the Pacific, or Saltpeter War (saltpeter is the term for potassium nitrate found in guano and it was used both as fertilizer and to manufacture gunpowder). The Chilean victory gained resource-rich coastal territory from Peru and Bolivia.

With outright slavery on its way out the door in the capitalist countries, only this form of indentured debt-slavery labor could dredge up enough working people to save industrialized Western capitalism as we know it. The global asymmetries that developed were that the Western capitalist nations became more powerful, while the poorer nations, those in the Global South, became less powerful.

From Feeding the World to Chemical Weapons to Killing Our Water

The Great War (World War I) began in 1914. Two years earlier in 1912, German scientists Fritz Haber and Carl Bosch developed the Haber-Bosch Process for taking nitrogen from the air and converting it to ammonia, from which it can then be made into the fertilizer ammonium nitrate. This process replaced the need for the seabird guano of the Peru islands and other locales. It allowed the industrial West to make synthetic fertilizers and feed the world. It also enabled Germany to make high explosives for use in the World Wars that followed. Haber in 1918 and Bosch in 1931 were both awarded Nobel Prizes in chemistry. Without this process, it is estimated that worldwide today we would only be able to feed two-thirds of the Earth's present population.[20]

Fritz Haber was considered a German patriot who developed the first chemical weapons used in World War I. The Hague Convention of 1899 had banned the use of "asphyxiating or deleterious gasses." Haber was behind the German development of gas warfare from start to finish. On April 12, 1915, in Ypres, Belgium, the wind shifted to blow toward the entrenched Allied troops. German "gas troops" opened pressurized canisters and released 150 tons of chlorine gas. The four-mile-wide yellow cloud rode the wind toward the French and Algerian soldiers deployed at Ypres. Scores of soldiers died and many more were injured. A Canadian soldier who witnessed the event a little too closely described what he experienced: "Passive curiosity turned to active torment.... A burning sensation in the head, red-hot needles in the lungs, the throat seized as by a strangler."[21] The psychological effect was tremendous and before too long, both sides were using the previously banned chemical gas warfare.

Fritz Haber was an ardent believer in the use of chemical weapons, saying they were no worse than bullets or artillery shells. He was quoted as saying that "innumerable human lives would be saved" with their use. His wife, Clara Immerwahr, a respected chemist in her own right, disagreed. A week after Haber first deployed the chlorine gas in Ypres, Clara Immerwahr used her husband's service revolver to take her own life.[22]

Ocean Dead Zones

Shipping huge quantities of bird guano across the globe to restore depleted fields had disrupted the normal metabolism of nature. Both transporting guano from the Global South to the Capitalist North in the nineteenth century and the Haber Bosch Process that replaced guano in the twentieth century have resulted in increased nitrogen and phosphorus runoffs that eventually make their way into fresh water and then the oceans. This increase then causes the creation of "dead zones" in our oceans. When there is too much nitrogen and phosphorus in either fresh water or the oceans, it causes an overstimulation of growth in aquatic plants and algae. This excessive growth then uses up the dissolved oxygen in the water, blocking sunlight from reaching deeper waters. This process of creating dead zones is called eutrophication. Dead zones get their name from the conditions they create, hypoxic (low-oxygen) areas in the world's oceans and lakes. Since most organisms need oxygen to live, few organisms can survive in hypoxic conditions, giving the dead zones their ghoulish moniker.

The U.S. Government Water Science School relates that the dead zones, or eutrophic events as they call them, have increased as a direct result of the "rapid rise of intensive agricultural practices, industrial activities, and population growth." This then causes the discharge of large amounts of nitrogen and phosphorous into our air, soil, and water, nearly two times as much nitrogen and three times as much phosphorus as would naturally occur.[23] *National Geographic* reports:

> Scientists have identified 415 dead zones worldwide. Hypoxic areas have increased dramatically during the past 50 years, from about 10 documented cases in 1960 to at least 169 in 2007. The majority of the world's dead zones are located along the eastern coast of the United States, and the coastlines of the Baltic States, Japan, and the Korean Peninsula.[24]

A 2007 study from the Virginia Institute of Marine Science recorded 405 dead zones in coastal waters worldwide, affecting 95,000 square miles, roughly the size of New Zealand. The world's largest dead zone is in U.S. coastal waters at the mouth of the Mississippi River in the Gulf of Mexico, covering 8,500 square miles, an area about the size of New Jersey.[25]

Debt Slavery: Past and Present

Debt slavery, also known as bonded labor or peonage, is the pledge of a person's labor as security for the repayment of a debt or obligation in which the terms of repayment are not clearly stated or understood. The person holding the debt thus has control over the debt slave, who at best finds it, extremely difficult and usually at worst impossible, to escape the debt.

When done in the Pacific Islands the creation of debt slaves was called the "pig trade" and "blackbirding", while in more refined circles it came to be referred to as "indentured servitude." The capitalist system obtained cheap labor around the world by using all manner of coercion up to and including outright kidnapping to entrap poor people in this system from which there was no legal means of escape. Ideally, signing a person to a contract that compels one to repay the cost of passage across the sea could be done in a reputable way, and the indentured servant could be freed from the contract in a reasonable length of time. But far too often this did not happen. Interest on the debt and the necessity to also pay for food, lodging, and tools needed to do the work they did, usually ensured that the debt and bondage continued until death.

Debt slavery is what they were consigned to then, and it is what we are consigned to today. I fully understand that comparing debt slavery today in the U.S. to the debt slavery of Asian and Pacific Island labor in the guano fields is a stretch. The magnitude of difference cannot be imagined. What is the same though, is our inability to extricate ourselves from the system. The workers on the guano islands could not escape the system themselves without leaping to their death or just wearing down to the point they could no longer breathe.

Expert Witness: Johann Wolfgang von Goethe

At least the guano workers knew they were enslaved, today the Earth's peoples have almost no knowledge of the workings of the bank-created debt-money system that enslaves us all. The great German writer Johann Wolfgang von Goethe's observation from the early nineteenth century, "None are more hopelessly enslaved than those who falsely believe they are free,"[26] perfectly captures the lack of knowledge of the American people on how our money is created and how our entire society is enslaved by the bank-created debt-money system.[27]

Today, money is absolutely necessary for modern society to exist. Because we and our government were conned more than a century ago into the creation of the Federal Reserve System and into gifting the power and privilege to create our money to private banks as debt, we as individuals and collectively (through our government) must forever remain in debt. The fact that some of us can get out of debt is certainly beneficial for those of us who can, but that good fortune cannot and does not befall us all. A large number of American people must go deeper into debt, pumping money into the overall system, from which only the fortunate few are able to escape. Or we can change to a system of publicly created money.

Bootstrap Pulling

When the first draft of the *People, Planet & Power of Money Project* was sent to test readers for their input, I received responses from two people who had worked hard and lived within their means. They were having trouble understanding the justification, for a system of publicly created money that would bail out those in debt, who had not lived within their means. This also reflected the values I was raised with—we should all pull ourselves up by the bootstraps. But within the debt-money system, everybody can't get out of debt; only a limited number of fortunate people can extricate themselves from debt. Both people and government must remain in debt, and that overall level of debt must steadily increase for society to have a money supply and be able to function within the bank-created debt-money system.

Although publicly created money will certainly offer a lifeline to those in our society who need it the most, it will also offer numerous benefits to everyone. First and foremost, publicly created money is not a right or left, conservative or progressive issue. Yes, publicly created money can provide some much-needed help for the majority of Americans now under tremendous financial pressure representing half or more of our people. In addition, it is the only hope to properly fund real climate and other environmental action. Publicly created money is also the only way forward to repaying our national debt.

Fiscal responsibility and repayment of the national debt are at the heart of conservatism. “The validity of the public debt of the United States, authorized by law…shall not be questioned,”[28] states the U.S. Constitution in the 14th Amendment. Yet it is an absolute impossibility to repay our federal debt within the bank-created debt-money system. The way the federal debt is handled now, old debt is repaid by taking out new debt. This is not really a repayment of debt but more of a transfer of debt from one creditor to another, all the while it steadily increases.

Answering my test readers and others who question the fairness of a publicly created money system which helps everyone, but certainly could help some more than others; let’s consider that everyone does not now possess the boots to pull themselves up by their own bootstraps. Think of publicly created money as a shoe store that provides work boots with straps for everyone, so that we can all pull ourselves up by our own bootstraps.

Foot Washing with Father Jerry Zawada

Although I was raised as a Catholic, including 12 years in Catholic schools, the Catholic Church and I parted ways as I grew into an adult. I believe a person’s religion should be reflective of their understanding of the world and if there is a difference, they should part ways. Many of my family members and friends remain practicing Catholics and I respect them for their beliefs, as I do anyone who sincerely subscribes to any religion. It is just not for me.

Soon after we started our weekly Saturday vigil against the Iraq and Afghanistan Wars which lasted from July 2005 until the outbreak of Covid Pandemic in early 2020, we were occasionally joined by a quiet unassuming man, Franciscan priest Father Jerry Zawada. He never gave a lecture; he never used the bullhorn to give out anti-war information to passing motorists and he never told you anything about what he had done or was currently doing without us absolutely prying it out of him. But every time I saw Father Jerry he always wanted to know what I had been doing.

Father Jerry was born in 1937 in Gary, Indiana, as one of 7 children in a family of Polish immigrants. He and several of his siblings were sent to live with other families during the Great Depression, because that was the only way many large families could survive it. He was ordained a Franciscan priest in Chicago in 1964. He first served as a priest in the Philippines and then came home to serve among the poor and gang members on Chicago's North Side. He was very candid in telling us that he had suffered severe depression for years, because he believed himself to be inadequate in his vocation to lessen the suffering of others. I remember him telling us that his depression was so severe that he was unable to function for a time, not only as a priest but just as a member of society. An immigrant from El Salvador working as a maid in the seminary where Father Jerry was housed shared her story with him. She was a school teacher who fought for the rights of the poor in El Salvador. She was arrested, raped and tortured by the Salvadoran military. After hearing this immigrant woman's heart-breaking story, it became clear to Father Jerry that his true vocation was to be a witness with the poor and downtrodden.

Expert Witness: Father Jerry Zawada

Father Jerry explains his rescue from depression:

> And it dawned on me almost like a light, I could not, not do something. I didn't have to take away anybody's pain. I just needed to walk with them and learn from them and maybe somehow, I describe it in my religious terms as seeing the face of Christ, and working along those lines just learning from them, accompanying them in their plight and then hopefully to work with others for some type of resolution and relief.[29]

Long before we met him and exactly 25 years to the day that Father Jerry had been ordained, he found himself in a new church, an open-air church, so to speak. It was a summer day in June, 1989 and Father Jerry, with the assistance of a lay member of his activist congregation, was in the midst of the Missouri Peace Planting Campaign against nuclear weapons in northwest Missouri. Father Jerry was performing the Catholic Mass on the top of a nuclear missile silo. I recall Father Jerry reluctantly telling us some of the details from this particular escapade. He and his friend were quite surprised that they were able to enter the nuclear facility and gain access to the missile silo at all. Father Jerry and his companion thought they would be instantly arrested when they started to cut the wire on the first perimeter fence. They also broke through two additional wire perimeter fences, but no one saw them or seemed to care what they were doing until they climbed on the silo.

> We sang. We prayed. We joined hands. When the military did come to take possession of us, we even invited them to join us if they so felt, to pray. And it was very meaningful, the whole thing; we did a lot of good things, symbolic things.[30]

Father Jerry and his friend were arrested, convicted, and served 25 months in a federal prison for this powerful statement against the insanity of nuclear weapons. But that was hardly the only time he spent in jail in service to peace and social justice. He was arrested, prosecuted and served six months in prison for crossing the line into Fort Benning (Fort Moore), Georgia in protest against the Army's School of the Americas, now known as Western Hemisphere Institute for Security Cooperation (WHINSEC). Its mission, regardless of which name, has been to train soldiers from all across Latin America on the use of violence against their own people.[31]

Always on the edge with the Catholic hierarchy, Father Jerry began to spend more of his time in the American southwestern states Arizona and New Mexico, rather than the Midwest. There he was active in helping immigrants survive in the desert after they had come across our border. I can think of a certain political party that would have issues with his work assisting immigrants, but he was doing the work of Jesus and not Donald Trump, caring for the least amongst us. He was also involved in anti-war, anti-drone, and anti-nuclear weapons activism at southwestern Air Force Bases. He served additional time in jail for many other actions that I just can't remember. I think he said that he had served more than a total of six years in jail. But jail wasn't a bad place for Father Jerry, he always told us being in jail gave him the opportunity to offer comfort to the other prisoners.

Equality: Father Jerry—2, Catholic Church Hierarchy—0

Father Jerry's failure to obey arbitrary rules that were against his sense of justice and humanity put him squarely at odds with the Catholic church throughout his career. Finally in March 2014 the Vatican's Congregation for the Doctrine of Faith sent him a letter that removed him from priestly ministry and directed him to "a life of prayer and penance." He was told that he could not present himself in public as a priest or celebrate the sacraments publicly. His crime? Once in 2010 in a somewhat private setting and again in 2011 in a public setting in front of more than 300 peace and social justice activists at a School of the Americas Watch liturgy, he assisted Janice Sevre-Duszynska, a woman priest, as she said Mass.[32] Reverend Sevre-Duszynska had been ordained in 2008 through the Association of Roman Catholic Women Priests.[33]

Father Jerry's work was hardly confined to our country. He was in Iraq when President George W. Bush's Shock and Awe bombing campaign signaled the opening of the Iraq War. He was there to give comfort and witness to the Iraqi people as their country was being laid waste by America's military.

Not long before he died in 2017, Father Jerry told us that he was working on a book. The title was to be *You Can't Wash Feet from the Top of the Ladder*. He explained the meaning to me because I must have looked puzzled. He told me that if you want to really serve people, you must be prepared to go where you are needed the most, and to where no one else is prepared to go. And you can't do that from the top of the ladder, you need to be at the lowest rung or off the ladder completely to reach the feet of those who most need you. It doesn't seem like his book was ever finished, which is unfortunate.

After the Last Supper, Jesus took off his outer garments, wrapped a towel around his waist, poured water into a basin and proceeded to wash the feet of his disciples. He was the Lord God, and he was washing their feet? Like Father Jerry, I understand the act of foot-washing to be a powerful metaphor of humility and service. I hope those who are reluctant to publicly create money, because someone, somewhere, may benefit a little more from it than they do, find this helpful in reassessing their consideration of publicly created money.

All-Inclusive National Healthcare or Not?

My wife and I have Medicare and a private supplemental healthcare insurance plan. I also receive healthcare through the Veterans Administration (VA). As a member of the U.S. Air Force from 1966-70, I like my three brothers, Mike, Alex and John, and millions of our brothers and sisters who have served our nation in the military, benefitted from socialized medicine during our military service. While I currently enjoy these medical privileges, I am also deeply saddened that all our people are not able to have whatever vital healthcare they need without hopelessly putting themselves in debt that they are never able to repay.

I am of the belief that we should have an all-inclusive, all-encompassing national health care plan for all of our people. Publicly created money can provide for whatever shortage might come from funding such a plan with taxes. It is up to us the American people to use our political system to work through our differences and reach satisfactory solutions on these and other issues.

Bank-Created Debt-Money System—Bad for Society, Whether or Not...

But: the bank-created debt-money system is bad for society whether or not we get a national health care plan, repay our national debt, give our youths some relief from their student debt, or decide to tackle climate change head-on. The bank-created debt-money system is bad for society, whether or not we decide to rebuild our country's crumbling infrastructure or pay all of our workers a basic living wage. The bank-created debt-money system is bad for society, whether or not we decide to invest in revitalizing ocean dead zones and implement a sensible plastic policy. These are all policy issues that we can debate and work out within our democratic political framework. The problem today is that none of these policy issues can be solved within the present debt-money system. Only with publicly created money, combined with the industry and determination of the American people, will we have the money necessary to heal our planet and ourselves and ensure *Spaceship Earth's* survival.

Knowledge of the fraudulent, pernicious debt-money system is the key that opens the door for us to introduce a rational system of publicly created money. The debt-money system can only continue if the Money Power is successful at keeping the knowledge of publicly created money's history and potential from the people. The bank-created debt-money system's power lies in secrecy. Our hope for the future lies in spreading knowledge about it and the alternative—publicly created money.

Faced with the question of choosing what type of government, economic, and monetary systems we should have, I vote for democracy in all categories and hope you do too:

- A participatory democracy in which our citizens are active in determining policy.
- An economic system in which we make the collective decision to no longer settle for a system of winners and losers, but rather, push for a system in which we leave no one behind.
- An economic system of just the right mixture of capitalism and socialism, that above all, allows us as vigilant citizens to enact policies that offer the opportunity to live peacefully and sustainably within the natural system of our Mother Earth.

- A monetary system that lets us adjust as needed, to best answer the crises that will confront us in the future.
- And finally, a monetary system that is like the system most of us intuitively and mistakenly believe we have now.

Forming the Future by Defining Money

In Chapter 3, Danish Architect Bjarke Ingels explained that the Danish word for architecture means giving the future form. When Mr. Ingels does an architectural project, he first looks at the world ten years ago, one hundred years ago and one thousand years ago. And then imagines the world ten years into the future, one hundred years into the future, and one thousand years into the future. Our job today is to do the same with what different types of money have done in the past, so we can see what they will do in the future. To also look at the world today and determine what we would like it to look like in ten years, one hundred years and one thousand years.

Looking back in *History of Money 101* and to a lesser extent within these pages, we have described early systems of publicly created money beginning in the Fertile Crescent as agricultural accounting systems and then on to Greece and Rome, using iron and bronze that had little or no value as a commodity, but represented the value given it by the state, as a function of their legal systems. Rome for 500 years and Sparta for 300 years prospered and in Rome's case, became the dominant force in the ancient world using fiat, publicly created money systems. (*History of Money 101*, Chapters 2 and 3)

We also described how early colonial America struggled to survive without a money system and was forced to use all manner of things including fruit, vegetables and Native American wampum as money systems. Out of absolute necessity, the colonists, beginning in 1690 Massachusetts, eventually began to print fiat, paper, bills of credit, referred to as *Colonial Scrip* and use them as a system of money. Eventually all 13 original colonies used the colonial scrip to build infrastructure and prosper. And it was England's outlawing these publicly created bills of credit that was the leading cause of why the

American colonists decided to break away from England. (*History of Money 101*, Chapter 4)

The direct cause of the American Revolution, as stated by American monetary historian Alexander Del Mar and seconded by money historians Charles J. Bullock, Montroville Dickeson, Joseph Albert Earnst, William Graham Summer and Stephen Zarlenga, was our revolutionary government's creation in June 1775 of the *Continental Currency*, fiat, paper money. This declaration of monetary independence from the British Crown was the bridge too far, which England could not stand for. The bloody battles at Lexington and Concord, two months earlier, could have been overlooked. England had proposed loaning us money, but allowing the colonies to create our own money was not allowed. When Benjamin Franklin went to England the following year representing our Continental Congress, he turned down an offer in Parliament to replace our fiat, publicly created, Continental Currency with money created by the Bank of England and then lent to us. (*History of Money 101*, Chapter 5)

Without the Continental Currency, there would have been no American Revolution. The Continentals lasted for six years, before being abandoned by same Continental Congress that had created them. For six years they financed our fight for freedom, bringing us within 5 months of the final victory at Yorktown, before being abandoned by our Founders who were still deluded into thinking money must be gold and silver. The Continentals did lose their value, but this was due to the massive counterfeiting, done by both the British and criminal enterprises and the loss of confidence in them by our Founders. The cost paid for our freedom today computes to 44 cents per day, in 2023 dollars, over a 20-year period, that was paid by the 2½ million American colonists. Is American freedom worth 44 cents per day over a 20-year period? (*History of Money 101*, Chapter 5)

Fourscore and seven years later, President Lincoln and Congress created fiat, publicly created money called *Greenbacks* to fight and win the Civil War, freeing our enslaved people. Bank-created debt-money could have been used, but America was just recovering from the Panic of 1857-61 in which the banks had stopped converting their banknotes for gold, because they didn't have the gold in their vaults to do so. Fortunately, in 1861 we had enough sense to publicly create the Greenbacks and saved our country. Although the American people were quite happy with the Greenbacks, the banking interests had enough power to stop the creation of further Greenbacks and eventually go back to the flawed, dysfunctional system of bank-created debt-money. (*History of Money 101*, Chapters 8 and 9)

These examples of successful publicly created money systems are all covered in much greater detail in *History of Money 101*. Our job today is to imagine what a bank-created debt-money world looks like in ten years, one hundred years and one thousand years. And then to imagine a world in which we publicly create money, in ten years, one hundred years, one thousand years. Which future do we want for our children, grandchildren and great, great grandchildren? Which future do we want for *Spaceship Earth*?

Money is an exclusive, abstract, legal power of the state, which acts as a measure of value and a final means of payment, facilitating commerce, enabling all our people to have meaningful lives, and being there for society to confront the momentous crises of today and those which will inevitably arise in the future.

Such a system of money was represented in the NEED Act, put into Congress in 2011 and ignored. We have discussed updating it in some form as in the *NEED Act Revisited*. The Alliance for Just Money has written a revision, the American Monetary Reform Act of 2024. As *Spaceship Earth* continues her journey through the heavens, all life-forms are under attack by the reckless and careless behavior of humanity. Climate change, dying oceans and lakes, species and ecosystems, and the unrestrained production of indigestible plastic present challenges that our present economic/monetary system has been unable to satisfactorily answer. Likewise for the tremendous gap between billionaire class and the rest of humanity that has developed under the bank-created debt-money system.

Monetary reformers like myself, believe that a just, sovereign system of publicly created money is the keystone needed, upon which to build a sustainable future for *Spaceship Earth* and all her passengers. We humbly invite you to join us in our quest. Our job as citizens is to spread the word to our friends, families, and elected representatives; to educate them on the choice between a money system that is public and represents the combined efforts of us all, or one that is private, representing the debt we owe to our current masters—the bank-created debt-money system. Taking our marching orders from former Supreme Court Justice Louis Brandeis: "The most important political office is that of the private citizen."[34]

---

1. Livio, Mario, "Who's the Greatest Mathematician of them All?" HuffPost, June 25, 2014, https://www.huffpost.com/entry/whos-the-greatest-mathematician-of-themall_b_5526648
2. Foster, John Bellamy; Clark, Brett; York, Richard, *The Ecological Rift – Capitalism's War on the Earth,* Monthly Review Press, 2010, New York.
3. Willis, A.J., "The ecosystem: an evolving concept viewed historically," *Functional Ecology,* 1997 British Ecological Society, p. 268-271, https://besjournals.onlinelibrary.wiley.com/doi/pdf/10.1111/j.1365-2435.1997.00081.x
4. Merriam-Webster, "hegemony," https://www.merriam-webster.com/dictionary/hegemony
5. Foster, John Bellamy, *Marx's Ecology: Materialism and Nature*, Monthly Review Press, New York, 2000, p. 159.
6. Foster et al, *The Ecological Rift,* p.159
7. Foster et al, *The Ecological Rift,* Marx is quoted, pp. 123-126
8. Willis, A.J., "The ecosystem: an evolving concept viewed historically," *Functional Ecology,* 1997 British Ecological Society, p. 268-271, https://besjournals.onlinelibrary.wiley.com/doi/pdf/10.1111/j.1365-2435.1997.00081.x
9. Foster et al, *The Ecological Rift,* pp. 123-126
10. Foster et al, *The Ecological Rift,* p. 355
11. Bible Gateway, 2 Kings 6:25 NIV, http://web.mit.edu/jywang/www/cef/Bible/NIV/NIV_Bible/2KGS+6.html#:~:text=Bible%20Gateway%202%20Kings%206%20%3A%3A%20NIV&text=The%20company%20of%20the%20prophets,he%20-said%2C%20%22Go.%22
12. Foster et al, *The Ecological Rift,* p. 356
13. Vandermeer, John, *The Ecology of Agroecosystems,* Jones & Bartlett, Sudbury, MA, 2011, p. 149.
14. Foster et al, *The Ecological Rift,* p. 360
15. Foster et al, *The Ecological Rift*, p. 360
16. Agnew, Jeremy, *Alcohol and Opium in the Old West*, McFarland & Co, 2013, pp. 82-85
17. Foster et al, *The Ecological Rift,* p. 360
18. Duffield, Alexander, James, *Peru in the Guano Age*, E. Pickard Hall & J.H. Stacy, Oxford University, 1877, https://www.gutenberg.org/files/45998/45998-h/45998-h.htm

19. Foster et al, *The Ecological Rift,* p. 405
20. Flavell-While, Claudia, "Fritz Haber and Carl Bosch -- Feed the World," May 1, 2010, The Chemical Engineer, https://www.thechemicalengineer.com/features/cewctw-fritz-haber-and-carl-bosch-feed-the-world/
21. Andrews, Evan, "The Nobel Laureate Who Pioneered Chemical Warfare," History.-com, Aug 31, 2018, https://www.history.com/news/the-nobel-laureate-who-pioneered-chemical-warfare#:~:text=With%20the%20bald%2C%20cigar%2Dchomping,gas%20on%20the%20Allied%20trenches
22. *Ibid.*
23. USGS Water Science School, "Water and Nitrogen," https://www.usgs.gov/special-topic/water-science-school/science/nitrogen-and-water?qt-science_center_objects=0#qt-science_center_objects
24. National Geographic Resource Library, "Dead Zone," https://www.nationalgeographic.org/encyclopedia/dead-zone/
25. Virginia Institute of Marine Science, "Dead Zones," https://www.vims.edu/research/topics/dead_zones/index.php
26. Brainy Quote "Johann Wolfgang von Goethe," https://www.brainyquote.com/quotes/johann_wolfgang_von_goeth_134023
27. Free Self-Help Legal Information for Missouri Residents, "Slavery Isn't Over They Just Changed What They Call It," Court.rchp.com, https://court.rchp.com/history/truth-of-how-slavery-started-the-black-slave-trade-and-racism/slavery-isnt-over-they-just-changed-what-they-called-it/
28. Constitution Annotated, "Public Debt Clause," 14th Amendment Section 4, https://constitution.congress.gov/browse/essay/amdt14-S4-1-1/ALDE_00000849/#:~:text=S4.-,1.1%20Public%20Debt%20Clause,rebellion%2C%20shall%20not%20be%20questioned
29. Roewe, Brian, "Jerry Zawada, quiet, powerful presence in peace movement, dies," National Catholic Reporter, July 27, 2017, https://www.ncronline.org/jerry-zawada-quiet-powerful-presence-peace-movement-dies
30. *Ibid.*
31. School of the Americas Watch, "Memoria Y Resistencia: Close the School of the Americas," https://soaw.salsalabs.org/fortmoore2023
32. Roewe, Brian, "Jerry Zawada, quiet, powerful presence in peace movement, dies," National Catholic Reporter, July 27, 2017.
33. Association of Roman Catholic Women Priests, "A Renewed Priestly Ministry in a Community of Equals," https://arcwp.org/
34. Brandeis University, "Our Namesake: Louis D. Brandeis," https://www.brandeis.edu/about/louis-brandeis.html#:~:text=Justice%20Brandeis%20believed%20a%20democratic,wrote%20early%20in%20his%20career

Epilogue

The future of our people and planet is to be determined and you can help. Reviews are the best way to get the word out that the three books in the *People, Planet & the Power of Money Project* are worth reading: *Money Creation 101, History of Money 101, and Spaceship Earth 101.* An honest, heartfelt rating and/or review on Amazon.com is the best first step you can take to help spread the word about publicly created money.

An African proverb, "If you want to go fast, go alone. If you want to go far, go together,"[1] perfectly describes the futility of trying to achieve monetary reform alone. We all need to support each other to advance the cause of a just system of money. Your efforts to talk about the debt-money system and a publicly created money system with others will greatly contribute to achieving the end goal of a money system that works for our people and our planet.

None of this is complicated and there is no reason for us to make it so. We want our government to create our money, the banks to only loan money that already exists, and the Federal Reserve System to be just that, federal and a part of our democratic government. Our existing, bank-created debt-money system is intentionally inscrutable for the simple reason that those who benefit from this system know that if we understood it, we would rid ourselves of it in a New York minute. The debt-money system's power lies in the fact that it is complex and difficult for us to get our heads around. This complexity has allowed the economics profession to be cowed into meekly going along with the present debt-money system.

Fortunately, Jaromir Benes, Joseph Huber, Michael Kumhof, Michael McLeay, Amar Radia, Thomas Ryland, Richard Werner, Kaoru Yamaguchi, and Stephen Zarlenga, are but a few of the brave economists and monetary researchers, who have stepped up to the plate and spoken truth to the Monetary Power. Their resolute fearlessness, fortitude and endurance in the last two decades has made it easier for us today to take the debate for publicly created money to the public and from there to our elected representatives.

While I see publicly created money as the ultimate social justice, that does not mean that publicly created money has a political bias. All those who are appalled at a government swimming in debt, as a result of our money being created as debt, should join the fight for publicly created money. Achieving a system of publicly created money will then enable us to democratically determine what sort of social safety net we have. Conversely, keeping the debt-money system in place ensures that there will never be enough money to go around for either our people or our planet.

---

1. Goldberg, Joel, "It Takes A Village To Determine The Origins Of An African Proverb," NPR, WBEZ Chicago, July 30, 2016, https://www.npr.org/sections/goatsandsoda/2016/07/30/487925796/it-takes-a-village-to-determine-the-origins-of-an-african-proverb

Acknowledgments

While writing the *People, Planet & Power of Money Project*, I went to my daughter for advice. She had written and published a book in 2020 and it became, and continues to be after two years in print, an Amazon best seller—*One Truth, One Law: I AM, I Create*, by Erin Werley.[1] For other budding authors I will forward her advice: first, push to get through with a rough draft. Then get the first draft into the hands of beta readers, people who will read your book and give you advice from a reader's perspective. I finally finished the first draft and was ready to go over it again when Erin said to stop and find some beta readers.

Several friends had offered to perform the same service, but Erin cautioned against that route. If I really wanted to make the book better, I needed the opinions of unbiased readers from different backgrounds, not of my friends. I ended up with seven beta readers who read and reviewed my first draft. To be honest, I had been more than a tad glib when informing them that I had a thick skin and to please let me know what I needed to fix. When the beta reader reviews came in, it was more than just a little difficult to hear their criticism. This despite Erin telling me that when she received her own beta reader reports she abandoned her book for months before she could face rewriting it. In *One Truth, One Law*'s first year and a half it has been an Amazon best seller with over 2,400 Amazon reviews. It brings tears to my eyes when I read them and think that our daughter has helped so many people and was able to do so after being so discouraged at first that she almost didn't rewrite and publish it at all.

Thank you so much to my beta readers: Jeffrey Hopkins, Mishel G. Salazar, Derek Scott Calum Sayer, Marie Rose daSilva, Nicholas

Summers, Kristen Waller, and Laura Wilson. Without your insight and advice, which was not always easy for me to admit to myself I should follow, the three books of the *People, Planet & the Power of Money Project* would certainly not exist in its present form.

Money Creation 101, *History of Money 101* and *Spaceship Earth 101* would simply not exist at all without the inquisitive mind of Stephen Zarlenga, beloved, deceased, former Director of the American Monetary Institute and author of *The Lost Science of Money*. He is the modern-day Father of Publicly Created Money. Stephen, Bob Poteat, Jamie Walton, and Steven Walsh at the American Monetary Institute drafted the American Monetary Act. It was then rewritten by the Congressional Legislative Counsel to conform to all other existing legislation and put into Congress by Dennis Kucinich and John Conyers as the NEED Act. The shoulders I have stood on in writing *People, Planet & the Power of Money* include a long list of monetary reformers at the American Monetary Institute and the Alliance for Just Money. Their names are not listed because there are too many and I cannot trust my faulty 79-year-old memory to include all of my many friends and colleagues.

Professor Kaoru Yamaguchi, Dr. Michael Kumhof, Dr. Joseph Huber, Dr. Richard A. Werner, Michael McLeay, Amar Radia, Thomas Ryland, and the entire Monetary Directorate at the Bank of England must be cited for their courage in standing up to the Money Power and risking censure for bravely revealing the bank-created, debt-money system. I believe that Dr. Yamaguchi was the only one of these who had to pay by losing his job for speaking truth to power. Thankfully, after years of being shunned by other universities, he is now teaching at the University of Ankara, Turkey.

After rewriting the *People, Planet and the Power of Money Project* using my beta readers' suggestions, an editor was needed. I found myself discouraged in the search process until the power of the universe brought developmental editor Morgan Day to the project. Morgan helped me to reorganize that rough first draft so as to better tell the story of the struggle over millennia for publicly created money. Morgan believed in *People, Planet & the Power of Money* and it was her idea to rearrange the material into the present three books. I will remain forever in her debt.

Our daughter's own commitments made her unavailable to help with publishing *Spaceship Earth 101*. Thankfully, we were able to enlist the services of Polly Letofsky and her assistant Amanda Miller at My Word Publishing to get us seamlessly to the finish line. In full disclosure, much of what little I did learn in school in the way of grammar all those years ago has long since been forgotten. Fortunately, Polly enlisted copy editor James Hallman to come to the rescue. The book cover was beautifully designed by Write Bright Publishing and the interior was exquisitely designed by Bryan Canter. Melissa McQueen of Creative Reflections Web Design was able to completely redo my author's webpage, making it much easier for readers to learn about *Spaceship Earth 101*. I remain eternally thankful for the extraordinary efforts of all these vital crew members.

Spaceship Earth 101 was originally written under another title without a conscious thought of Earth as a spaceship that economist Kenneth Boulding presented in 1966. Although I had heard of his term and concept when I was younger, I had long since forgotten about it. It was only after the first drafts of the books were finished and I was talking with my brother Mike that he said that the third book reminded him of Dr. Boulding's *Spaceship Earth*. Mike had given Dr. Boulding a tour of the Indiana University campus in the 1960s when Mike was a graduate business student there and Dr. Boulding came to give a talk on *Spaceship Earth*.

Colleague, graphic artist, and musician Elliott Next has proclaimed our planet "a self-contained biological, technological, analytical, ecosystem traveling through space"—a living *Spaceship Earth* ecosystem, and it is high time we begin treating it as such. Thank you, brother Mike, Elliott, and Dr. Boulding for your help in illuminating the perilous nature of our journey.

---

1. Werley, Erin, *One Truth, One Law: I AM, I Create*, MadLeo Publishing, Hammond, IN, 2020, My Book

In Memoriam: American Altar Boy, Michael Alexander Egnatz

My big brother Mike departed *Spaceship Earth* on January 1, 2024, just days shy of what would have been his 80th birthday.

Stargazer & poet, intrepid & inquisitive, Mike was a Navy lieutenant and pilot, serving during the Vietnam War. He was the oldest of the nine Egnatz children and my one big brother. Throughout our lives, we were there for each other, as sounding boards to interpret the world with our thoughts and ideas on how to make it a better place for all the different lifeforms that call it home.

Although Mike's later life was marked by severe challenges, he answered them all with amazing grace, wit and humility. He used his poetry, under the pseudonym American Altar Boy, to examine the difficulties faced by our people and planet through the lens of his own personal life.

Mike christened *Spaceship Earth* and I miss him dearly.

In Caelis (Heaven)

By American Altar Boy, Michael Alexander Egnatz

Through
Clear Cold,
End December
Half Moon Dawn,
Dark Horizon
Slowly Brightens
to OUR STAR'S Ascendency.

Winter, Black, Bare, Branches,
Strain, Dawn Light,
Strain, Sun Light,
As Our, perfect,
BRIGHT,
ORANGE BALL,
RISES,
Through
WINTER's BLEAK HORIZON.

While,
This,
HELIO~Tropic, Soul
Thankfully,
Warmingly, Marvels
at the,
Silent Celestial Mechanics~
"God's one and only voice, is silence."

Herman Melville
American Altar Boy, December 12, 2018

Thanks & Free Offer

Thank you for taking the time to consider these topics that are of such important to our country and our society.

If you thought the insights in this book were valuable, please leave a review on Amazon.com. Reviews are extremely valuable to authors and other readers alike.

FREE OFFER

Scan the QR code below to receive a supplemental article on Linking Social Justice to Monetary Reform.

Resources

- 350.org—350.org
- Alliance For Just Money—monetaryalliance.org
- American Monetary Institute—monetary.org
- International Movement for Monetary Reform—internationalmoneyreform.org
- Move to Amend—movetoamend.org
- Nick Egnatz Author Website—nickegnatz.com
- Project Drawdown—drawdown.org
- Rethinking Economics—rethinkeconomics.org

Subchapter Index

About the Author

Nick Egnatz is a Vietnam vet, anti-war, social justice, and environmental activist who focusing his research on the origins of the American money system. A regular speaker at the American Monetary Institute on the subject of on Monetary Reform. In 2007, Nick was named Northwest Indiana Citizen of the Year by the National Association of Social Workers for his anti-war and social justice activism. Nick is a founding member of the Alliance for Just Money and currently serves as a trustee for the American Monetary Institute.

www.ingramcontent.com/pod-product-compliance
Lightning Source LLC
LaVergne TN
LVHW100252210926
848480LV00003B/905

* 9 7 9 8 2 1 8 4 9 1 2 0 8 *